John Osborne's plays include: *Look Back in Anger* (1956), *The Entertainer* (1957) and *Inadmissible Evidence* (1965). His collected prose, *Damn You, England* was published in 1994 and the two volumes of his autobiography, *A Better Class of Person* (1929–1956) and *Almost a Gentleman* (1955–1966) were published in 1981 and 1991 respectively. John Osborne was born in 1929 and died at Christmas 1994.

JOHN OSBORNE
Plays Three

Luther
A Patriot for Me,
and
Inadmissible Evidence

Introduced by the author

faber and faber
LONDON · BOSTON

This collection first published in 1998
by Faber and Faber Limited
3 Queen Square London WC1N 3AU

Photoset by Parker Typesetting Service, Leicester
Printed and bound in England by Mackays of Chatham PLC, Chatham, Kent

A CIP record for this book
is available from the British Library
ISBN 0-571-17847-2

2 4 6 8 10 9 7 5 3 1

CONTENTS

INTRODUCTION

By the autumn of 1960 I had to overcome my natural indolence and start writing again, to prove to myself that my nerve was only faltering not failed. I wanted to write a play about the interior religious life. I was not yet reconciled to an inheritance of the perpetual certainty of doubt. This effort alone linked easily with the uncertainty of faith, and Martin Luther's explosive revelation of its precedence over good works was irresistible.

Justification by faith and not works, the notion that good intentions are not enough, seemed like justification for any anarchy I might have imposed on my own actions, some key to plunder. Applied, or reduced, to daily experience, it might be a case for the supremacy of imagination over doing good, of sceptics over the 'carers', or the undissembling over the radical pharisees. It pointed the way to resolving the severest doubt of Christian faith, which, to me, was its taint of insurance, of guarantee. In whatever form faith revealed itself, it was emphatically not the same as certainty. 'Oh, Lord, help thou my unbelief.' A modest request, surely, reasonable and dignified.

I was in no hurry to finish *Luther*, although my head was buzzing with visual images as much as history and argument – the frightening *Garden of Earthly Delights* of Bosch and Bach. My prevarication in completing the play was only partly encouraged by a determination not to be goaded into a precipitate denial of the popular rumour of my creative death. I was excited by the way in which I had, I believed, resolved the 'technical problem'. I was at least certain that I had infused some vitality into that moribund genre, the English 'historical' play. I was confident that it had enough brawn of language. I forgot that no one *listens*. It was not my writing arm that was holding me back from the lists but my exposed inner and religious uncertainties.

Through George Devine's intervention I met Trevor Huddleston. I can't remember the exact circumstances that brought them together, but Huddleston was the very sort of radical populist the Royal Court's few followers and many detractors wished to see sweeping up the steps of Sloane Square. He had roused attention with *Nought for your Comfort*, a best-selling polemic about South Africa, his adopted homeland. He was a member of the Anglican Community of the Resurrection and a commanding figure even to foot-slogging unbelievers like George.

He had been Novice Master of the Community at Mirfield and suggested I might care to stay there. I took the train to Huddersfield and for the next week relished a kind of indolence in a setting of minimal rigour. It was a shivering rub-down of the senses. Only plainsong rose above the muffled wind of croaking birdsong. The silence observed in all communal rooms was broken by the sounds of sandalled feet on stone, utensils on wood and the single bell ringing the offices of prime, terce, sext, none and compline. It was as bracing as the view from my small window.

The only office I attended was compline. This end to the day seemed to invoke not only rest but a sense of soothed watchfulness, which I might do well to remember, as in the antiphon to the *nunc dimittis*: 'Take ye heed, watch ye all and pray, for ye know not when the time is. Watch thee, therefore, because ye know not when the Master of the house cometh, at even, or at midnight, or at cockcrow, or in the morning; lest coming suddenly, peradventure, he should find you sleeping.'

When *Luther* and I got back from Yorkshire, Devine's rumbustious excitement was not his gruff demeanour of everyday. He lifted his arms aloft and cast a fine growl. 'By God, boysie, you've done it! You've done it again!' I never saw him so thoroughly justified and joyful, like a man acquitted by a torn jury. 'I always say to them: it may take time and a lot of sweat but when Johnny finally does bring one out, he really *shits* it out!'

He must have known that the part of young Luther's friend, the Vicar-General Staupitz, was a tentative tribute to a possibly romanticized account of our relationship, or my own view of it. The mentor's combination of sympathy and rigour spoke through Staupitz in a clear voice: 'I've never had any patience with all your mortifications. The only wonder is that you haven't killed yourself with your prayers, and watchings, yes, and even your reading too. All those trials and temptations you go through, they're meat and drink to you.'

How right he was.

From *Almost a Gentleman*,
by John Osborne (Faber and Faber, 1991)

LUTHER

CHARACTERS

KNIGHT
PRIOR
MARTIN
HANS
LUCAS
WEINAND
TETZEL
STAUPITZ
CAJETAN
MILTITZ
LEO
ECK
KATHERINE
HANS, THE YOUNGER
AUGUSTINIANS, DOMINICANS,
HERALD, EMPEROR, PEASANTS, ETC.

CONTENTS

ACT ONE

ACT TWO

ACT THREE

NOTE

At the opening of each act, the Knight appears. He grasps a banner and briefly barks the time and place of the scene following at the audience, and then retires.

The first performance of *Luther* was given at the Theatre Royal, Nottingham, on June 26th, 1961, by the English Stage Company. It was directed by Tony Richardson and the décor was by Jocelyn Herbert. The part of Luther was played by Albert Finney.

ACT ONE

SCENE ONE

The Cloister Chapel of the Eremites of St. Augustine. Erfurt, Thuringia, 1506. MARTIN *is being received into the Order. He is kneeling in front of the* PRIOR *in the presence of the assembled convent.*

PRIOR: Now you must choose one of two ways: either to leave us now, or give up this world, and consecrate and devote yourself entirely to God and our Order. But I must add this: once you have committed yourself, you are not free, for whatever reason, to throw off the yoke of obedience, for you will have accepted it freely, while you were still able to discard it.

(The habit and hood of the Order are brought in and blessed by the PRIOR.*)*

PRIOR: He whom it was your will to dress in the garb of the Order, oh Lord, invest him also with eternal life.

(He undresses MARTIN.*)*

The Lord divest you of the former man and of all his works. The Lord invest you with the new man.

(The CHOIR *sings as* MARTIN *is robed in the habit and hood. The long white scapular is thrown over his head and hung down, before and behind; then he kneels again before the* PRIOR*, and, with his hand on the statutes of the Order, swears the oath.)*

MARTIN: I, brother Martin, do make profession and promise obedience to Almighty God, to Mary the Sacred Virgin, and to you, my brother Prior of this cloister, in the name of the Vicar General of the order of Eremites of the holy Bishop of St. Augustine and his successors, to live without property and in chastity according to the Rule of our Venerable Father Augustine until death.

(The PRIOR *wishes a prayer over him, and* MARTIN *prostrates himself with arms extended in the form of a cross.)*

PRIOR: Lord Jesus Christ, our leader and our strength, by the fire of humility you have set aside this servant, Martin, from the rest of Mankind. We humbly pray that this fire will also cut him off from carnal intercourse and from the community of those things done on earth by men, through the sanctity shed from heaven upon him, and that you will bestow on him grace to remain yours, and merit eternal life. For it is not he who begins, but he who endures will be saved. Amen.

(*The* CHOIR *sings Veni Creator Spiritus (or perhaps Great Father Augustine). A newly lighted taper is put into* MARTIN'S *hands, and he is led up the altar steps to be welcomed by the monks with the kiss of peace. Then, in their midst, he marches slowly with them behind the screen and is lost to sight.*

The procession disappears, and, as the sound of voices dies away, two men are left alone in the congregation. One of them, HANS, *gets up impatiently and moves down-stage. It is* MARTIN'S FATHER, *a stocky man wired throughout with a miner's muscle, lower-middle class, on his way to become a small, primitive capitalist; bewildered, full of pride and resentment. His companion,* LUCAS, *finishes a respectful prayer and joins him.*)

HANS: Well?

LUCAS: Well?

HANS: Don't 'well' me you feeble old ninny, what do you think?

LUCAS: Think? Of what?

HANS: Yes, think man, think, what do you think, pen and ink, think of all that?

LUCAS: Oh –

HANS: Oh! Of all these monks, of Martin and all the rest of it, what do you think? You've been sitting in this arse-aching congregation all this time, you've been watching, haven't you? What about it?

LUCAS: Yes, well, I must say it's all very impressive.

HANS: Oh, yes?

LUCAS: No getting away from it.

HANS: Impressive?

LUCAS: Deeply. It was moving and oh –

HANS: What?

LUCAS: You must have felt it, surely. You couldn't fail to.

HANS: Impressive! I don't know what impresses me any longer.

LUCAS: Oh, come on –

HANS: Impressive!

LUCAS: Of course it is, and you know it.

HANS: Oh, you – you can afford to be impressed.

LUCAS: It's surely too late for any regrets, or bitterness, Hans. It obviously must be God's will, and there's an end of it.

HANS: That's exactly what it is – an end of it! Very fine for you, my old friend, very fine indeed. You're just losing a son-in-law, and you can take your pick of plenty more of those where he comes from. But what am I losing? I'm losing a son; mark: a son.

LUCAS: How can you say that?

HANS: How can I say it? I do say it, that's how. Two sons to the plague, and now another. God's eyes! Did you see that haircut? Brother Martin!

LUCAS: There isn't a finer order than these people, not the Dominicans or Franciscans –

HANS: Like an egg with a beard.

LUCAS: You said that yourself.

HANS: Oh, I suppose they're Christians under their damned cowls.

LUCAS: There are good, distinguished men in this place, and well you know it.

HANS: Yes – good, distinguished men –

LUCAS: Pious, learned men, men from the University like Martin.

HANS: Learned men! Some of them can't read their own names.

LUCAS: So?

HANS: So! I – I'm a miner. I don't need books. You can't see to read books under the ground. But Martin's a scholar.

LUCAS: He most certainly is.

HANS: A Master of Arts! What's he master of now? Eh? Tell me.

LUCAS: Well, there it is. God's gain is your loss.

HANS: Half these monks do nothing but wash dishes and beg in the streets.

LUCAS: We should be going, I suppose.

HANS: He could have been a man of stature.

LUCAS: And he will, with God's help.

HANS: Don't tell me. He could have been a lawyer.

LUCAS: Well, he won't now.

HANS: No, you're damn right he won't. Of stature. To the Archbishop, or the Duke, or –

LUCAS: Yes.

HANS: Anyone.

LUCAS: Come on.

HANS: Anyone you can think of.

LUCAS: Well, I'm going.

HANS: Brother Martin!

LUCAS: Hans.

HANS: Do you know why? Lucas: Why? What made him do it?
(*He has ceased to play a role by this time and he asks the question simply as if he expected a short, direct answer.*)
What made him do it?
(*LUCAS grasps his forearm.*)

LUCAS: Let's go home.

HANS: Why? That's what I can't understand. Why? Why?

LUCAS: Home. Let's go home.
(*They go off. The convent bell rings. Some monks are standing at a refectory table. After their prayers, they sit down, and, as they eat in silence, one of the Brothers reads from a lectern. During this short scene, MARTIN, wearing a rough apron over his habit, waits on the others.*)

READER: What are the tools of Good Works?
First, to love Lord God with all one's heart, all one's soul, and all one's strength. Then, one's neighbour as oneself. Then not to kill.

    Not to commit adultery
    Not to steal
    Not to covet
    Not to bear false witness

To honour all men
To deny yourself, in order to follow Christ
To chastise the body
Not to seek soft living
To love fasting
To clothe the naked
To visit the sick
To bury the dead
To help the afflicted
To console the sorrowing
To prefer nothing to the love of Christ

Not to yield to anger
Not to nurse a grudge
Not to hold guile in your heart
Not to make a feigned peace
To fear the Day of Judgment
To dread Hell
To desire eternal life with all your spiritual longing
To keep death daily before your eyes
To keep constant vigilance over the actions of your life
To know for certain that God sees you everywhere
When evil thoughts come into your heart, to dash them
at once on the love of Christ and to manifest them to
your spiritual father
To keep your mouth from evil and depraved talk
Not to love much speaking
Not to speak vain words or such as produce laughter
To listen gladly to holy readings
To apply yourself frequently to prayer
Daily in your prayer, with tears and sighs to confess your
past sins to God
Not to fulfil the desires of the flesh
To hate your own will

Behold, these are the tools of the spiritual craft. If we
employ these unceasingly day and night, and render
account of them on the Day of Judgment, then we shall

receive from the Lord in return that reward that He
Himself has promised: Eye hath not seen nor ear heard
what God hath prepared for those that love him. Now this
is the workshop in which we shall diligently execute all
these tasks. May God grant that you observe all these rules
cheerfully as lovers of spiritual beauty, spreading around
you by the piety of your deportment the sweet odour of
Christ.

(*The convent bell rings. The* MONKS *rise, bow their heads in
prayer, and then move upstage to the steps where they kneel.*
MARTIN, *assisted by another brother, stacks the table and clears
it. Presently, they all prostrate themselves, and, beneath flaming
candles, a communal confession begins.* MARTIN *returns and
prostrates himself downstage behind the rest. This scene
throughout is urgent, muted, almost whispered, confidential,
secret, like a prayer.*)

BROTHER: I confess to God, to Blessed Mary and our holy
Father Augustine, to all the saints, and to all present that I
have sinned exceedingly in thought, word and deed by my
own fault. Wherefore I pray Holy Mary, all the saints of
God and you all assembled here to pray for me. I confess I
did leave my cell for the Night Office without the Scapular
and had to return for it. Which is a deadly infringement of
the first degree of humility, that of obedience without
delay. For this failure to Christ I abjectly seek forgiveness
and whatever punishment the Prior and community is
pleased to impose on me.

MARTIN: I am a worm and no man, a byword and a laughing
stock. Crush out the worminess in me, stamp on me.

BROTHER: I confess I have three times made mistakes in the
Oratory, in psalm singing and Antiphon.

MARTIN: I was fighting a bear in a garden without flowers,
leading into a desert. His claws kept making my arms bleed
as I tried to open a gate which would take me out. But the
gate was no gate at all. It was simply an open frame, and I
could have walked through it, but I was covered in my own
blood, and I saw a naked woman riding on a goat, and the
goat began to drink my blood, and I thought I should faint

with the pain and I awoke in my cell, all soaking in the devil's bath.

BROTHER: Let Brother Norbert remember also his breakage while working in the kitchen.

BROTHER: I remember it, and confess humbly.

BROTHER: Let him remember also his greater transgression in not coming at once to the Prior and community to do penance for it, and so increasing his offence.

MARTIN: I am alone. I am alone, and against myself.

BROTHER: I confess it. I confess it, and beg your prayers that I may undergo the greater punishment for it.

MARTIN: How can I justify myself?

BROTHER: Take heart, you shall be punished, and severely.

MARTIN: How can I be justified?

BROTHER: I confess I have failed to rise from my bed speedily enough. I arrived at the Night Office after the Gloria of the 94th Psalm, and though I seemed to amend the shame by not standing in my proper place in the choir, and standing in the place appointed by the Prior for such careless sinners so that they may be seen by all, my fault is too great and I seek punishment.

MARTIN: I was among a group of people, men and women, fully clothed. We lay on top of each other in neat rows about seven or eight across. Eventually, the pile was many people deep. Suddenly, I panicked – although I was on top of the pile – and I cried: what about those underneath? Those at the very bottom, and those in between? We all got up in an orderly way, without haste, and when we looked, those at the bottom were not simply flattened by the weight, they were just their clothes, they were just their clothes, neatly pressed and folded on the ground. They were their clothes, neatly pressed and folded on the ground.

BROTHER: I did omit to have a candle ready at the Mass.

BROTHER: Twice in my sloth, I have omitted to shave, and even excused myself, pretending to believe my skin to be fairer than that of my Brothers, and my beard lighter and my burden also. I have been vain and slothful, and I beg forgiveness and ask penance.

MARTIN: If my flesh would leak and dissolve, and I could live as bone, if I were forged bone, plucked bone and brain, warm hair and a bony heart, if I were all bone, I could brandish myself without terror, without any terror at all – I could be indestructible.

BROTHER: I did ask for a bath, pretending to myself that it was necessary for my health, but as I lowered my body into the tub, it came to me that it was inordinate desire and that it was my soul that was soiled.

MARTIN: My bones fail. My bones fail, my bones are shattered and fall away, my bones fail and all that's left of me is a scraped marrow and a dying jelly.

BROTHER: Let Brother Paulinus remember our visit to our near sister house, and lifting his eyes repeatedly at a woman in the town who dropped alms into his bag.

BROTHER: I remember, and I beg forgiveness.

BROTHER: Then let him remember also that though our dear Father Augustine does not forbid us to see women, he blames us if we should desire them or wish to be the object of their desire. For it is not only by touch and by being affectionate that a man excites disorderly affection in a woman. This can be done also even by looks. You cannot maintain that your mind is pure if you have *wanton* eyes. For a wanton eye is a wanton heart. When people with impure hearts manifest their inclinations towards each other through the medium of looks, even though no word is spoken, and when they take pleasure in their desire for each other, the purity of their character has gone even though they may be undefiled by any unchaste act. He who fixes his eyes on a woman and takes pleasure in her glance, must not think that he goes unobserved by his brothers.

MARTIN: I confess that I have offended grievously against humility, being sometimes discontented with the meanest and worst of everything. I have not only failed to declare myself to myself lower and lower and of less account than all other men, but I have failed in my most inmost heart to believe it. For many weeks, many weeks it seemed to me, I was put to cleaning the latrines. I did it, and I did it vigorously, not tepidly, with all my poor strength, without whispering or objections to anyone. But although I fulfilled my task, and I did it well, sometimes there were murmurings in my heart. I prayed that it would cease, knowing that God, seeing my murmuring heart, must reject my work, and it was as good as not done. I sought out my master, and he punished me, telling me to fast for two days. I have fasted for three, but, even so, I can't tell if the murmurings are really gone, and I ask for your prayers, and I ask for your prayers that I may be able to go on fulfilling the same task.

BROTHER: Let Brother Martin remember all the degrees of humility; and let him go on cleaning the latrines.

(*The convent bell rings. After lying prostrate for a few moments, all the* BROTHERS, *including* MARTIN, *rise and move to the* CHOIR. *The office begins, versicle, antiphon and psalm, and* MARTIN *is lost to sight in the ranks of his fellow* MONKS. *Presently, there is a quiet, violent moaning, just distinguishable amongst the voices. It becomes louder and wilder, the cries more violent, and there is some confusion in* MARTIN'S *section of the* CHOIR. *The singing goes on with only a few heads turned. It seems as though the disturbance has subsided.* MARTIN *appears, and staggers between the stalls. Outstretched hands fail to restrain him, and he is visible to all, muscles rigid, breath suspended, then jerking uncontrollably as he is seized in a raging fit. Two* BROTHERS *go to him, but* MARTIN *writhes with such ferocity, that they can scarcely hold him down. He tries to speak, the effort is frantic, and eventually, he is able to roar out a word at a time.*)

MARTIN: Not! Me! I am *not*!

(*The attack reaches its height, and he recoils as if he had bitten his tongue and his mouth were full of blood and saliva. Two more* MONKS *come to help, and he almost breaks away from them, but the effort collapses, and they are able to drag him away, as he is about to vomit. The Office continues as if nothing had taken place.*)

(*End of Act One – Scene One.*)

A knife, like a butcher's, hanging aloft, the size of a garden fence.
The cutting edge of the blade points upwards. Across it hangs the
torso of a naked man, his head hanging down. Below it, an
enormous round cone, like the inside of a vast barrel, surrounded by
darkness. From the upstage entrance, seemingly far, far away, a
dark figure appears against the blinding light inside, as it grows
brighter. The figure approaches slowly along the floor of the vast
cone, and stops as it reaches the downstage opening. It is MARTIN,
haggard and streaming with sweat.

MARTIN: I lost the body of a child, a child's body, the eyes of a
child; and at the first sound of my own childish voice. I lost
the body of a child; and I was afraid, and I went back to
find it. But I'm still afraid. I'm afraid, and there's an end of
it! But *I* mean . . . (*Shouts.*) . . . Continually! For instance
of the noise the Prior's dog makes on a still evening when
he rolls over on his side and licks his teeth. I'm afraid of
the darkness, and the hole in it; and I see it sometime of
every day! And some days more than once even, and
there's no bottom to it, no bottom to my breath, and I
can't reach it. Why? Why do you think? There's a bare fist
clenched to my bowels and they can't move, and I have to
sit sweating in my little monk's house to open them. The
lost body of a child, hanging on a mother's tit, and close to
the warm, big body of a man, and I can't find it.
(*He steps down, out of the blazing light within the cone, and*
goes to his cell down L. *Kneeling by his bed, he starts to try and*
pray but he soon collapses. From down R. *appears a procession*
of MONKS, *carrying various priest's vestments, candles and*
articles for the altar, for MARTIN *is about to perform his very*
first Mass. Heading them is BROTHER WEINAND. *They pass*
MARTIN'S *cell, and, after a few words, they go on, leaving*
BROTHER WEINAND *with* MARTIN, *and disappear into what*
is almost like a small house on the upstage left of the stage: a
bagpipe of the period, fat, soft, foolish and obscene looking.)

BRO. WEINAND: Brother Martin! Brother Martin!

MARTIN: Yes.

BRO. WEINAND: Your father's here.

MARTIN: My father?

BRO. WEINAND: He asked to see you, but I told him it'd be
  better to wait until afterwards.

MARTIN: Where is he?

BRO. WEINAND: He's having breakfast with the Prior.

MARTIN: Is he alone?

BRO. WEINAND: No, he's got a couple of dozen friends at least,
  I should say.

MARTIN: Is my mother with him?

BRO. WEINAND: No.

MARTIN: What did he have to come for? I should have told him
  not to come.

BRO. WEINAND: It'd be a strange father who didn't want to be
  present when his son celebrated his first Mass.

MARTIN: I never thought he'd come. Why didn't he tell me?

BRO. WEINAND: Well, he's here now, anyway. He's also given
  twenty guilden to the chapter as a present, so he can't be
  too displeased with you. ·

MARTIN: Twenty guilden.

BRO. WEINAND: Well, are you all prepared?

MARTIN: That's three times what it cost him to send me to the
  University for a year.

BRO. WEINAND: You don't look it. Why, you're running all
  over with sweat again. Are you sick? Are you?

MARTIN: No.

BRO. WEINAND: Here, let me wipe your face. You haven't
  much time. You're sure you're not sick?

MARTIN: My bowels won't move, that's all. But that's nothing
  out of the way.

BRO. WEINAND: Have you shaved?

MARTIN: Yes. Before I went to confession. Why, do you think I
  should shave again?

BRO. WEINAND: No. I don't. A few overlooked little bristles
  couldn't make that much difference, any more than a few
  imaginary sins. There, that's better.

MARTIN: What do you mean?

BRO. WEINAND: You were sweating like a pig in a butcher's

shop. You know what they say, don't you? Wherever you find a melancholy person, there you'll find a bath running for the devil.

MARTIN: No, no, what did you mean about leaving a few imaginary sins?

BRO. WEINAND: I mean there are plenty of priests with dirty ears administering the sacraments, but this isn't the time to talk about that. Come on, Martin, you've got nothing to be afraid of.

MARTIN: How do you know?

BRO. WEINAND: You always talk as if lightning were just about to strike behind you.

MARTIN: Tell me what you meant.

BRO. WEINAND: I only meant the whole convent knows you're always making up sins you've never committed. That's right – well, isn't it? No sensible confessor will have anything to do with you.

MARTIN: What's the use of all this talk of penitence if I can't feel it?

BRO. WEINAND: Father Nathin told me he had to punish you only the day before yesterday because you were in some ridiculous state of hysteria, all over some verse in Proverbs or something.

MARTIN: "Know thou the state of thy flocks."

BRO. WEINAND: And all over the interpretation of one word apparently. When will you ever learn? Some of the brothers laugh quite openly at you, you and your over-stimulated conscience. Which is wrong of them, I know, but you must be able to see why?

MARTIN: It's the single words that trouble me.

BRO. WEINAND: The moment you've confessed and turned to the altar, you're beckoning for a priest again. Why, every time you break wind they say you rush to a confessor.

MARTIN: Do they say that?

BRO. WEINAND: It's their favourite joke.

MARTIN: They say that, do they?

BRO. WEINAND: Martin! You're protected from many of the

world's evils here. You're expected to master them, not be obsessed by them. God bids us hope in His everlasting mercy. Try to remember that.

MARTIN: And you tell me this! What have I gained from coming into this sacred Order? Aren't I still the same? I'm still envious, I'm still impatient, I'm still passionate?

BRO. WEINAND: How can you ask a question like that?

MARTIN: I do ask it. I'm asking you! What have I gained?

BRO. WEINAND: In any of this, all we can ever learn is how to die.

MARTIN: That's no answer.

BRO. WEINAND: It's the only one I can think of at this moment. Come on.

MARTIN: All you teach me in this sacred place is how to doubt –

BRO. WEINAND: Give you a little praise, and you're pleased for a while, but let a little trial of sin and death come into your day and you crumble, don't you?

MARTIN: But that's all you've taught me, that's really all you've taught me, and all the while I'm living in the Devil's worm-bag.

BRO. WEINAND: It hurts me to watch you like this, sucking up cares like a leech.

MARTIN: You *will* be there beside me, won't you?

BRO. WEINAND: Of course, and, if anything at all goes wrong, or if you forget anything, we'll see to it. You'll be all right. But nothing will – you won't make any mistakes.

MARTIN: But what if I do, just one mistake. Just a word, one word – one sin.

BRO. WEINAND: Martin, kneel down.

MARTIN: Forgive me, Brother Weinand, but the truth is this –

BRO. WEINAND: Kneel.

(MARTIN *kneels.*)

MARTIN: It's this, just this. All I can feel, all I can feel is God's hatred.

BRO. WEINAND: Repeat the Apostles' Creed.

MARTIN: He's like a glutton, the way he gorges me, he's a glutton. He gorges me, and then spits me out in lumps.

17

BRO. WEINAND: After me. 'I believe in God the Father
  Almighty, maker of Heaven and Earth . . .
MARTIN: I'm a trough, I tell you, and he's swilling about in me.
  All the time.
BRO. WEINAND: 'And in Jesus Christ, His only Son Our
  Lord . . .
MARTIN: 'And in Jesus Christ, His only Son Our Lord . . .
BRO. WEINAND: 'Who was conceived by the Holy Ghost, born
  of the Virgin Mary, suffered under Pontius Pilate . . .
MARTIN: (*Almost unintelligibly*) 'Was crucified, dead and buried;
  He descended into Hell; the third day He rose from the
  dead. He ascended into Heaven, and sitteth on the right
  hand of God the Father Almighty; from thence He shall
  come to judge the quick and the dead.' And every sunrise
  sings a song for death.
BRO. WEINAND: 'I believe –
MARTIN: 'I believe –
BRO. WEINAND: Go on.
MARTIN: 'I believe in the Holy Ghost; the holy Catholic
  Church; the Communion of Saints; the forgiveness of
  sins;
BRO. WEINAND: Again!
MARTIN: The forgiveness of sins.
BRO. WEINAND: What was that again?
MARTIN: I believe in the forgiveness of sins.
BRO. WEINAND: Do you? Then remember this: St. Bernard
  says that when we say in the Apostles' Creed 'I believe in
  the forgiveness of sins' each one must believe that *his* sins
  are forgiven. Well? –
MARTIN: I wish my bowels would open. I'm blocked up like an
  old crypt.
BRO. WEINAND: Try to remember, Martin?
MARTIN: Yes, I'll try.
BRO. WEINAND: Good. Now, you must get yourself ready.
  Come on, we'd better help you.
  (*Some* BROTHERS *appear from out of the bagpipe with the
  vestments, etc. and help* MARTIN *put them on.*)
MARTIN: How much did you say my father gave to the chapter?

BRO. WEINAND: Twenty guilden.

MARTIN: That's a lot of money to my father. He's a miner, you know.

BRO. WEINAND: Yes, he told me.

MARTIN: As tough as you can think of. Where's he sitting?

BRO. WEINAND: Near the front. I should think. Are you nearly ready?

(*The Convent bell rings. A procession leads out from the bagpipe.*)

MARTIN: Thank you, Brother Weinand.

BRO. WEINAND: For what? Today would be an ordeal for any kind of man. In a short while, you will be handling, for the first time, the body and blood of Christ. God bless you, my son.

(*He makes the sign of the cross, and the other* BROTHERS *leave.*)

MARTIN: Somewhere, in the body of a child, Satan foresaw in me what I'm suffering now. That's why he prepares open pits for me, and all kinds of tricks to bring me down, so that I keep wondering if I'm the only man living who's baited, and surrounded by dreams, and afraid to move.

BRO. WEINAND: (*Really angry by now*) You're a fool. You're really a fool. God isn't angry with you. It's you who are angry with Him.

(*He goes out. The* BROTHERS *wait for* MARTIN, *who kneels.*)

MARTIN: Oh, Mary, dear Mary, all I see of Christ is a flame and raging on a rainbow. Pray to your Son, and ask Him to still His anger, for I can't raise my eyes to look at Him. Am I the only one to see all this, and suffer?

(*He rises, joins the procession and disappears off with it. As the Mass is heard to begin offstage, the stage is empty. Then the light within the cone grows increasingly brilliant, and, presently* MARTIN *appears again. He enters through the far entrance of the cone, and advances towards the audience. He is carrying a naked child. Presently, he steps down from the cone, comes downstage, and stands still.*)

MARTIN: And so, the praising ended – and the blasphemy began.

(*He returns, back into the cone, the light fades as the Mass comes to its end.*)
(*End of Act One – Scene Two.*)

SCENE THREE

The Convent refectory. Some monks are sitting at table with HANS *and* LUCAS. LUCAS *is chatting with the* BROTHERS *eagerly, but* HANS *is brooding. He has drunk a lot of wine in a short time, and his brain is beginning to heat.*

HANS: What about some more of this, eh? Don't think you can get away with it, you know, you old cockchafer. I'm getting me twenty guilden's worth before the day's out. After all, it's a proud day for all of us. That's right, isn't it?

LUCAS: It certainly is.

BRO. WEINAND: Forgive me, I wasn't looking. Here –
(*He fills* HANS'S *glass.*)

HANS: (*Trying to be friendly*) Don't give me that. You monks don't miss much. Got eyes like gimlets and ears like open drains. Tell me – Come on, then, what's your opinion of Brother Martin?

BRO. WEINAND: He's a good, devout monk.

HANS: Yes. Yes, well, I suppose you can't say much about each other, can you? You're more like a team, in a way. Tell me, Brother – would you say that in this monastery – or, any monastery you like – you were as strong as the weakest member of the team?

BRO. WEINAND: No, I don't think that's so.

HANS: But wouldn't you say then – I'm not saying this in any criticism, mind, but because I'm just interested, naturally, in the circumstances – but wouldn't you say that one bad monk, say for instance, one really monster sized, roaring great bitch of a monk, if he really got going, really going, couldn't he get his order such a reputation that eventually, it might even have to go into – what do they call it now – liquidation. That's it. Liquidation. Now, you're an educated man, you understand Latin and Greek and Hebrew –

BRO. WEINAND: Only Latin, I'm afraid, and a very little Greek.

HANS: (*Having planted his cue for a quick, innocent boast*) Oh, really. Martin knows Latin and Greek, and now he's half-way through Hebrew too, they tell me.

BRO. WEINAND: Martin is a brilliant man. We are not all as gifted as he is.

HANS: No, well, anyway what would be your opinion about this?

BRO. WEINAND: I think my opinion would be that the Church is bigger than those who are in her.

HANS: Yes, yes, but don't you think it could be discredited by, say, just a few men?

BRO. WEINAND: Plenty of people have tried, but the Church is still there. Besides, a human voice is small and the world's very large. But the Church reaches out and is heard everywhere.

HANS: Well, what about this chap Erasmus, for instance?

BRO. WEINAND: (*Politely. He knows* HANS *knows nothing about him*) Yes?

HANS: Erasmus. (*Trying to pass the ball.*) Well, what about *him*, for instance? What do you think about him?

BRO. WEINAND: Erasmus is apparently a great scholar, and respected throughout Europe.

HANS: (*Resenting being lectured*) Yes, of course, *I* know who he is, I don't need you to tell me that, what I said was: what do you think about him?

BRO. WEINAND: Think about him?

HANS: Good God, you won't stand still a minute and let yourself be saddled, will you? Doesn't he criticize the Church or something?

BRO. WEINAND: He's a scholar, and, I should say, his criticisms could only be profitably argued about by other scholars.

LUCAS: Don't let him get you into an argument. He'll argue about anything, especially if he doesn't know what he's talking about.

HANS: I know what I'm talking about, I was merely asking a question –

LUCAS: Well, you should be asking questions on a day like today. Just think of it, for a minute, Hans –

HANS: What do you think I'm doing? You soppy old woman!

LUCAS: It's a really 'once only' occasion, like a wedding, if you like.

HANS: Or a funeral. By the way, what's happened to the corpse? Eh? Where's Brother Martin?

BRO. WEINAND: I expect he's still in his cell.

HANS: Well, what's he doing in there?

BRO. WEINAND: He's perfectly all right, he's a little – disturbed.

HANS: (*Pouncing delightedly*) Disturbed! Disturbed! What's he disturbed about?

BRO. WEINAND: Celebrating one's first Mass can be a great ordeal for a sensitive spirit.

HANS: Oh, the bread and the wine and all that?

BRO. WEINAND: Of course; there are a great many things to memorize as well.

LUCAS: Heavens, yes. I don't know how they think of it all.

HANS: I didn't think he made it up as he went along! But doesn't he know we're still here? Hasn't anybody told him we're all waiting for him?

BRO. WEINAND: He won't be much longer – you see. Here, have some more of our wine. He simply wanted to be on his own for a little while before he saw anyone.

HANS: I should have thought he had enough of being on his own by now.

LUCAS: The boy's probably a bit – well, you know, anxious about seeing you again too.

HANS: What's he got to be anxious about?

LUCAS: Well, apart from anything else, it's nearly three years since he last saw you.

HANS: I saw *him*. He didn't see me.

(*Enter* MARTIN.)

LUCAS: There you are, my boy. We were wondering what had happened to you. Come and sit down, there's a good lad. Your father and I have been punishing the convent wine cellar, I'm afraid. Bit early in the day for me, too.

HANS: Speak for yourself, you swirly-eyed old gander. We're
    not *started* yet, are we?

LUCAS: My dear boy, are you all right? You're so pale.

HANS: He's right though. Brother Martin! Brother Lazarus they
    ought to call you!
    (*He laughs and* MARTIN *smiles at the joke with him.* MARTIN
    is cautious, HANS *too, but manoeuvring for position.*)

MARTIN: I'm all right, thank you. Lucas.

HANS: Been sick, have you?

MARTIN: I'm much better now, thank you, father.

HANS: (*Relentless*) Upset tummy, is it? That's what it is? Too
    much fasting I expect. (*Concealing concern.*) You look like
    death warmed up, all right.

LUCAS: Come and have a little wine. You're allowed that, aren't
    you? It'll make you feel better.

HANS: I know that milky look. I've seen it too many times. Been
    sick have you?

LUCAS: Oh, he's looking better already. Drop of wine'll put the
    colour back in there. You're all right, aren't you, lad?

MARTIN: Yes, what about you –

LUCAS: That's right. Of course he is. He's all right.

HANS: Vomit all over your cell, I expect. (*To* BROTHER
    WEINAND.) But he'll have to clear that up himself, won't
    he?

LUCAS: (*To* MARTIN) Oh you weren't were you? Poor old lad,
    well, never mind, no wonder you kept us waiting.

HANS: Can't have his mother coming in and getting down on
    her knees to mop it all up.

MARTIN: I managed to clean it up all right. How are *you*,
    father?

HANS: (*Feeling an attack, but determined not to lose the initiative*)
    Me? Oh, I'm all right. I'm all right, aren't I, Lucas?
    Nothing ever wrong with me. Your old man's strong
    enough. But then that's because we've got to be, people
    like Lucas and me. Because if *we* aren't strong, it won't
    take any time at all before we're knocked flat on our backs,
    or flat on our knees, or flat on something or other. Flat on
    our backs and finished, and we can't afford to be finished

because if we're finished, that's it, that's the end, so we just
have to stand up to it as best we can. But that's life, isn't it?

MARTIN: I'm never sure what people mean when they say that.

LUCAS: Your father's doing very well indeed, Martin. He's got
his own investment in the mine now, so he's beginning to
work for himself if you see what I mean. That's the way
things are going everywhere now.

MARTIN: (*To* HANS) You must be pleased.

HANS: I'm pleased to make money. I'm pleased to break my
back doing it.

MARTIN: How's mother?

HANS: Nothing wrong there either. Too much work and too
many kids for too long, that's all. (*Hiding embarrassment.*)
I'm sorry she couldn't come, but it's a rotten journey as
you know, and all that, so she sent her love to you. Oh,
yes, and there was a pie too. But I was told (*at* BROTHER
WEINAND) I couldn't give it to you, but I'd have to give it
to the Prior.

MARTIN: That's the rule about gifts, father. You must have
forgotten?

HANS: Well, I hope you get a piece of it anyway. She took a lot
of care over it. Oh yes, and then there was Lucas's girl, she
asked to be remembered to you.

MARTIN: Oh, good. How is she?

HANS: Didn't she, Lucas? She asked specially to be
remembered to Martin, didn't she?

LUCAS: Oh she often talks about you, Martin. Even now. She's
married you know.

MARTIN: No, I didn't know.

LUCAS: Oh, yes, got two children, one boy and a girl.

HANS: That's it – two on show on the stall, and now another
one coming out from under the counter again – right,
Lucas?

LUCAS: Yes, oh, she makes a fine mother.

HANS: And what's better than that? There's only one way of
going 'up you' to Old Nick when he does come for you
and that's when you show him your kids. It's the one thing
– that is, if you've been lucky, and the plagues kept away

from you – you can spring it out from under the counter at him. *That* to you! Then you've done something for yourself forever – forever and ever. Amen. (*Pause.*) Come along, Brother Martin, don't let your guests go without. Poor old Lucas is sitting there with a glass as empty as a nun's womb, aren't you, you thirsty little goosey?

MARTIN: Oh, please, I'm sorry.

HANS: That's right, and don't forget your old dad. (*Pause.*) Yes, well, as I say, I'm sorry your mother couldn't come, but I don't suppose she'd have enjoyed it much, although I dare say she'd like to have watched her son perform the Holy Office. Isn't a mother supposed to dance with her son after the ceremony? Like Christ danced with *his* mother? Well, I can't see her doing that. I suppose you think *I'm* going to dance with you instead.

MARTIN: You're not obliged to, father.

HANS: It's like giving a bride away, isn't it?

MARTIN: Not unlike.

(*They have been avoiding any direct contact until now, but now they look at each other, and both relax a little.*)

HANS: (*Encouraged*) God's eyes! Come to think of it, you look like a woman, in all that!

MARTIN: (*With affection*) Not any woman you'd want, father.

HANS: What do *you* know about it, eh? Eh? What do you know about it? (*He laughs but not long.*) Well, Brother Martin.

MARTIN: Well? (*Pause.*) Have you had some fish? Or a roast, how about that, that's what you'd like, isn't it?

HANS: Brother Martin, old Brother Martin. Well, Brother Martin, you had a right old time up there by that altar for a bit, didn't you? I wouldn't have been in your shoes, I'll tell you. All those people listening to you, every word you're saying, watching every little tiny movement, watching for one little lousy mistake. I couldn't keep my eyes off it. We all thought you were going to flunk it for one minute there, didn't we, Lucas?

LUCAS: Well, we had a couple of anxious moments –

HANS: Anxious moments! I'll say there were. I thought to myself, 'he's going to flunk it, he can't get through it, he's

going to flunk it'. What was that bit, you know, the worst
bit where you stopped and Brother –

MARTIN: Weinand.

HANS: Weinand, yes, and he very kindly helped you up. He was
actually holding you up at one point, wasn't he?

MARTIN: Yes.

BRO. WEINAND: It happens often enough when a young priest
celebrates Mass for the first time.

HANS: Looked as though he didn't know if it was Christmas or
Wednesday. We thought the whole thing had come to a
standstill for a bit, didn't we? Everyone waiting and
nothing happening. What was that bit, Martin, what was it?

MARTIN: I don't remember.

HANS: Yes, you know, the bit you really flunked.

MARTIN: (*Rattling it off*) Receive, oh Holy Father, almighty and
eternal God, this spotless host, which I, thine unworthy
servant, offer unto thee for my own innumerable sins of
commission and omission, and for all here present and all
faithful Christians, living and dead, so that it may avail for
their salvation and everlasting life. When I entered the
monastery, I wanted to speak to God directly, you see.
Without any embarrassment, I wanted to speak to him
myself, but when it came to it, I dried up – as I always
have.

LUCAS: No, you didn't, Martin, it was only for a few moments,
besides –

MARTIN: Thanks to Brother Weinand. Father, why do you hate
me being here?

(HANS *is outraged at a direct question.*)

HANS: Eh? What do you mean? I don't hate you being here.

MARTIN: Try to give me a straight answer if you can, father. I
should like you to tell me.

HANS: What are you talking about, Brother Martin, you don't
know what you're talking about. You've not had enough
wine, that's your trouble.

MARTIN: And don't say I could have been a lawyer.

HANS: Well, so you could have been. You could have been
better than that. You could have been a burgomaster, you

could have been a magistrate you could have been a chancellor, you could have been anything! So what! I don't want to talk about it. What's the matter with you! Anyway, I certainly don't want to talk about it in front of complete strangers.

MARTIN: You make me sick.

HANS: Oh, do I? Well, thank you for that, Brother Martin! Thank you for the truth, anyway.

MARTIN: No, it isn't the truth. It isn't the truth at all. You're drinking too much wine – and I'm . . .

HANS: Drinking too much wine! I could drink this convent piss from here till Gabriel's horn – and from all accounts, that'll blow about next Thursday – so what's the difference? (*Pause.* HANS *drinks.*) Is this the wine you use? Is it? Well? I'm asking a straight question myself now. Is this the wine you use? (*To* MARTIN.) Here, have some.
(MARTIN *takes it and drinks.*)
You know what they say?

MARTIN: No, what do they say?

HANS: I'll tell you:
Bread thou art and wine thou art
And always shall remain so.
(*Pause.*)

MARTIN: My father didn't mean that. He's a very devout man, I know.
(*Some of the* BROTHERS *have got up to leave.*)
(*To* LUCAS.) Brother Weinand will show you over the convent. If you've finished, that is.

LUCAS: Yes, oh yes, I'd like that. Yes, I've had more than enough, thank you. Right, well, let's go, shall we, Brother Weinand? I'll come back for you, shall I. Hans, you'll stay here?

HANS: Just as you like.

LUCAS: (*To* MARTIN) You're looking a bit better now, lad. Good-bye, my boy, but I'll see you before I go, won't I?

MARTIN: Yes, of course.
(*They all go, leaving* MARTIN *and* HANS *alone together. Pause.*)

HANS: Martin, I didn't mean to embarrass you.

MARTIN: No, it was my fault.

HANS: Not in front of everyone.

MARTIN: I shouldn't have asked you a question like that. It was a shock to see you suddenly, after such a long time. Most of my day's spent in silence you see, except for the Office; and I enjoy the singing, as you know, but there's not much speaking, except to one's confessor. I'd almost forgotten what your voice sounded like.

HANS: Tell me, son – what made you get all snarled up like that in the Mass?

MARTIN: You're disappointed, aren't you?

HANS: I want to know, that's all. I'm a simple man, Martin, I'm no scholar, but I can understand all right. But you're a learned man, you speak Latin and Greek and Hebrew. You've been trained to remember ever since you were a tiny boy. Men like you don't just forget their words!

MARTIN: I don't understand what happened. I lifted up my head at the host, and, as I was speaking the words, I heard them as if it were the first time, and suddenly – (*Pause.*) they struck at my life.

HANS: I don't know. I really don't. Perhaps your father and mother are wrong, and God's right, after all. Perhaps. Whatever it is you've got to find, you could only find out by becoming a monk; maybe that's the answer.

MARTIN: But you don't believe that. Do you?

HANS: No; no I don't.

MARTIN: Then say what you mean.

HANS: All right, if that's what you want, I'll say just what I mean. I think a man murders himself in these places.

MARTIN: (*Retreating at once*) I am holy. I kill no one but myself.

HANS: I don't care. I tell you it gives me the creeps. And that's why I couldn't bring your mother, if you want to know.

MARTIN: The Gospels are the only mother I've ever had.

HANS: (*Triumphantly*) And haven't you ever read in the Gospels, don't you know what's written in there? 'Thou shalt honour thy father and thy mother.'

MARTIN: You're not understanding me, because you don't want to.

HANS: That's fine talk, oh yes, fine, holy talk, but it won't wash, Martin. It won't wash because you can't ever, however you try, you can't ever get away from your body because that's what you live in, and it's all you've got to die in, and you can't get away from the body of your father and your mother! We're bodies, Martin, and so are you, and we're bound together for always. But you're like every man who was ever born into this world, Martin. You'd like to pretend that you made yourself, that it was *you* who made you – and not the body of a woman and another man.

MARTIN: Churches, kings and fathers – why do they ask so much, and why do they all of them get so much more than they deserve?

HANS: You think so. Well, I think I deserve a little more than you've given me –

MARTIN: I've given you! I don't have to give you! I *am* –that's all I need to give to you. That's your big reward, and that's all you're ever going to get, and it's more than any father's got a right to. You wanted me to learn Latin, to be a Master of Arts, be a lawyer. All you want is me to justify *you*! Well, I can't, and, what's more, I won't. I can't even justify myself. So just stop asking me what have I accomplished, and what have I done for you. I've done all for you I'll ever do, and that's live and wait to die.

HANS: Why do you blame *me* for everything?

MARTIN: I don't blame you. I'm just not grateful, that's all.

HANS: Listen, I'm not a specially good man, I know, but I believe in God and in Jesus Christ, His Son, and the Church will look after me, and I can make some sort of life for myself that has a little joy in it somewhere. But where is your joy? You wrote to me once, when you were at the University that only Christ could light up the place you live in, but what's the point? What's the point if it turns out the place you're living in is just a hovel? Don't you think it mightn't be better not to see at all?

MARTIN: I'd rather be able to see.

HANS: You'd rather see!

MARTIN: You really are disappointed, aren't you? Go on.

HANS: And why? I see a young man, learned and full of life, my son, abusing his youth with fear and humiliation. You think you're facing up to it in here, but you're not; you're running away, you're running away and you can't help it.

MARTIN: If it's so easy in here, why do you think the rest of the world isn't knocking the gates down to get in?

HANS: Because they haven't given up, that's why.

MARTIN: Well, there it is: you think I've given up.

HANS: Yes, there it is. That damned monk's piss has given me a headache.

MARTIN: I'm sorry.

HANS: Yes, we're all sorry, and a lot of good it does any of us.

MARTIN: I suppose fathers and sons always disappoint each other.

HANS: I worked for you, I went without for you.

MARTIN: Well?

HANS: Well! (*Almost anxiously.*) And if I beat you fairly often, and pretty hard sometimes I suppose, it wasn't any more than any other boy, was it?

MARTIN: No.

HANS: What do you think it is makes you different? Other men are all right, aren't they? You were stubborn, you were always stubborn, you've always had to resist, haven't you?

MARTIN: You've disappointed me too, and not just a few times, but at some time of every day I ever remember hearing or seeing you, but, as you say, maybe that was also no different from any other boy. But I loved you the best. It was always *you* I wanted. I wanted your love more than anyone's, and if anyone was to hold me, I wanted it to be you. Funnily enough, my mother disappointed me the most, and I loved her less, much less. She made a gap which no one could have filled, but all she could do was make it bigger, bigger and more unbearable.

HANS: I don't know what any of that means; I really don't. I'd better be going, Martin. I think it's best; and I dare say you've got your various duties to perform.

MARTIN: She beat me once for stealing a nut, your wife. I remember it so well, she beat me until the blood came, I was so surprised to see it on my finger-tips; yes, stealing a nut, that's right. But that's not the point. I had corns on my backside already. Always before, when I was beaten for something, the pain seemed outside of me in some way, as if it belonged to the rest of the world, and not only me. But, on that day, for the first time, the pain belonged to me and no one else, it went no further than *my* body, bent between *my* knees and *my* chin.

HANS: You know what, Martin, I think you've always been scared – ever since you could get up off your knees and walk. You've been scared for the good reason that that's what you most like to be. Yes, I'll tell you. I'll tell you what! Like that day, that day when you were coming home from Erfurt, and the thunderstorm broke, and you were so piss-scared, you lay on the ground and cried out to St. Anne because you saw a bit of lightning and thought you'd seen a vision.

MARTIN: I saw it all right.

HANS: And you went and asked her to save you – on condition that you became a monk.

MARTIN: I saw it.

HANS: Did you? So it's still St. Anne is it? I thought you were blaming your mother and me for your damned monkery!

MARTIN: Perhaps I should.

HANS: And perhaps sometime you should have another little think about that heavenly vision that wangled you away into the cloister.

MARTIN: What's that?

HANS: I mean: I hope it really was a vision. I hope it wasn't a delusion and some trick of the devil's. I really hope so, because I can't bear to think of it otherwise. (*Pause.*) Good-bye son. I'm sorry we had to quarrel. It shouldn't have turned out like this at all today.
(*Pause.*)

MARTIN: Father – why did you give your consent?

HANS: What, to your monkery, you mean?

31

MARTIN: Yes. You could have refused, but why didn't you?
HANS: Well, when your two brothers died with the plague . . .
MARTIN: You gave me up for dead, didn't you?
HANS: Good-bye, son. Here – have a glass of holy wine.
(*He goes out.* MARTIN *stands, with the glass in his hand and looks into it. Then he drinks from it slowly, as if for the first time. He sits down at the table and sets the glass before him.*)
MARTIN: But – but what if it isn't true?
(*Curtain.*)
(*End of Act One.*)
DÉCOR NOTE
After the intense private interior of Act One, with its outer darkness and rich, personal objects, the physical effect from now on should be more intricate, general, less personal; sweeping, concerned with men in time rather than particular man in the unconscious; caricature not portraiture, like the popular woodcuts of the period, like DÜRER. Down by the apron in one corner there is now a heavily carved pulpit.

ACT TWO

SCENE ONE

The market place, Jüterbög, 1517. The sound of loud music, bells as a procession approaches the centre of the market place, which is covered in the banners of welcoming trade guilds. At the head of the slow-moving procession, with its lighted tapers and to the accompaniment of singing, prayers and the smoke of incense, is carried the Pontiff's bull of grace on a cushion and cloth of gold. Behind this the arms of the Pope and the Medici. After this, carrying a large red wooden cross, comes the focus of the procession, JOHN TETZEL, *Dominican, inquisitor and most famed and successful indulgence vendor of his day. He is splendidly equipped to be an ecclesiastical huckster, with alive, silver hair, the powerfully calculating voice, range and technique of a trained orator, the terrible, riveting charm of a dedicated professional able to winkle coppers out of the pockets of the poor and desperate.*

The red cross is taken from TETZEL *and established prominently behind him, and, from it are suspended the arms of the Pope.*

TETZEL: Are you wondering who I am, or what I am? Is there anyone here among you, any small child, any cripple, or any sick idiot who hasn't heard of me, and doesn't know why I am here? No? No? Well, speak up then if there is? What, no one? Do you all know me then? Do you all know who I am? If it's true, it's very good, and just as it should be. Just as it should be, and no more than that! However, however – just in case – just in case, mind, there is one blind, maimed midget among you today who can't hear, I will open his ears and wash them out with sacred soap for him! And, as for the rest of you. I know I can rely on you all to listen patiently while I instruct him. Is that right? Can I go on? I'm asking you, is that right, can I go on? I say 'can I go on'?
(Pause.)
Thank you. And what is there to tell this blind, maimed

33

midget who's down there somewhere among you? No, don't look round for him, you'll only scare him and then he'll lose his one great chance, and it's not likely to come again, or if it does come, maybe it'll be too late. Well, what's the good news on this bright day? What's the information you want? It's this! Who is this friar with his red cross? Who sent him, and what's he here for? Don't try to work it out for yourself because I'm going to tell you now, this very minute. I am John Tetzel, Dominican, inquisitor, sub-commissioner to the Archbishop of Mainz, and what I bring you is indulgences. Indulgences made possible by the red blood of Jesus Christ, and the red cross you see standing up here behind me is the standard of those who carry them. Look at it! Go on, look at it! What else do you see hanging from the red cross? Well, what do they look like? Why, it's the arms of his holiness, because why? Because it's him who sent me here. Yes, my friend, the Pope himself has sent me with indulgences for you! Fine, you say, but what are indulgences? And what are they to me? What are indulgences? They're only the most precious and noble of God's gifts to men, that's all they are! Before God, I tell you I wouldn't swap my privilege at this moment with that of St. Peter in Heaven because I've already saved more souls with my indulgences than he could ever have done with all his sermons. You think that's bragging, do you? Well, listen a little more carefully, my friend, because this concerns *you*! Just look at it this way. For every mortal sin you commit, the Church says that after confession and contrition, you've got to do penance – either in this life or in purgatory – for seven years. Seven years! Right? Are you with me? Good. Now then, how many mortal sins are committed by you – by you – in a single day? Just think for one moment: in one single day of your life. Do you know the answer? Oh, not so much as one a day. Very well then, how many in a month? How many in six months? How many in a year? And how many in a whole lifetime? Yes, you needn't shuffle your feet – it doesn't bear thinking about, does it? You couldn't even add up all those years without a merchant's clerk to do it for you! Try and add up all the years of torment piling up! What about it? And isn't there anything you can do about this terrible situation you're in? Do you really want to know? Yes! There is something, and that something I have here with me now up here, letters, letters of indulgence. Hold up the letters so that everyone can see them. Is there anyone so small he can't see? Look at them, all properly sealed, an indulgence in every envelope, and one of them can be yours today, now, before it's too late! Come on, come up as close as you like, you won't squash me so easily. Take a good look. There isn't any one sin so big that one of these letters can't remit it. I challenge any one here, one member of this audience, to present me with a sin, anything, any kind of a sin, I don't care what it is, that I can't settle for him with one of these precious little envelopes. Why, if any one had ever offered violence to the blessed Virgin Mary, Mother of God, if he'd only pay up – as long as he paid up all he could – he'd find himself forgiven. You think I'm exaggerating? You do, do you? Well, I'm authorized to go even further than that. Not only am I empowered to give you these letters of pardon for the sins you've already committed, I can give you pardon for those sins you haven't even committed (*pause . . . then slowly*) but, which, however you *intend* to commit! But, you ask – and it's a fair question – but, you ask, why is our Holy Lord prepared to distribute such a rich grace to me? The answer, my friends, is all too simple. It's so that we can restore the ruined church of St. Peter and St. Paul in Rome! So that it won't have its equal anywhere in the world. This great church contains the bodies not only of the holy apostles Peter and Paul, but of a hundred thousand martyrs and no less than forty-six popes! To say nothing of the relics like St. Veronica's handkerchief, the burning bush of Moses and the very rope with which Judas Iscariot hanged himself! But, alas, this fine old building is threatened with destruction, and all these things with it, if a sufficient restoration fund isn't raised, and raised soon. (*With passionate irony.*) . . . Will anyone dare to say that the cause is not a good one? (*Pause.*) . . . Very well, and won't you, for as little as one quarter of a florin, my friend, buy yourself one of these letters, so that in the hour of death, the gate through which sinners enter the world of torment shall be closed against you, and the gate leading to the joy of paradise be flung open for you? And, remember this, these letters aren't just for the living but for the dead too. There can't be one amongst you who hasn't at least one dear one who has departed – and to who knows what? Why, these letters are for them too. It isn't even necessary to repent. So don't hold back, come forward, think of your dear ones, think of yourselves! For twelve groats, or whatever it is we think you can afford, you can rescue your father from agony and yourself from certain disaster. And if you only have the coat on your back to call your own, then strip it off, strip it off now so that you too can obtain grace. For remember: As soon as your money rattles in the box and the cash bell rings, the soul flies out of purgatory and sings! So, come on then. Get your money out! What is it then, have your wits flown away with your faith? Listen then, soon, I shall take down the cross, shut the gates of heaven, and put out the brightness of this sun of grace that shines on you here today. (*He flings a large coin into the open strong box, where it rattles furiously.*)

The Lord our God reigns no longer. He has resigned all power to the Pope. In the name of the Father, and of the Son and of the Holy Ghost. Amen.

(*The sound of coins clattering like rain into a great coffer as the light fades.*)

(*End of Act Two – Scene One.*)

SCENE TWO

The Eremite Cloister, Wittenberg. 1517. Seated beneath a single pear tree is JOHANN VON STAUPITZ, *Vicar General of the Augustinian Order. He is a quiet, gentle-voiced man in late middle age, almost*

*stolidly contemplative. He has profound respect for Martin,
recognizing in him the powerful potential of insight, sensitivity,
courage and, also heroics that is quite outside the range of his own
endeavour. However, he also understands that a man of his own
limitations can offer a great deal to such a young man at this point in
his development, and his treatment of Martin is a successful
astringent mixture of sympathy and ridicule. Birds sing as he reads in
the shade, and* MARTIN *approaches, prostrating himself.* STAUPITZ
motions him to his feet.

MARTIN: (*Looking up*) The birds always seem to fly away the
    moment I come out here.

STAUPITZ: Birds, unfortunately, have no faith.

MARTIN: Perhaps it's simply that they don't like me.

STAUPITZ: They haven't learned yet that you mean them no
    harm, that's all.

MARTIN: Are you treating me to one of your allegories?

STAUPITZ: Well, you recognized it, anyway.

MARTIN: I ought to. Ever since I came into the cloister, I've
    become a craftsman allegory maker myself. Only last week
    I was lecturing on Galatians Three, verse three, and I
    allegorized going to the lavatory.

STAUPITZ: (*Quoting the verse*) 'Are ye so foolish, that ye have
    begun in the spirit, you would now end in the flesh.'

MARTIN: That's right. But allegories aren't much help in
    theology – except to decorate a house that's been already
    built by argument.

STAUPITZ: Well, it's a house you've been able to unlock for a
    great many of us. I never dreamed when I first came here
    that the University's reputation would ever become what it
    has, and in such a short time, and it's mostly due to you.

MARTIN: (*Very deliberately turning the compliment*) If ever a man
    could get to heaven through monkery, that man would be
    me.

STAUPITZ: I don't mean that. You know quite well what I
    mean. I'm talking about your scholarship, and what you
    manage to do with it, not your monkishness as you call it.
    I've never had any patience with all your mortifications.
    The only wonder is that you haven't killed yourself with

37

your prayers, and watchings, yes and even your reading too. All these trials and temptations you go through, they're meat and drink to you.

MARTIN: (*Patient*) Will you ever stop lecturing me about this?

STAUPITZ: Of course not, why do you think you come here – to see me in the garden when you could be inside working?

MARTIN: Well, if it'll please you, I've so little time, what with my lectures and study, I'm scarcely able to carry out even the basic requirements of the Rule.

STAUPITZ: I'm delighted to hear it. Why do you think you've always been obsessed with the Rule? No, I don't want to hear all your troubles again. I'll tell you why: you're obsessed with the Rule because it serves very nicely as a protection for you.

MARTIN: What protection?

STAUPITZ: You know perfectly well what I mean, Brother Martin, so don't pretend to look innocent. Protection against the demands of your own instincts, that's what. You see, you think you admire authority, and so you do, but unfortunately, you can't submit to it. So, what you do, by your exaggerated attention to the Rule, you make the authority ridiculous. And the reason you do that is because you're determined to substitute that authority with something else – yourself. Oh, come along, Martin, I've been Vicar General too long not to have made that little discovery. Anyway, you shouldn't be too concerned with a failing like that. It also provides the strongest kind of security.

MARTIN: Security? I don't feel *that*.

STAUPITZ: I dare say, but you've got it all the same, which is more than most of us have.

MARTIN: And how have I managed to come by this strange security?

STAUPITZ: Quite simply: by demanding an impossible standard of perfection.

MARTIN: I don't see what work or merit can come from a heart like mine.

STAUPITZ: Oh, my dear, dear friend, I've sworn a thousand

times to our holy God to live piously, and have I been able to keep my vows? No, of course I haven't. Now I've given up making solemn promises because I know I'm not able to keep them. If God won't be merciful to me for the love of Christ when I leave this world, then I shan't stand before Him on account of all my vows and good works, I shall perish, that's all.

MARTIN: You think I lavish too much attention on my own pain, don't you?

STAUPITZ: Well, that's difficult for me to say, Martin. We're very different kinds of men, you and I. Yes, you do lavish attention on yourself, but then a large man is worth the pains he takes. Like St. Paul, some men must say 'I die daily'.

MARTIN: Tell me, Father, have you never felt humiliated to find that you belong to a world that's dying?

STAUPITZ: No, I don't think I have.

MARTIN: Surely, this must be the last age of time we're living in. There can't be any more left but the black bottom of the bucket.

STAUPITZ: Do you mean the Last Judgment?

MARTIN: No. I don't mean that. The Last Judgment isn't to come. It's here and now.

STAUPITZ: Good. That's a little better, anyway.

MARTIN: I'm like a ripe stool in the world's straining anus, and at any moment we're about to let each other go.

STAUPITZ: There's nothing new in the world being damned, dying or without hope. It's always been like that, and it'll stay like it. What's the matter with you? What are you making funny faces for?

MARTIN: It's nothing, Father, just a – a slight discomfort.

STAUPITZ: Slight discomfort? What are you holding your stomach for? Are you in pain?

MARTIN: It's all right. It's gone now.

STAUPITZ: I don't understand you. What's gone now? I've seen you grabbing at yourself like that before. What is it?

MARTIN: I'm – constipated.

STAUPITZ: Constipated? There's always something the matter

with you, Brother Martin. If it's not the gripes, insomnia, or faith and works, it's boils or indigestion or some kind of belly-ache you've got. All these severe fasts –

MARTIN: That's what my father says.

STAUPITZ: Your father sounds pretty sensible to me.

MARTIN: He is, and you know, he's a theologian too. I've discovered lately.

STAUPITZ: I thought he was a miner.

MARTIN: So he is, but he made a discovery years and years ago that took me sweat and labour to dig out of the earth for myself.

STAUPITZ: Well, that's no surprise. There's always some chunk of truth buried down away somewhere which lesser men will always reach with less effort.

MARTIN: Anyway, he always knew that works alone don't save any man. Mind you, he never said anything about faith coming first.

STAUPITZ: (*Quoting*) 'Oh, well, that's life, and nothing you can do's going to change it.'

MARTIN: The same speech.

STAUPITZ: You can't change human nature.

MARTIN: Nor can you.

STAUPITZ: That's right, Martin, and you've demonstrated it only too well in your commentaries on the Gospels and St. Paul. But don't overlook the fact that your father's taken a vow of poverty too, even though it's very different from your own. And he took it the day he told himself and told *you*, that he was a complete man, or at least, a contented man.

MARTIN: A hog waffling in its own crap is contented.

STAUPITZ: Exactly.

MARTIN: My father, faced with an unfamiliar notion is like a cow staring at a new barn door. Like those who look on the cross and see nothing. All they hear is the priest's forgiveness.

STAUPITZ: One thing I promise you, Martin. You'll never be a spectator. You'll always take part.

MARTIN: How is it you always manage somehow to comfort me?

STAUPITZ: I think some of us are not much more than pretty
modest sponges, but we're probably best at quenching big
thirsts. How's your tummy?

MARTIN: Better.

STAUPITZ: One mustn't be truly penitent because one
anticipates God's forgiveness, but because one already
possesses it. You have to sink to the bottom of your black
bucket because that's where God judges you, and then
look to the wounds of Jesus Christ. You told me once that
when you entered the cloister, your father said it was like
giving away a bride, and again your father was right. You
are a bride and you should hold yourself ready like a
woman at conception. And when grace comes and your
soul is penetrated by the spirit, you shouldn't pray or exert
yourself, but remain passive.

MARTIN: (*Smiles*) That's a hard role.

STAUPITZ: (*Smiles too*) Too hard for you, I dare say. Did you
know the Duke's been complaining to me about you?

MARTIN: Why, what have I done?

STAUPITZ: Preaching against indulgences again.

MARTIN: Oh that – I was very mild.

STAUPITZ: Yes, well I've heard your mildness in the pulpit.
When I think sometimes of the terror it used to be for you,
you used to fall up the steps with fright. Sheer fright! You
were too frightened to become a Doctor of Theology, and
you wouldn't be now if I hadn't forced you. 'I'm too weak,
I'm not strong enough. I shan't live long enough!' Do you
remember what I said to you?

MARTIN: 'Never mind, the Lord still has work in heaven, and
there are always vacancies.'

STAUPITZ: Yes, and the Duke paid all the expenses of your
promotion for you. He was very cross when he spoke to
me, I may say. He said you even made some reference to
the collection of holy relics in the Castle Church, and most
of those were paid for by the sale of indulgences, as you
know. Did you say anything about them?

MARTIN: Well, yes, but not about those in the Castle Church. I
did make some point in passing about someone who

claimed to have a feather from the wing of the angel
Gabriel.

STAUPITZ: Oh yes, I heard about him.

MARTIN: And the Archbishop of Mainz, who is supposed to
have a flame from Moses' burning bush.

STAUPITZ: Oh dear, you shouldn't have mentioned that.

MARTIN: And I just finished off by saying how does it happen
that Christ had twelve apostles and eighteen of them are
buried in Germany?

STAUPITZ: Well, the Duke says he's coming to your next
sermon to hear for himself, so try to keep off the subject, if
you possibly can. It's All Saints' Day soon, remember, and
all those relics will be out on show for everyone to gawp at.
The Duke's a good chap, and he's very proud of his
collection, and it doesn't help to be rude about it.

MARTIN: I've tried to keep off the subject because I haven't
been by any means sure about it. Then I did make a few
mild protests in a couple of sermons, as I say.

STAUPITZ: Yes, yes, but what did you actually say?

MARTIN: That you can't strike bargains with God. There's a
Jewish, Turkish, Pelagian heresy if you like.

STAUPITZ: Yes, more mildness. Go on.

MARTIN: I said, oh it was an evil sanction because only *you*
could live *your* life, and only you can die your death. It
can't be taken over for you. Am I right?

STAUPITZ: (*Doubtfully*) Yes, what's difficult to understand is
why your sermons are so popular.

MARTIN: Well, there are plenty who sit out there stiff with
hatred, I can tell you. I can see their faces, and there's no
mistaking them. But I wanted to tell you something –

STAUPITZ: Yes?

MARTIN: About all this. The other day a man was brought to
me, a shoemaker. His wife had just died, and I said to him,
'What've you done for her?' so he said, 'I've buried her and
commended her soul to God.' 'But haven't you had a
Mass said for the repose of her soul?' 'No,' he said, 'what's
the point? She entered heaven the moment she died.' So I
asked him, 'How do you know that?' And he said, 'Well,

I've got proof, that's why.' And out of his pocket he took a letter of indulgence.

STAUPITZ: Ah.

MARTIN: He threw it at me, and said, 'And if you still maintain that a Mass is necessary, then my wife's been swindled by our most holy father the Pope. Or, if not by him, then by the priest who sold it to me.'

STAUPITZ: Tetzel.

MARTIN: Who else?

STAUPITZ: That old tout!

MARTIN: There's another story going around about him which is obviously true because I've checked it at several sources. It seems that a certain Saxon nobleman had heard Tetzel in Juterbög. After Tetzel had finished his usual performance, he asked him if he'd repeat what he'd said at one stage, that he – Tetzel I mean – had the power of pardoning sins that men intended to commit. Tetzel was very high and mighty, you know what he's like, and said, 'What's the matter, weren't you listening? Of course I can give pardon not only for sins already committed but for sins that men *intend* to commit.' 'Well, then, that's fine,' says this nobleman, 'because I'd like to take revenge on one of my enemies. You know, nothing much, I don't want to kill him or anything like that. Just a little slight revenge. Now, if I give you ten guilden, will you give me a letter of indulgence that will justify me – justify me freely and completely?' Well, it seems Tetzel made a few stock objections, but eventually agreed on thirty guilden, and they made a deal. The man went away with his letter of indulgence, and Tetzel set out for the next job, which was Leipzig. Well half-way between Leipzig and Treblen, in the middle of a wood, he was set on by a band of thugs, and beaten up. While he's lying there on the grass in a pool of his own blood, he looks up and sees that one of them is the Saxon nobleman and that they're making off with his great trunk full of money. So, the moment he's recovered enough, he rushes back to Juterbörg, and takes the nobleman to court. And what does the nobleman do?

43

Takes out the letter of indulgence and shows it to Duke George himself – case dismissed!

STAUPITZ: (*Laughing*) Well, I leave you to handle it. But try and be careful. Remember, *I* agree with all you say, but the moment someone disagrees or objects to what you're saying, *that* will be the moment when you'll suddenly recognize the strength of your belief!

MARTIN: Father, I'm never sure of the words till I hear them out loud.

STAUPITZ: Well, that's probably the meaning of the Word. The Word is me, and I am the Word. Anyway, try and be a little prudent. Look at Erasmus: he never really gets into any serious trouble, but he still manages to make his point.

MARTIN: People like Erasmus get upset because I talk of pigs and Christ in the same breath. I must go. (*Clutches himself unobtrusively.*)

STAUPITZ: Well, you might be right. Erasmus is a fine scholar, but there are too many scholars who think they're better simply because they insinuate in Latin what you'll say in plain German. What's the matter, are you having that trouble again? Good heavens! Martin – just before you go: a man with a strong sword will draw it at some time, even if it's only to turn it on himself. But whatever happens, he can't just let it dangle from his belt. And, another thing, don't forget – you began this affair in the name of Our Lord Jesus Christ. You must do as God commands you, of course, but remember, St. Jerome once wrote about a philosopher who destroyed his own eyes so that it would give him more freedom to study. Take care of your eyes, my son, and do something about those damned bowels!

MARTIN: I will. Who knows? If I break wind in Wittenberg, they might smell it in Rome.

(*Exit. Church bells.*)

(*End of Act Two – Scene Two.*)

The steps of the Castle Church, Wittenberg, October 31st, 1517. From inside the Church comes the sound of Matins being sung. Sitting on the steps is a child, dirty, half-naked and playing intently by himself. MARTIN enters with a long roll of paper. It is his ninety-five theses for disputation against indulgences. As he goes up the steps, he stops and watches the child, absorbed in his private fantasy. He is absorbed by the child, who doesn't notice him at first, but, presently, as soon as the boy becomes aware of an intruder, he immediately stops playing and looks away distractedly in an attempt to exclude outside attention. MARTIN hesitates briefly, then puts out his hand to the child, who looks at it gravely and deliberately, then slowly, not rudely, but naturally, gets up and skips away sadly out of sight. MARTIN watches him, then walks swiftly back down the steps to the pulpit and ascends it.

MARTIN: My text is from the Epistle of Paul the Apostle to the
    Romans, chapter one, verse seventeen: 'For therein is the
    righteousness of God revealed from faith to faith.'
    (*Pause.*)
    We are living in a dangerous time. You may not think so,
    but it could be that this is the most dangerous time since
    the light first broke upon the earth. It may not be true, but
    it's very probably true – but, what's most important is that
    it's an assumption we are obliged to make. We Christians
    seem to be wise outwardly and mad inwardly, and in this
    Jerusalem we have built there are blasphemies flourishing
    that make the Jews no worse than giggling children. A man
    is not a good Christian because he understands Greek and
    Hebrew. Jerome knew five languages, but he's inferior to
    Augustine, who knew only one. Of course, Erasmus
    wouldn't agree with me, but perhaps one day the Lord will
    open his eyes for him. But listen! A man without Christ
    becomes his own shell. We are content with shells. Some
    shells are whole men and some are small trinkets. And,
    what are the trinkets? Today is the eve of All Saints, and
    the holy relics will be on show to you all; to the hungry
    ones whose lives are made satisfied by trinkets, by an

45

imposing procession and the dressings up of all kinds of dismal things. You'll mumble for magic with lighted candles to St. Anthony for your erysipelas; to St. Valentine for your epilepsy; to St. Sebastian for the pestilence; to St. Laurentis to protect you from fire, to St. Appolonia if you've got the toothache, and to St. Louis to stop your beer from going sour. And tomorrow you'll queue for hours outside the Castle Church so that you can get a cheap-rate glimpse of St. Jerome's tooth, or four pieces each of St. Chrysostom and St. Augustine, and six of St. Bernard. The deacons will have to link hands to hold you back while you struggle to gawp at four hairs from Our Lady's head, at the pieces of her girdle and her veil stained with her Son's blood. You'll sleep outside with the garbage in the streets all night so that you can stuff your eyes like roasting birds on a scrap of swaddling clothes, eleven pieces from the original crib, one wisp of straw from the manger and a gold piece specially minted by three wise men for the occasion. Your emptiness will be frothing over at the sight of a strand of Jesus' beard, at one of the nails driven into His hands, and at the remains of the loaf at the Last Supper. Shells for shells, empty things for empty men. There are some who complain of these things, but they write in Latin for scholars. Who'll speak out in rough German? Someone's got to bell the cat! For you must be made to know that there's no security, there's no security at all, either in indulgences, holy busywork or anywhere in this world. It came to me while I was in my tower, what they call the monk's sweathouse, the jakes, the john or whatever you're pleased to call it. I was struggling with the text I've given you: 'For therein is the righteousness of God revealed, from faith to faith; as it is written, the just shall live by faith.' And seated there, my head down, on that privy just as when I was a little boy, I couldn't reach down to my breath for the sickness in my bowels, as I seemed to sense beneath me a large rat, a heavy, wet, plague rat, slashing at my privates with its death's teeth. (*He kneads his knuckles into his abdomen, as if he were*

suppressing pain. His face runs with sweat.)
I thought of the righteousness of God, and wished his
gospel had never been put to paper for men to read; who
demanded my love and made it impossible to return it.
And I sat in my heap of pain until the words emerged and
opened out. 'The just shall live by faith.' My pain
vanished, my bowels flushed and I could get up. I could
see the life I'd lost. No man is just because he does just
works. The works are just if the man is just. If a man
doesn't believe in Christ, not only are his sins mortal, but
his good works. This I know; reason is the devil's whore,
born of one stinking goat called Aristotle, which believes
that good works make a good man. But the truth is that the
just shall live by faith alone. I need no more than my sweet
redeemer and mediator, Jesus Christ, and I shall praise
Him as long as I have voice to sing; and if anyone doesn't
care to sing with me, then he can howl on his own. If we
are going to be deserted, let's follow the deserted Christ.
(*He murmurs a prayer, descends from the pulpit, then walks up
the steps to the Church door, and nails his theses to it. The
singing from within grows louder as he walks away.*)
(*End of Act Two – Scene Three.*)

SCENE FOUR

*The Fugger Palace, Augsburg. October 1518. As a backcloth a
satirical contemporary woodcut, showing, for example, the Pope
portrayed as an ass playing the bagpipes, or a cardinal dressed up as
a court fool. Or perhaps Holbein's cartoon of Luther with the Pope
suspended from his nose. However, there is a large area for the
director and designer to choose from.*

Seated at a table is THOMAS DE VIO, *known as Cajetan,
Cardinal of San Sisto, General of the Dominican Order, as well as
its most distinguished theologian, papal legate, Rome's highest
representative in Germany. He is about fifty, but youthful, with a
shrewd broad outlook, quite the opposite of the vulgar bigotry of*
TETZEL, *who enters.*

TETZEL: He's here.

CAJETAN: So I see.

TETZEL: What do you mean?

CAJETAN: You look so cross. Is Staupitz with him?

TETZEL: Yes. At least *he's* polite.

CAJETAN: I know Staupitz. He's a straightforward, four-square kind of a man, and probably very unhappy at this moment. From all accounts, he has a deep regard for this monk – which is all to the good from our point of view.

TETZEL: He's worried all right, you can see that. These Augustinians, they don't have much fibre.

CAJETAN: What about Dr. Luther? What's he got to say for himself?

TETZEL: Too much. I said to him if our Lord the Pope were to offer you a good Bishopric and a plenary indulgence for repairing your church, you'd soon start singing a different song.

CAJETAN: Dear, oh, dear, and what did he say to that?

TETZEL: He asked me –

CAJETAN: Well?

TETZEL: He asked me how was my mother's syphilis.

CAJETAN: It's a fair question in the circumstances. You Germans, you're a crude lot.

TETZEL: He's a pig.

CAJETAN: I've no doubt. After all, it's what your country's most famous for.

TETZEL: That's what I said to him – you're not on your own ground here, you know. These Italians they're different. They're not just learned, they're subtle, experienced antagonists. You'll get slung in the fire after five minutes.

CAJETAN: And?

TETZEL: He said, 'I've only been to Italy once, and they didn't look very subtle to me. They were lifting their legs on street corners like dogs.'

CAJETAN: I hope he didn't see any cardinals at it. Knowing some of them as I do, it's not impossible. Well, let's have a look at this foul-mouthed monk of yours.

TETZEL: What about Staupitz?

CAJETAN: Let him wait in the corridor. It'll help him to worry.
TETZEL: Very well, your eminence. I hope he behaves properly. I've spoken to him.

(TETZEL *goes out and returns presently with* MARTIN *who advances, prostrates himself, his face to the ground before* CAJETAN. CAJETAN *makes a motion and* MARTIN *rises to a kneeling position, where* CAJETAN *studies him.*)

CAJETAN: (*Courteous*) Please stand up, Dr. Luther. So you're the one they call the excessive doctor. You don't look excessive to me. Do you feel very excessive?

MARTIN: (*Conscious of being patronized*) It's one of those words which can be used like a harness on a man.

CAJETAN: How do you mean?

MARTIN: I mean it has very little meaning beyond traducing him.

CAJETAN: Quite. There's never been any doubt in my mind that you've been misinterpreted all round, and, as you say, traduced. Well, what a surprise you are! Here was I expecting to see some doddering old theologian with dust in his ears who could be bullied into a heart attack by Tetzel here in half an hour. And here you are, as gay and sprightly as a young bull. How old are you, my son?

MARTIN: Thirty-four, most worthy father.

CAJETAN: Tetzel, he's a boy – you didn't tell me! And how long have you been wearing your doctor's ring?

MARTIN: Five years –

CAJETAN: So you were only twenty-nine! Well, obviously, everything I've heard about you is true – you must be a remarkable young man. I wouldn't have believed there was one doctor in the whole of Germany under fifty. Would you, Brother John?

TETZEL: Not as far as I know.

CAJETAN: I'm certain there isn't. What is surprising, frankly, is that they allowed such an honour to be conferred on anyone so young and inexperienced as a man must inevitably be at twenty-nine.

(*He smiles to let his point get home.*)

Your father must be a proud man.

MARTIN: (*Irritated*) Not at all, I should say he was disappointed and constantly apprehensive.

CAJETAN: Really? Well, that's surely one of the legacies of parenthood to offset the incidental pleasures. Now then, to business. I was saying to Tetzel, I don't think this matter need take up very much of our time. But, before we do start, there's just one thing I would like to say, and that is I was sorry you should have decided to ask the Emperor for safe conduct. That was hardly necessary, my son, and it's a little – well, distressing to feel you have such an opinion of us, such a lack of trust in your mother church, and in those who have, I can assure you, your dearest interests at heart.

MARTIN: (*Out-manoeuvred*) I –

CAJETAN: (*Kindly*) But never mind all that now, that's behind us, and, in the long run, it's unimportant, after all, isn't it? Your Vicar General has come with you, hasn't he?

MARTIN: He's outside.

CAJETAN: I've known Staupitz for years. You have a wonderful friend there.

MARTIN: I know. I – have great love for him.

CAJETAN: And he certainly has for you, I know. Oh my dear, dear son, this is such a ridiculous, unnecessary business for us all to be mixed up in. It's such a tedious, upsetting affair, and what purpose is there in it? Your entire order in Germany has been brought into disgrace. Staupitz is an old man, and he can't honestly be expected to cope. Not now. I have my job to do, and, make no mistake, it isn't all honey for an Italian legate in your country. You know how it is, people are inclined to resent you. Nationalist feeling and all that – which I respect – but it does complicate one's task to the point where this kind of issue thrown in for good measure simply makes the whole operation impossible. You know what I mean? I mean, there's your Duke Frederick, an absolutely fair, honest man, if ever there was one, and one his holiness values and esteems particularly. Well, he instructed me to present him with the Golden Rose of Virtue, so you can see . . . As well as even more indulgences for his Castle Church. But what happens now? Because of all this unpleasantness and the uproar it's caused throughout Germany, the Duke's put in an extremely difficult position about accepting it. Naturally, he wants to do the right thing by everyone. But he's not going to betray you or anything like that, however much he's set his heart on that Golden Rose, even after all these years. And, of course he's perfectly right. I know he has the greatest regard for you and for some of your ideas – even though, as he's told me – he doesn't agree with a lot of them. No, I can only respect him for all that. So, you see, my dear son, what a mess we are in. Now, what are we going to do? Um? The Duke is unhappy. I am unhappy, his holiness is unhappy and, you, my son, you are unhappy.

MARTIN: (*Formal, as if it were a prepared speech*) Most worthy father, in obedience to the summons of his papal holiness, and in obedience to the orders of my gracious lord, the Elector of Saxony, I have come before you as a submissive and dutiful son of the holy Christian church, and acknowledge that I have published the proposition and theses ascribed to me. I am ready now to listen most obediently to my indictment, and if I have been wrong, to submit to your instruction in the truth.

CAJETAN: (*Impatient*) My son, you have upset all Germany with your dispute about indulgences. I know you're a very learned doctor of the Holy Scriptures, and that you've already aroused some supporters. However, if you wish to remain a member of the Church, and to find a gracious father in the Pope, you'd better listen. I have here, in front of me, three propositions which, by the command of our holy father, Pope Leo the Tenth, I shall put to you now. First, you must admit your faults, and retract all your errors and sermons. Secondly, you must promise to abstain from propagating your opinions at any time in the future. And, thirdly, you must behave generally with greater moderation, and avoid anything which might cause offence or grieve and disturb the Church.

MARTIN: May I be allowed to see the Pope's instruction?

CAJETAN: No, my dear son, you may not. All you are required to do is confess your errors, keep a strict watch on your words, and not go back like a dog to his vomit. Then, once you have done that, I have been authorized by our most holy father to put everything to rights again.

MARTIN: I understand all that. But I'm asking you to tell me where I have erred.

CAJETAN: If you insist. (*Rattling off, very fast.*) Just to begin with, here are two propositions you have advanced, and which you will have to retract before anything else. First, the treasure of indulgences does not consist of the sufferings and torments of our Lord Jesus Christ. Second, the man who receives the holy sacrament must have faith in the grace that is presented to him. Enough?

MARTIN: I rest my case entirely on Holy Scriptures.

CAJETAN: The Pope alone has power and authority over all those things.

MARTIN: Except Scripture.

CAJETAN: Including Scripture. What do you mean?

TETZEL: Only the Pope has the right of deciding in matters of Christian faith. He alone and no one else has the power to interpret the meaning of Scripture, and to approve or condemn the views of other men, whoever they are – scholars, councils or the ancient fathers. The Pope's judgement cannot err, whether it concerns the Christian faith or anything that has to do with the salvation of the human race.

MARTIN: That sounds like your theses.

TETZEL: Burned in the market place by your students in Wittenberg – thank you very much –

MARTIN: I assure you, I had nothing to do with that.

CAJETAN: Of course. Brother John wasn't suggesting you had.

MARTIN: I can't stop the mouth of the whole world.

TETZEL: Why, your heresy isn't even original. It's no different from Wyclif or Hus.

CAJETAN: True enough, but we mustn't try to deprive the learned doctor of his originality. An original heresy may have been thought of by someone else before you. In fact, I shouldn't think such a thing as an original heresy exists. But it is original so long as it originated in *you*, the virgin heretic.

TETZEL: The time'll come when you'll have to defend yourself before the world, and then every man can judge for himself who's the heretic and schismatic. It'll be clear to everyone, even those drowsy snoring Christians who've never smelled a Bible. They'll find out for themselves that those who scribble books and waste so much paper just for their own pleasure, and are contemptuous and shameless, end up by condemning themselves. People like you always go too far, thank heaven. You play into our hands. I give you a month, Brother Martin, to roast yourself.

MARTIN: You've had your thirty pieces of silver. For the sake of Christ, why don't you betray someone?

CAJETAN: (*To* TETZEL) Perhaps you should join Staupitz.

TETZEL: Very well, your eminence.

(*He bows and goes out.*)

CAJETAN: In point of fact, he gets eighty guilden a month plus expenses.

MARTIN: What about his vow of poverty?

CAJETAN: Like most brilliant men, my son, you have an innocent spirit. I've also just discovered that he has managed to father two children. So there goes another vow. Bang! But it'll do him no good, I promise you. You've made a hole in that drum for him. I may say there's a lot of bad feelings among the Dominicans about you. I should know – because I'm their General. It's only natural, they're accustomed to having everything their own way. The Franciscans are a grubby, sentimental lot, on the whole, and mercifully ignorant as well. But your people seem to be running alive with scholars and would-be politicians.

MARTIN: I'd no idea that my theses would ever get such publicity.

CAJETAN: Really now!

MARTIN: But it seems they've been printed over and over again, and circulated well, to an extent I'd never dreamed of.

CAJETAN: Oh yes, they've been circulated and talked about wherever men kneel to Christ.

MARTIN: Most holy father, I honour the Holy Roman Church, and I shall go on doing so. I have sought after the truth, and everything I have said I still believe to be right and true and Christian. But I am a man, and I may be deceived, so I am willing to receive instruction where I have been mistaken –

CAJETAN: (*Angrily*) Save your arrogance, my son, there'll be a better place to use it. I can have you sent to Rome and let any of your German princes try to stop me! He'll find himself standing outside the gates of heaven like a leper.

MARTIN: (*Stung*) I repeat, I am here to reply to all the charges you may bring against me –

CAJETAN: No, you're not –

MARTIN: I am ready to submit my theses to the universities of Basle, Freibourg, Louvain or Paris –

CAJETAN: I'm afraid you've not grasped the position. I'm not here to enter into a disputation with you, now or at any other time. The Roman Church is the apex of the world, secular and temporal, and it may constrain with its secular arm any who have once received the faith and gone astray. Surely I don't have to remind you that it is not bound to use reason to fight and destroy rebels. (*He sighs.*) My son, it's getting late. You must retract. Believe me, I simply want to see this business ended as quickly as possible.

MARTIN: Some interests are furthered by finding truth, others by destroying it. I don't care – what pleases or displeases the Pope. He is a man.

CAJETAN: (*Wearily*) Is that all?

MARTIN: He seems a good man, as Popes go. But it's not much for a world that sings out for reformation. I'd say that's a hymn for everyone.

CAJETAN: My dear friend, think, think carefully, and see if you can't see some way out of all this. I am more than prepared to reconcile you with the Church, and the sovereign bishop. Retract, my son, the holy father prays for it –

MARTIN: But won't you discuss –

CAJETAN: Discuss! I've not *discussed* with you, and I don't
intend to. If you want a disputation, I dare say Eck will
take care of you –

MARTIN: John Eck? The Chancellor of Ingolstadt?

CAJETAN: I suppose you don't think much of him?

MARTIN: He knows theology.

CAJETAN: He has a universal reputation in debate.

MARTIN: It's understandable. He has a pedestrian style and a
judicial restraint and that'll always pass off as wisdom to
most men.

CAJETAN: You mean he's not original, like you –

MARTIN: I'm not an original man, why I'm not even a teacher,
and I'm scarcely even a priest. I know Jesus Christ doesn't
need my labour or my services.

CAJETAN: All right, Martin, I *will* argue with you if you want me
to, or, at least, I'll put something to you, because there is
something more than your safety or your life involved,
something bigger than you and I talking together in this
room at this time. Oh, it's fine for someone like you to
criticize and start tearing down Christendom, but tell me
this, just tell me this: what will you build in its place?

MARTIN: A withered arm is best amputated, an infected place is
best scoured out, and so you pray for healthy tissue and
something sturdy and clean that was crumbling and full of
filth.

CAJETAN: Can't you see? My son, you'll destroy the perfect
unity of the world.

MARTIN: Someone always prefers what's withered and infected.
But it should be cauterized as honestly as one knows how.

CAJETAN: And how honest is that? There's something I'd like to
know: suppose you *did* destroy the Pope. What do you
think would become of you?

MARTIN: I don't know.

CAJETAN: Exactly, you wouldn't know what to do because you
need him, Martin, you need to hunt him more than he
needs his silly wild boar. Well? There have always been
Popes, and there always will be, even if they're called
something else. They'll have them for people like *you*.

55

You're not a good old revolutionary, my son, you're just a common rebel, a very different animal. You don't fight the Pope because he's too big, but because for your needs he's not big enough.

MARTIN: My General's been gossiping –

CAJETAN: (*Contemptuous*) I don't need Staupitz to explain you to me. Why, some deluded creature might even come to you as a leader of their revolution, but you don't want to break rules, you want to make them. You'd be a master breaker and maker and no one would be able to stand up to you, you'd hope, or ever sufficiently repair the damage you did. I've read some of your sermons on faith. Do you know all they say to me?

MARTIN: No.

CAJETAN: They say: I am a man struggling for certainty, struggling insanely like a man in a fit, an animal trapped to the bone with doubt.

(MARTIN *seems about to have a physical struggle with himself.*) Don't you see what could happen out of all this? Men could be cast out and left to themselves for ever, helpless and frightened!

MARTIN: Your eminence, forgive me. I'm tired after my journey – I think I might faint soon –

CAJETAN: That's what would become of them without their Mother Church – with all its imperfections, Peter's rock, without it they'd be helpless and unprotected. Allow them their sins, their petty indulgences, my son, they're unimportant to the comfort we receive –

MARTIN: (*Somewhat hysterical*) Comfort! It – doesn't concern me!

CAJETAN: We live in thick darkness, and it grows thicker. How will men find God if they are left to themselves each man abandoned and only known to himself?

MARTIN: They'll have to try.

CAJETAN: I beg of you, my son, I beg of you. Retract.
(*Pause.*)

MARTIN: Most holy father, I cannot.
(*Pause.*)

CAJETAN: You look ill. You had better go and rest. (*Pause.*)
  Naturally, you will be released from your order.
MARTIN: I –
CAJETAN: Yes?
MARTIN: As you say, your eminence. Will you refer this matter
  to the Pope for his decision?
CAJETAN: Assuredly. Send in Tetzel.
  (MARTIN *prostrates himself, and then kneels.* CAJETAN *is
  distressed but in control.*)
  You know, a time will come when a man will no longer be
  able to say, 'I speak Latin and am a Christian' and go his
  way in peace. There will come frontiers, frontiers of all
  kinds – between men – and there'll be no end to them.
  (MARTIN *rises and goes out.* TETZEL *returns.*)
TETZEL: Yes?
CAJETAN: No, of course he didn't – that man hates himself.
  And if he goes to the stake, Tetzel, you can have the
  pleasure of inscribing it: he could only love others.
  (*End of Act Two – Scene Four.*)

SCENE FIVE

*A hunting lodge at Magliana in Northern Italy, 1519. Suspended the
arms, the brass balls, of the Medici.* KARL VON MILTITZ, *a young
Chamberlain of the Pope's household is waiting. There are cries off,
and sounds of excitement.* POPE LEO THE TENTH *enters with a*
HUNTSMAN, *dogs and* DOMINICANS. *He is richly dressed in
hunting clothes and long boots. He is indolent, cultured, intelligent,
extremely restless, and well able to assimilate the essence of anything
before anyone else. While he is listening, he is able to play with a live
bird with apparent distraction. Or shoot at a board with a crossbow.
Or generally fidget.* MILTITZ *kneels to kiss his toe.*

LEO: I should forget it. I've got my boots on. Well? get on with
  it. We're missing the good weather.
  (*He sits and becomes immediately absorbed in his own play, as
  it seems.* MILTITZ *has a letter, which he reads.*)
MILTITZ: 'To the most blessed father Leo the tenth, sovereign

57

bishop, Martin Luther, Augustine Friar, wishes eternal salvation. I am told that there are vicious reports circulating about me, and that my name is in bad odour with your holiness. I am called a heretic, apostate, traitor and many other insulting names. I cannot understand all this hostility, and I am alarmed by it. But the only basis of my tranquillity remains, as always, a pure and peaceful conscience. Deign to listen to me, most holy father, to me who is like a child.

(LEO *snorts abstractedly.*)

'There have always been, as long as I can remember, complaints and grumbling in the taverns about the avarice of the priests and attacks on the power of the keys. And this has been happening throughout Germany. When I listened to these things my zeal was aroused for the glory of Christ, so I warned not one, but several princes of the Church. But, either they laughed in my face or ignored me. The terror of your name was too much for everyone. It was then I published my disputation, nailing it on the door of the Castle Church here in Wittenberg. And now, most holy father, the whole world has gone up in flames. Tell me what I should do? I cannot retract; but this thing has drawn down hatred on me from all sides, and I don't know where to turn to but to you. I am far too insignificant to appear before the world in a matter as great as this.

(LEO *snaps his fingers to glance at this passage in the letter. He does so and returns it to* MILTITZ *who continues reading.*)

'But in order to quieten my enemies and satisfy my friends I am now addressing myself to you most holy father and speak my mind in the greater safety of the shadow of your wings. All this respect I show to the power of the keys. If I had not behaved properly it would have been impossible for the most serene Lord Frederick, Duke and Elector of Saxony, who shines in your apostolic favour, to have endured me in his University of Wittenberg. Not if I am as dangerous as is made out by my enemies. For this reason, most holy father, I fall at the feet of your holiness, and submit myself to you, with all I have and all that I am.

Declare me right or wrong. Take my life, or give it back to me, as you please. I shall acknowledge your voice as the voice of Jesus Christ. If I deserve death, I shall not refuse to die. The earth is God's and all within it. May He be praised through all eternity, and may He uphold you for ever. Amen. Written the day of the Holy Trinity in the year 1518, Martin Luther, Augustine Friar.'

(They wait for LEO *to finish his playing and give them his full attention. Presently, he gets up and takes the letter from* MILTITZ. *He thinks.)*

LEO: Double faced German bastard! Why can't he say what he means? What else?

MILTITZ: He's said he's willing to be judged by any of the Universities of Germany, with the exception of Leipzig, Erfurt and Frankfurt, which he says are not impartial. He says it's impossible for him to appear in Rome in person.

LEO: I'm sure.

MILTITZ: Because his health wouldn't stand up to the rigours of the journey.

LEO: Cunning! Cunning German bastard! What does Staupitz say for him?

MILTITZ: *(Reading hastily from another letter)* 'The reverend father, Martin Luther, is the noblest and most distinguished member of our university. For many years, we have watched his talents –'

LEO: Yes, well we know all about that. Write to Cajetan. Take this down. We charge you to summon before you Martin Luther. Invoke for this purpose, the aid of our very dear son in Christ, Maximilian, and all the other princes in Germany, together with all communities, universities, potentates ecclesiastic and secular. And, once you get possession of him, keep him in safe custody, so that he can be brought before us. If, however, he should return to his duty of his own accord and begs forgiveness, we give you the power to receive him into the perfect unity of our Holy Mother the Church. But, should he persist in his obstinacy and you cannot secure him, we authorize you to outlaw him in every part of Germany. To banish and excommunicate him. As well as all prelates, religious orders, universities, counts, and dukes who do not assist in apprehending him. As for the laymen, if they do not immediately obey your orders, declare them infamous, deprived of Christian burial and stripped of anything they may hold either from the apostolic see or from any lord whatsoever. There's a wild pig in our vineyard, and it must be hunted down and shot. Given under the seal of the Fisherman's Ring, etcetera. That's all.

(He turns quickly and goes out.)

(End of Act Two – Scene Five.)

SCENE SIX

The Elster Gate, Wittenberg. 1520. Evening. A single bell. As a backcloth the bull issued against Luther. Above it a fish-head and bones. The bull is slashed with the reflection of the flames rising round the Elster Gate where the books of canon law, the papal decretals, are burning furiously. MONKS *come to and fro with more books and documents, and hurl them on the fire.* MARTIN *enters and ascends the pulpit.*

MARTIN: I have been served with a piece of paper. Let me tell you about it. It has come to me from a latrine called Rome, that capital of the devil's own sweet empire. It is called the papal bull and it claims to excommunicate me, Dr. Martin Luther. These lies they rise up from paper like fumes from the bog of Europe; because papal decretals are the devil's excretals. I'll hold it up for you to see properly. You see the signature? Signed beneath the seal of the Fisherman's Ring by one certain midden cock called Leo, an over-indulged jakes' attendant to Satan himself, a glittering worm in excrement, known to you as his holiness the Pope. You may know him as the head of the Church. Which he may still be: like a fish is the head of a cat's dinner; eyes without sight clutched to a stick of sucked bones. God has told me: there can be no dealings between this cat's dinner and me. And, as for this bull, it's going to roast, it's going to roast and so are the balls of the Medici!

(*He descends and casts the bull into the flames. He begins to shake, as if he were unable to breathe; as if he were about to have another fit. Shaking, he kneels.*)

Oh, God! Oh, God! Oh, thou my God, my God, help me against the reason and wisdom of the world. You must – there's only you – to do it. Breathe into me. Breathe into me, like a lion into the mouth of a stillborn cub. This cause is not mine but yours. For myself, I've no business to be dealing with the great lords of this world. I want to be still, in peace, and alone. Breathe into me, Jesus. I rely on no man, only on you. My God, my God do you hear me? Are you dead? Are you dead? No, you can't die, you can only hide yourself, can't you? Lord, I'm afraid. I am a child, the lost body of a child. I am stillborn. Breathe into me, in the name of Thy Son, Jesus Christ, who shall be my protector and defender, yes, my mighty fortress, breathe into me. Give me life, oh Lord. Give me life.

(MARTIN *prays as the deep red light of the flames flood the darkness around him.*)

(*End of Act Two.*)

ACT THREE

SCENE ONE

The Diet of Worms, April 18th, 1521. A gold front-cloth, and on it, in the brightest sunshine of colour, a bold, joyful representation of this unique gathering of princes, electors, dukes, ambassadors, bishops, counts, barons, etc. Perhaps Luther's two-wheeled wagon which brought him to Worms. The mediaeval world dressed up for the Renaissance.

Devoid of depth, such scenes are stamped on a brilliant ground of gold. Movement is frozen, recession in space ignored and perspective served by the arrangement of figures, or scenes, one above the other. In this way, landscape is dramatically substituted by objects in layers. The alternative is to do the opposite, in the manner of, say, Altdorfer. Well in front of the cloth is a small rostrum with brass rails sufficient to support one man. If possible, it would be preferable to have this part of the apron projected a little into the audience. Anyway, the aim is to achieve the maximum in physical enlargement of the action, in the sense of physical participation in the theatre, as if everyone watching had their chins resting on the sides of a boxing-ring. Also on the apron, well to the front are several chairs. On one side is a table with about twenty books on it. The table and books may also be represented on the gold cloth. The rostrum has a small crescent of chairs round it. From all corners of the auditorium comes a fanfare of massed trumpets, and, approaching preferably from the auditorium up steps to the apron, come a few members of the Diet audience (who may also be represented on the gold cloth). Preceded by a HERALD, *and seating themselves on the chairs, they should include* THE EMPEROR CHARLES THE FIFTH *(in front of the rostrum),* ALEANDER, THE PAPAL NUNCIO; ULRICH VON HUTTEN, KNIGHT; THE ARCHBISHOP OF TRIER *and* HIS SECRETARY, JOHN VON ECK, *who sit at the table with the books. The trumpets cease, and they wait.* MARTIN *appears from the stage, and ascends the rostrum centre.*

ECK: (*Rising*) Martin Luther, you have been brought here by

His Imperial Majesty so that you may answer two questions. Do you publicly acknowledge being the author of the books you see here? When I asked you this question yesterday, you agreed immediately that the books were indeed your own. Is that right?

(MARTIN *nods in agreement.*)

When I asked you the second question, you asked if you might be allowed time in which to consider it. Although such time should have been quite unnecessary for an experienced debater and distinguished doctor of theology like yourself, His Imperial Majesty was graciously pleased to grant your request. Well, you have had your time now, a whole day and a night, and so I will repeat the question to you. You have admitted being the author of these books. Do you mean to defend all these books, or will you retract any of them?

(ECK *sits.* MARTIN *speaks quietly, conversationally, hardly raising his voice throughout, and with simplicity.*)

MARTIN: Your serene highness, most illustrious princes and gracious lords, I appear before you by God's mercy, and I beg that you will listen patiently. If, through my ignorance, I have not given anyone his proper title or offended in any way against the etiquette of such a place as this, I ask your pardon in advance for a man who finds it hard to know his way outside the few steps from wall to wall of a monk's cell. We have agreed these books are all mine, and they have all been published rightly in my name. I will reply to your second question. I ask your serene majesty and your gracious lordships to take note that not all my books are of the same kind. For instance, in the first group, I have dealt quite simply with the values of faith and morality, and even my enemies have agreed that all this is quite harmless, and can be read without damaging the most fragile Christian. Even the bull against me, harsh and cruel as it is, admits that some of my books are offensive to no one. Perhaps it's the strange nature of such a questionable compliment, that the bull goes on to condemn these with the rest, which it considers offensive. If I'm to begin withdrawing these books, what should I be doing? I should be condemning those very things my friends and enemies are agreed on. There is a second group of books I have written, and these all attack the power of the keys, which has ravaged Christendom. No one can deny this, the evidence is everywhere and everyone complains of it. And no one has suffered more from this tyranny than the Germans. They have been plundered without mercy. If I were to retract those books now, I should be issuing a licence for more tyranny, and it is too much to ask of me.

I have also written a third kind of book against certain, private distinguished and, apparently – highly established – individuals. They are all defenders of Rome and enemies of my religion. In these books, it's possible that I have been more violent than may seem necessary, or, shall I say, tasteful in one who is, after all, a monk. But then, I have never set out to be a saint and I've not been defending my own life, but the teaching of Christ. So you see, again I'm not free to retract, for if I did, the present situation would certainly go on just as before. However, because I am a man and not God, the only way for me to defend what I have written is to employ the same method used by my Saviour. When He was being questioned by Annas, the high priest, about His teaching, and He had been struck in the face by one of the servants, He replied: 'If I have spoken lies tell me what the lie is.' If the Lord Jesus Himself, who could not err, was willing to listen to the arguments of a servant, how can I refuse to do the same? Therefore, what I ask, by the Mercy of God, is let someone expose my errors in the light of the Gospels. The moment you have done this, I shall ask you to let me be the first to pick up my books and hurl them in the fire.

I think this is a clear answer to your question. I think I understand the danger of my position well enough. You have made it very clear to me. But I can still think of nothing better than the Word of God being the cause of all the dissension among us. For Christ said, 'I have not come to bring peace, but a sword. I have come to set a man against his father.' We also have to be sure that the reign of this noble, young Princes Charles, so full of promise, should not end in the misery of Europe. We must fear God alone. I commend myself to your most serene majesty and to your lordships, and humbly pray that you will not condemn me as your enemy. That is all.

ECK: (*Rising*) Martin, you have not answered the question put to you. Even if it were true that some of your books are innocuous – a point which, incidentally, we don't concede – we still ask that you cut out these passages which are blasphemous; that you cut out the heresies or whatever could be construed as heresy, and, in fact, that you delete any passage which might be considered hurtful to the Catholic faith. His sacred and imperial majesty is more than prepared to be lenient, and, if you will do these things, he will use his influence with the supreme pontiff to see that the good things in your work are not thrown out with the bad. If, however, you persist in your attitude, there can be no question that all memory of you will be blotted out, and everything you have written, right or wrong, will be forgotten.

You see, Martin, you return to the same place as all other heretics – to Holy Scripture. You demand to be contradicted from Scripture. We can only believe that you must be ill or mad. Do reasons have to be given to anyone who cares to ask a question? Any question? Why, if anyone who questioned the common understanding of the Church on any matter he liked to raise, and had to be answered irrefutably from the Scriptures, there would be nothing certain or decided in Christendom. What would the Jews and Turks and Saracens say if they heard us *debating* whether what we have always believed is true or not? I beg you, Martin, not to believe that you, and you alone, understand the meaning of the Gospels. Don't rate your own opinion so highly, so far beyond that of many other sincere and eminent men. I ask you: don't throw doubt on the most holy, orthodox faith, the faith founded by the most perfect legislator known to us, and spread by His apostles throughout the world, with their blood and miracles. This faith has been defined by sacred councils and confirmed by the Church. It is your heritage, and we are forbidden to dispute it by the laws of the emperor and the pontiff. Since no amount of argument can lead to a final conclusion, they can only condemn those who refuse to submit to them. The penalties are provided and will be executed. I must, therefore, ask again, I must demand that you answer sincerely, frankly and unambiguously, yes or no: will you or will you not retract your books and the errors contained in them.

MARTIN: Since your serene majesty and your lordships demand a simple answer, you shall have it, without horns and without teeth. Unless I am shown by the testimony of the Scriptures – for I don't believe in popes or councils – unless I am refuted by Scripture and my conscience is captured by God's own word, I cannot and will not recant, since to act against one's conscience is neither safe nor honest. Here I stand; God help me; I can do no more. Amen.

(*End of Act Three – Scene One.*)

SCENE TWO

Wittenberg, 1525. A marching hymn, the sound of cannon and shouts of mutilated men. Smoke, a shattered banner bearing the cross and wooden shoe of the Bundschuh, emblem of the Peasants' Movement. A small chapel altar at one side of the stage opposite the pulpit. Centre is a small handcart, and beside it lies the bloody bulk of a peasant's corpse. Downstage stands the KNIGHT, *fatigued, despondent, stained and dirty.*

KNIGHT: There was excitement that day. In Worms – that day I mean. Oh, I don't mean now, not now. A lot's happened since then. There's no excitement like that any more. Not unless murder's your idea of excitement. I tell you, you can't have ever known the kind of thrill that monk set off amongst that collection of all kinds of men gathered together there – those few years ago. We all felt it, every one of us, just without any exception, you couldn't help it, even if you didn't want to, and, believe me, most of those people didn't want to. His scalp looked blotchy and itchy, and you felt sure, just looking at him, his body must be permanently sour and white all over, even whiter than his face and like a millstone to touch. He'd sweated so much by the time he'd finished, I could smell every inch of him even from where I was. But he fizzed like a hot spark in a trail of gunpowder going off in us, that dowdy monk, he went off in us, and nothing could stop it, and it blew up and there was nothing we could do, any of us, that was it. I just felt quite sure, quite certain in my own mind nothing could ever be the same again, just simply that. Something had taken place, something had changed and become something else, an event had occurred in the flesh, in the flesh and the breath – like, even like when the weight of that body slumped on its wooden crotch-piece and the earth grew dark. That's the kind of thing I mean by happen, and this also happened in very likely the same manner to all those of us who stood there, friends and enemies alike. I don't think, no I don't think even if I could speak and write like him, I could begin to give you an idea of what we thought, or what some of us thought, of what we might come to. Obviously, we couldn't have all felt quite the same way, but I wanted to burst my ears with shouting and draw my sword, no, not draw it, I wanted to pluck it as if it were a flower in my blood and plunge it into whatever he would have told me to.

(THE KNIGHT *is lost in his own thoughts, then his eyes catch the body of the peasant. He takes a swipe at the cart.*)
If one could only understand him. He baffles me, I just can't make him out. Anyway, it never worked out. (*To corpse.*) Did it, my friend? Not the way we expected anyway, certainly not the way *you* expected, but who'd have ever thought we might end up on different sides, him on one and us on the other. That when the war came between you and them, he'd be there beating the drum for

them outside the slaughter house, and beating it louder and better than anyone, hollering for *your* blood, cutting you up in your thousands, and hanging you up to drip away into the fire for good. Oh well, I suppose all those various groups were out for their different things, or the same thing really, all out for what we could get, and more than any of us had the right to expect. They were all the same, all those big princes and archbishops, the cut rate nobility and rich layabouts, honourable this and thats scrabbling like boars round a swill bucket for every penny those poor peasants never had. All those great abbots with their dewlaps dropped and hanging on their necks like goose's eggs, and then those left-over knights, like me for instance, I suppose, left-over men, impoverished, who'd seen better days and were scared and'd stick at nothing to try and make sure they couldn't get any worse. Yes. . . . Not one of them could read the words WAY OUT when it was written up for them, marked out clearly and unmistakably in the pain of too many men. Yes. They say, you know, that the profit motive – and I'm sure you know all about that one – they say that the profit motive was born with the invention of double entry book-keeping in the monasteries. Book-keeping! In the monasteries, and ages before any of us had ever got round to burning them down. But, you know, for men with such a motive, there is only really one entry. The profit is theirs, the loss is someone else's, and usually they don't even bother to write it up.

(*He nudges the corpse with his toe.*)

Well, it was your old loss wasn't it, dead loss, in fact, my friend, you could say his life was more or less a write-off right from the day he was born. Wasn't it? Um? And all the others like him, everywhere, now and after him.

(THE KNIGHT *starts rather weakly to load the body on to the cart.* MARTIN *enters, a book in his hands. They look at each other then* MARTIN *at the* PEASANT. THE KNIGHT *takes his book and glances at it, but he doesn't miss* MARTIN *shrink slightly from the peasant.*)

Another of yours?

(*He hands it back.*)

Do you think it'll sell as well as the others? (*Pause.*) I dare say it will. Someone's always going to listen to you. No?

(MARTIN *moves to go, but* THE KNIGHT *stops him.*)

Martin. Just a minute.

(*He turns and places his hand carefully, ritually, on the body in the cart. He smears the blood from it over* MARTIN.)

There we are. That's better.

(MARTIN *makes to move again, but again* THE KNIGHT *stops him.*)

You're all ready now. You even look like a butcher –

MARTIN: God is the butcher –

KNIGHT: Don't you?

MARTIN: Why don't you address your abuse to Him?

KNIGHT: Never mind – you're wearing His apron.

(MARTIN *moves to the stairs of the pulpit.*)

It suits you. (*Pause.*) Doesn't it? (*Pause.*) That day in Worms (*pause*) you were like a pig under glass weren't you? Do you remember it? I could smell every inch of you even where I was standing. All you've ever managed to do is convert everything into stench and dying and peril, but you could have done it, Martin, and you were the only one who could have ever done it. You could even have brought freedom and order in at one and the same time.

MARTIN: There's no such thing as an orderly revolution. Anyway, Christians are called to suffer, not fight.

KNIGHT: But weren't we all of us, all of us, without any exceptions to please any old interested parties, weren't we all redeemed by Christ's blood? (*Pointing to the peasant.*) Wasn't he included when the scriptures were being dictated? Or was it just you who was made free, you and the princes you've taken up with, and the rich burghers and –

MARTIN: Free? (*Ascends the pulpit steps.*) The princes blame me, you blame me and the peasants blame me –

KNIGHT: (*Following up the steps*) *You* put the water in the wine didn't you?

MARTIN: When I see chaos, then I see the devil's organ and then I'm afraid. Now, that's enough –

69

KNIGHT: You're breaking out again –

MARTIN: Go away –

KNIGHT: Aren't you?

(MARTIN *makes a sudden effort to push him back down the steps, but* THE KNIGHT *hangs on firmly.*)

MARTIN: Get back!

KNIGHT: Aren't you, you're breaking out again, you canting pig, I can smell you from here!

MARTIN: He heard the children of Israel, didn't He?

KNIGHT: Up to the ears in revelation, aren't you?

MARTIN: And didn't He deliver them out of the Land of Pharaoh?

KNIGHT: You canting pig, aren't you?

MARTIN: Well? Didn't He?

KNIGHT: Cock's wounds! Don't hold your Bible to my head, piggy, there's enough revelation of my own in there for me, in what I see for myself from here! (*Taps his forehead.*) Hold your gospel against that!

(THE KNIGHT *grabs* MARTIN's *hand and clamps it to his head.*)

You're killing the spirit, and you're killing it with the letter. You've been swilling about in the wrong place, Martin, in your own stink and ordure. Go on! You've got your hand on it, that's all the holy spirit there is, and it's all you'll ever get so feel it!

(*They struggle, but* THE KNIGHT *is very weak by now, and* MARTIN *is able to wrench himself away and up into the pulpit.*)

MARTIN: The world was conquered by the Word, the Church is maintained by the Word –

KNIGHT: Word? What Word? Word? That word, whatever that means, is probably just another old relic or indulgence, and you know what you did to those! Why, none of it might be any more than poetry, have you thought of that, Martin. Poetry! Martin, you're a poet, there's no doubt about that in anybody's mind, you're a poet, but do you know what most men believe in, in their hearts – because they don't see in images like you do – they believe in their hearts that Christ was a man as we are, and that He was a prophet and a teacher, and they also believe in their hearts that His supper is a plain meal like their own – if they're lucky enough to get it – a plain meal of bread and wine! A plain meal with no garnish and no word. And *you* helped them to begin to believe it!

MARTIN: (*Pause*) Leave me.

KNIGHT: Yes. What's there to stay for? I've been close enough to you for too long. I even smell like you.

MARTIN: (*Roaring with pain*) I smell because of my own argument, I smell because I never stop disputing with Him, and because I expect Him to keep His Word. Now then! If your peasant rebelled against that Word, that was worse than murder because it laid the whole country waste, and who knows now what God will make of us Germans!

KNIGHT: Don't blame God for the Germans, Martin! (*Laughs.*) Don't do that! You thrashed about more than anyone on the night they were conceived!

MARTIN: Christ! Hear me! My words pour from Your Body! They deserved their death, these swarming peasants! They kicked against authority, they plundered and bargained and all in Your name! Christ, believe me! (*To* THE KNIGHT.) I demanded it, I prayed for it, and I got it! Take that lump away! Now, drag it away with you!

(THE KNIGHT *prepares to trundle off the cart and corpse.*)

KNIGHT: All right, my friend. Stay with your nun then. Marry and stew with your nun. Most of the others have. Stew with her, like a shuddering infant in *her* bed. You think you'll manage?

MARTIN: (*Lightly*) At least my father'll praise me for *that*.

KNIGHT: Your father?

(THE KNIGHT *shrugs, pushes the cart wearily, and goes off.* MARTIN*'s head hangs over the edge of the pulpit.*)

MARTIN: I (*whispering*) trust you. . . . I trust you. . . . You've overcome the world. . . . I trust you. . . . You're all I wish to have . . . ever . . .

(*Slumped over the pulpit, he seems to be unconscious. Then he makes an effort to recover, as if he had collapsed in the middle of a sermon.*)

I expect you must . . . I'm sure you must remember –
Abraham. Abraham was – he was an old man . . . a . . .
very old man indeed, in fact, he was a hundred years old,
when what was surely, what must have been a miracle
happened, to a man of his years – a son was born to him. A
son. Isaac he called him. And he loved Isaac. Well, he
loved him with such intensity, one can only diminish it by
description. But to Abraham his little son was a miraculous
thing, a small, incessant . . . animal . . . astonishment. And
in the child he sought the father. But, one day, God said to
Abraham: Take your little son whom you love so much,
kill him, and make a sacrifice of him. And in that moment
everything inside Abraham seemed to shrivel once and for
all. Because it had seemed to him that God had promised
him life through his son. So then he took the boy and
prepared to kill him, strapping him down to the wood of
the burnt offering just as he had been told to do. And he
spoke softly to the boy, and raised the knife over his little
naked body, the boy struggling not to flinch or blink his
eyes. Never, save in Christ, was there such obedience as in
that moment, and, if God had blinked, the boy would have
died there, but the Angel intervened, and the boy was
released, and Abraham took him up in his arms again. In
the teeth of life we seem to die, but God says no – in the
teeth of death we live. If He butchers us, He makes us live.
(*Enter* THE KNIGHT, *who stands watching him, the
Bundschuh banner in his hands.*)
Heart of my Jesus save me; Heart of my Saviour deliver
me; Heart of my Shepherd guard me; Heart of my Master
teach me; Heart of my King govern me; Heart of my
Friend stay with me.
(*Enter* KATHERINE VON BORA, *his bride, accompanied by two*
MONKS. MARTIN *rises from the pulpit and goes towards her. A
simple tune is played on a simple instrument. She takes his
head, and they kneel together centre.* THE KNIGHT *watches.
Then he smashes the banner he has been holding, and tosses the
remains on to the altar.*)
(*End of Act Three – Scene Two.*)

72

SCENE THREE

*A hymn. The Eremite Cloister. Wittenberg. 1530. The refectory table,
and on it two places set, and the remains of two meals.* MARTIN *is
seated alone. The vigour of a man in his late thirties, and at the
height of his powers, has settled into the tired pain of a middle age
struggling to rediscover strength.*

KATHERINE *enters with a jug of wine. She is a big, pleasant-
looking girl, almost thirty.*

MARTIN: How is he?

KATHERINE: He's all right. He's just coming. Wouldn't let me
help him. I think he's been sick.

MARTIN: Poor old chap. After living all your life in a
monastery, one's stomach doesn't take too easily to your
kind of cooking.

KATHERINE: Wasn't it all right?

MARTIN: Oh, it was fine, just too much for an old monk's
shrivelled digestion to chew on, that's all.

KATHERINE: Oh, I see. *You're* all right, aren't you?

MARTIN: Yes, I'm all right, thank you, my dear. (*Smile.*) I
expect I'll suffer later though.

KATHERINE: You like your food, so don't make out you don't.

MARTIN: Well, I prefer it to fasting. Did you never hear the
story of the soldier who was fighting in the Holy Crusades?
No? Well, he was told by his officer that if he died in battle,
he would dine in Paradise with Christ; and the soldier ran
away. When he came back after the battle, they asked him
why he'd run away. 'Didn't you want to dine with Christ?'
they said. And he replied, 'No, I'm fasting today.'

KATHERINE: I've brought you some more wine.

MARTIN: Thank you.

KATHERINE: Should help you to sleep.

(STAUPITZ *enters, supporting himself with a stick.*)

MARTIN: There you are! I thought you'd fallen down the jakes –
right into the devil's loving arms.

STAUPITZ: I'm so sorry. I was – I was wandering about a bit.

MARTIN: Well, come and sit down. Katie's brought us some
more wine.

STAUPITZ: I can't get over being here again. It's so odd. This place was full of men. And now, now there's only you, you and Katie. It's very, very strange.

KATHERINE: I shouldn't stay up too long, Martin. You didn't sleep well again last night. I could hear you – hardly breathing all night.

MARTIN: (*Amused*) You could hear me hardly breathing?

KATHERINE: You know what I mean. When you don't sleep, it keeps me awake too. Good night, Dr. Staupitz.

STAUPITZ: Good night, my dear. Thank you for the dinner. It was excellent. I'm so sorry I wasn't able to do justice to it.

KATHERINE: That's all right. Martin's always having the same kind of trouble.

STAUPITZ: Yes? Well, he's not changed much then.

MARTIN: Not a bit. Even Katie hasn't managed to shift my bowels for me, have you?

KATHERINE: And if it's not that, he can't sleep.

MARTIN: Yes, Katie, you've said that already. I've also got gout, piles and bells in my ears. Dr. Staupitz has had to put up with all my complaints for longer than you have, isn't that right?

KATHERINE: Well, try not to forget what I said. (*She kisses* MARTIN*'s cheeks.*)

MARTIN: Good night, Katie.

(*She goes out.*)

STAUPITZ: Well, *you've* never been so well looked after.

MARTIN: It's a shame everyone can't marry a nun. They're fine cooks, thrifty housekeepers, and splendid mothers. Seems to me there are three ways out of despair. One is faith in Christ, the second is to become enraged by the world and make its nose bleed for it, and the third is the love of a woman. Mind you, they don't all necessarily work – at least, only part of the time. Sometimes, I'm lying awake in the devil's own sweat, and I turn to Katie and touch her. And I say: get me out, Katie, please, Katie, please try and get me out. And sometimes, sometimes she actually drags me out. Poor old Katie, fishing about there in bed with her great, hefty arms, trying to haul me out.

STAUPITZ: She's good.

MARTIN: Wine?

STAUPITZ: Not much. I must go to bed myself.

MARTIN: Help you sleep. You're looking tired.

STAUPITZ: Old. Our old pear tree's in blossom, I see. You've looked after it.

MARTIN: I like to get in a bit in the garden, if I can. I like to think it heals my bones somehow. Anyway, I always feel a bit more pleased with myself afterwards.

STAUPITZ: We'd a few talks under that tree.

MARTIN: Yes.

STAUPITZ: Martin, it's so still. I don't think I'd ever realized how eloquent a monk's silence really was. It was a voice. (*Pause.*) It's gone. (*He shakes his head, pause.*) How's your father these days?

MARTIN: Getting old too, but he's well enough.

STAUPITZ: Is he – is he pleased with you?

MARTIN: He was never pleased about anything I ever did. Not when I took my master's degree or when I got to be Dr. Luther. Only when Katie and I were married and she got pregnant. Then he was pleased.

STAUPITZ: Do you remember Brother Weinand?

MARTIN: I ought to. He used to hold my head between my knees when I felt faint in the choir.

STAUPITZ: I wonder what happened to him. (*Pause.*) He had the most beautiful singing voice.

MARTIN: My old friend, you're unhappy. I'm sorry. (*Pause.*) We monks were really no good to anyone, least of all to ourselves, every one of us rolled up like a louse in the Almighty's overcoat.

STAUPITZ: Yes. Well, you always have a way of putting it. I was always having to give you little lectures about the fanatic way you'd observe the Rule all the time.

MARTIN: Yes, and you talked me out of it, remember? (*Pause.*) Father are *you* pleased with me?

STAUPITZ: Pleased with you? My dear son, I'm not anyone or anything to be pleased with you any more. When we used to talk together underneath that tree you were like a child.

75

MARTIN: A child.

STAUPITZ: Manhood was something you had to be flung into, my son. You dangled your toe in it longer than most of us could ever bear. But you're not a frightened little monk any more who's come to his prior for praise or blame. Every time you belch now, the world stops what it's doing and listens. Do you know, when I first came to take over this convent, there weren't thirty books published every year. And now, last year it was more like six or seven hundred, and most of those published in Wittenberg too.

MARTIN: The best turn God ever did Himself was giving us a printing press. Sometimes I wonder what He'd have done without it.

STAUPITZ: I heard the other day they're saying the world's going to end in 1532.

MARTIN: It sounds as good a date as any other. Yes – 1532. That could easily be the end of the world. You could write a book about it, and just call it that – 1532.

STAUPITZ: I'm sorry, Martin. I didn't mean to come and see you after all this time and start criticizing. Forgive me. I'm getting old and a bit silly and frightened, that meal was just too much for me. It wasn't that I didn't –

MARTIN: Please – I'm sorry too. Don't upset yourself. I'm used to critics, John. They just help you to keep your muscles from getting slack. All those hollow cavillers, that subtle clown Erasmus, for instance. He ought to know better, but all he wants to do is to be able to walk on eggs without breaking any. As for that mandrill-arsed English baboon Henry, that leprous son of a bitch never had an idea of his own to jangle on a tombstone, let alone call himself Defender of the Faith.

(*Pause.* STAUPITZ *hasn't responded to his attempt at lightness.*)
Still, one thing for Erasmus, he didn't fool about with all the usual cant and rubbish about indulgences and the Pope and Purgatory. No, he went right to the core of it. He's still up to his ears with stuff about morality, and men being able to save themselves. No one does good, not anyone. God is true and one. But, and this is what he can't grasp,

76

He's utterly incomprehensible and beyond the reach of minds. A man's will is like a horse standing between two riders. If God jumps on its back, it'll go where God wants it to. But if Satan gets up there, it'll go where he leads it. And not only that, the horse can't choose its rider. That's left up to them, to those two. (*Pause.*) Why are you accusing me? What have I done?

STAUPITZ: I'm not accusing you, Martin. You know that. A just man is his own accuser. Because a just man judges as he is.

MARTIN: What's that mean? I'm not just?

STAUPITZ: You try. What else can you do?

MARTIN: You mean those damned peasants, don't you? You think I should have encouraged them!

STAUPITZ: I don't say that.

MARTIN: Well, what do you say?

STAUPITZ: You needn't have encouraged the princes. They were butchered and *you* got them to do it. And they had just cause, Martin. They did, didn't they?

MARTIN: I didn't say they hadn't.

STAUPITZ: Well then?

MARTIN: Do you remember saying to me, 'Remember, brother, you started this in the name of the Lord Jesus Christ'?

STAUPITZ: Well?

MARTIN: Father, the world can't be ruled with a rosary. They were a mob, a mob, and if they hadn't been held down and slaughtered, there'd have been a thousand more tyrants instead of half a dozen. It was a mob, and because it was a mob it was against Christ. No man can die for another, or believe for another or answer for another. The moment they try they become a mob. If we're lucky we can be persuaded in our own mind, and the most we can hope for is to die each one for himself. Do I have to tell you what Paul says? You read! 'Let every soul be subject unto the highest powers. For there is no power but of God: the powers that be are ordained of God. Whosoever therefore resisteth that power, resisteth the ordinance of God': that's

Paul, Father, and that's Scripture! 'And they that resist shall receive to themselves damnation.'

STAUPITZ: Yes, you're probably right.

MARTIN: 'Love worketh no ill to his neighbour: therefore love is the fulfilling of the law.'

STAUPITZ: Yes, well it seems to be all worked out. I must be tired.

MARTIN: It was worked out for me.

STAUPITZ: I'd better get off to bed.

MARTIN: They're trying to turn me into a fixed star, Father, but I'm a shifting planet. You're leaving me.

STAUPITZ: I'm not leaving you, Martin. I love you. I love you as much as any man has ever loved most women. But we're not two protected monks chattering under a pear tree in a garden any longer. The world's changed. For one thing, you've made a thing called Germany; you've unlaced a language and taught it to the Germans, and the rest of the world will just have to get used to the sound of it. As we once made the body of Christ from bread, you've made the body of Europe, and whatever our pains turn out to be, they'll attack the rest of the world too. You've taken Christ away from the low mumblings and soft voices and jewelled gowns and the tiaras and put Him back where He belongs. In each man's soul. We owe so much to you. All I beg of you is not to be too violent. In spite of everything, of everything you've said and shown us, there *were* men, *some* men who did live holy lives here once. Don't – don't believe you, only you are right.

(STAUPITZ *is close to tears, and* MARTIN *doesn't know what to do.*)

MARTIN: What else can I do? What can I do?

(*He clutches at his abdomen.*)

STAUPITZ: What is it?

MARTIN: Oh, the old trouble, that's all. That's all.

STAUPITZ: Something that's puzzled me, and I've always meant to ask you.

MARTIN: Well?

STAUPITZ: When you were before the Diet in Worms, and they

asked you those two questions – why did you ask for that extra day to think over your reply?

MARTIN: Why?

STAUPITZ: You'd known what your answer was going to be for months. Heaven knows, you told me enough times. Why did you wait?

(*Pause.*)

MARTIN: I wasn't certain.

STAUPITZ: And were you? Afterwards?

MARTIN: I listened for God's voice, but all I could hear was my own.

STAUPITZ: *Were* you sure?

(*Pause.*)

MARTIN: No.

(STAUPITZ *kisses him.*)

STAUPITZ: Thank you, my son. May God bless you. I hope you sleep better. Goodnight.

MARTIN: Goodnight, Father.

(STAUPITZ *goes out, and* MARTIN *is left alone. He drinks his wine.*)

MARTIN: Oh, Lord, I believe. I believe. I do believe. Only help my unbelief.

(*He sits slumped in his chair.* KATHERINE *enters. She is wearing a nightdress, and carries in her arms* HANS, *their young son.*)

KATHERINE: He was crying out in his sleep. Must have been dreaming again. Aren't you coming to bed?

MARTIN: Shan't be long, Katie. Shan't be long.

KATHERINE: All right, but try not to be too long. You look – well, you don't look as well as you should.

(*She turns to go.*)

MARTIN: Give him to me.

KATHERINE: What?

MARTIN: Give him to me.

KATHERINE: What do you mean, what for? He'll get cold down here.

MARTIN: No, he won't. Please, Katie. Let me have him.

KATHERINE: You're a funny man. All right, but only for five

minutes. Don't just sit there all night. He's gone back to sleep now. He'll be having another dream if you keep him down here.

MARTIN: Thank you, Katie.

KATHERINE: There! Keep him warm now! He's *your* son.

MARTIN: I will. Don't worry.

KATHERINE: Well, make sure you do. (*Pausing on way out.*) Don't be long now, Martin.

MARTIN: Good night, Kate.

(*She goes out, leaving* MARTIN *with the sleeping child in his arms.*)

(*Softly.*) What was the matter? Was it the devil bothering you? Um? Was he? Old nick? Up you, old nick. Well, don't worry. One day you might even be glad of him. So long as you can show him your little backside. That's right, show him your backside and let him have it. So try not to be afraid. The dark isn't quite as thick as all that. You know, my father had a son, and he'd to learn a hard lesson, which is a human being is a helpless little animal, but he's not created by his father, but by God. It's hard to accept you're anyone's son, and you're not the father of yourself. So, don't have dreams so soon, my son. *They'll* be having *you* soon enough.

(*He gets up.*)

You should have seen me at Worms. I was almost like you that day, as if I'd learned to play again, to play, to play out in the world, like a naked child. 'I have come to set a man against his father,' I said, and they listened to me. Just like a child. Sh! We must go to bed, mustn't we? A little while, and you *shall* see me. Christ said that, my son. I hope that'll be the way of it again. I hope so. Let's just hope so, eh? Eh? Let's just hope so.

(MARTIN *holds the child in his arms, and then walks off slowly.*)

The End.

A PATRIOT FOR ME

CHARACTERS

ALFRED REDL
AUGUST SICZYNSKI
STEINBAUER
LUDWIG MAX VON KUPFER
LT.-COL. LUDWIG VON MÖHL
ADJUTANT
MAXIMILIAN VON TAUSSIG
ALBRECHT
ANNA
HILDE
STANITSIN
COL. MISCHA OBLENSKY
GEN. CONRAD VON HÖTZENDORF
COUNTESS SOPHIA DELYANOFF
JUDGE ADVOCATE JAROSLAW KUNZ
YOUNG MAN IN CAFÉ
PAUL
BARON VON EPP
FERDY
FIGARO
LT. STEFAN KOVACS
MARIE-ANTOINETTE
TSARINA
LADY GODIVA
DR SCHOEPFER
2ND LT. VICTOR JERZABEK
ORDERLY
MISCHA LIPSCHUTZ
MITZI HEIGEL
MINISTER
KUPFER'S SECONDS, PRIVATES,
WAITERS AT ANNA'S, OFFICERS,

WHORES, FLUNKEYS, HOFBURG GUESTS,
CAFÉ WAITERS, GROUP AT TABLE,
BALL GUESTS, SHEPHERDESSES,
BOY, HOTEL WAITERS

The first performance of *A Patriot for Me* was given at the Royal Court Theatre, Sloane Square, London, on 30th June 1965, by the English Stage Society, by arrangement with the English Stage Company. It was directed by Anthony Page and the décor was by Jocelyn Herbert. The musical adviser was John Addison.

The cast was as follows:

ALFRED REDL	Maximilian Schell
AUGUST SICZYNSKI	John Castle
STEINBAUER	Rio Fanning
LUDWIG MAX VON KUPFER	Frederick Jaeger
KUPFER'S SECONDS	Lew Luton, Richard Morgan
PRIVATES	Tim Pearce, David Schurmann, Thick Wilson
LT.-COL. LUDWIG VON MÖHL	Clive Morton
ADJUTANT	Timothy Carlton
MAXIMILIAN VON TAUSSIG	Edward Fox
ALBRECHT	Sandor Eles
WAITERS AT ANNA'S	Peter John, Domy Reiter
OFFICERS	Timothy Carlton, Lew Luton, Hal Hamilton, Richard Morgan
WHORES	Dona Martyn, Virginia Wetherell, Jackie Daryl, Sandra Hampton
ANNA	Laurel Mather
HILDE	Jennifer Jayne
STANITSIN	Desmond Perry
COL. MISCHA OBLENSKY	George Murcell
GEN. CONRAD VON HÖTZENDORF	Sebastian Shaw
COUNTESS SOPHIA DELYANOFF	Jill Bennett
JUDGE ADVOCATE JAROSLAW KUNZ	Ferdy Mayne
FLUNKEYS	John Forbes, Richard

	Morgan,
	Peter John, Timothy Carlton
HOFBURG GUESTS	Cyril Wheeler, Douglas Sheldon, Bryn Bartlett, Dona Martyn, Virginia Wetherell, Jackie Daryl, Sandra Hampton, Laurel Mather
CAFÉ WAITERS	Anthony Roye, Domy Reiter, Bryn Bartlett, Cyril Wheeler
GROUP AT TABLE	Dona Martyn, Laurel Mather, Bryn Bartlett, Cyril Wheeler
YOUNG MAN IN CAFÉ	Paul Robert
PAUL	Douglas Sheldon
PRIVATES	Richard Morgan, David Schurmann, Tim Pearce, Thick Wilson
BARON VON EPP	George Devine
FERDY	John Forbes
FIGARO	Thick Wilson
LT. STEFAN KOVACS	Hal Hamilton
MARIE-ANTOINETTE	Lew Luton
TSARINA	Domy Reiter
LADY GODIVA	Peter John
BALL GUESTS	Cyril Wheeler, Richard Morgan, Timothy Carlton, John Castle, Edward Fox, Paul Robert, Douglas Sheldon, Tim Pearce
FLUNKEY	David Schurmann
SHEPHERDESSES	Franco Derosa, Robert Kidd
DR SCHOEPFER	Vernon Dobtcheff
BOY	Franco Derosa
2ND LT. VICTOR JERZABEK	Tim Pearce

HOTEL WAITERS	Bryn Bartlett, Lew Luton
ORDERLY	Richard Morgan
MISCHA LIPSCHUTZ	David Schurmann
MITZI HEIGEL	Virginia Wetherell
MINISTER	Anthony Roye
VOICES OF DEPUTIES	Clive Morton, Sebastian Shaw, George Devine, Vernon Dobtcheff, Cyril Wheeler
MUSICAL DIRECTOR	Tibor Kunstler
MUSICIANS	Reg Richman (Bass), Michael Zborowski (Piano), Ray Webb (Guitar)

ACT ONE

SCENE ONE

A Gymnasium. Of the 7th Galician Infantry Regiment at Lemburg, Galicia, 1890. It appears to be empty. From the high windows on one side, the earliest morning light shows up the climbing bars that run from floor to ceiling. From this, a long, thick rope hangs. Silhouetted is a vaulting horse. The lonely, slow tread of one man's boots is heard presently on the harsh floor. A figure appears. At this stage, his features can barely be made out. It is ALFRED REDL, *at this time Lieutenant. He has close cropped hair, a taut, compact body, a moustache. In most scenes he smokes long black cheroots, like Toscanas. On this occasion, he takes out a shabby cigarette case, an elegant amber holder, inserts a cigarette and lights it thoughtfully. He looks up at the window, takes out his watch and waits. It is obvious he imagines himself alone. He settles down in the half light. A shadow crosses his vision.*

REDL: Who's there? (*Pause.*) Who is it? Come on! Hey!

VOICE: Redl?

REDL: Who is it?

VOICE: Yes. I see you now.

REDL: Siczynski? Is it? Siczynski?

VOICE: Thought it was you. Yes.

> (*A figure appears,* PAUL SICZYNSKI. *He is a strong, very handsome young man about the same age as* REDL, *but much more boyish looking.* REDL *already has the stamp of an older man.*)

SICZYNSKI: Sorry.

REDL: Not at all.

SICZYNSKI: I startled you.

REDL: Well: we're both early.

SICZYNSKI: Yes.

REDL: Still. Not all that much. Cigarette?

(SICZYNSKI *takes one.* REDL *lights it for him.*)

SICZYNSKI: (*Smiles*) I haven't the style for that. Von Kupfer has
though. Expect he's snoozing away now. (*Looks at his
watch.*) Being wakened by his servant.
Um?

REDL: He gave a champagne supper at Anna's.

SICZYNSKI: Who was invited?

REDL: Half the garrison, I imagine.

SICZYNSKI: Did you go?

REDL: I'm your second . . .

SICZYNSKI: Is that what prevented you being asked?

REDL: It would have stopped me going.

SICZYNSKI: Well, then, he'll have stayed there till the last
moment, I should think. Perhaps he'll have been worn
down to nothing by one of those strapping Turkish
whores.

REDL: I doubt it.

SICZYNSKI: His spine cracked in between those thighs.
Snapped. . . . All the way up. No, you're most likely right.
You're right.

REDL: He's popular: I suppose.

SICZYNSKI: Yes. Unlikeable too.

REDL: Yes. He's a good, what's he, he's a good officer.

SICZYNSKI: He's a gentleman. And adjutant, adjutant mark
you, of a field battery at the ripe old age of twenty-one.
He's not half the soldier you are.

REDL: Well . . .

SICZYNSKI: And now he's on his way to the War College.

REDL: (*Quick interest*) Oh?

SICZYNSKI: Of course. If you'd been in his boots, you'd have
been in there and out again by this time, you'd be a major
at least, by now. (*Pause.*) Sorry – didn't mean to rub it in.

REDL: Kupfer. Ludwig Max Von Kupfer . . . it's cold.

SICZYNSKI: Cigarette smoke's warm.
(*Pause.*)

REDL: How are you?

SICZYNSKI: Cold.

REDL: Here.

SICZYNSKI: Cognac? Your health. Here's to the War College. And you.

REDL: Thank you.

SICZYNSKI: Oh, you will. Get in, I mean. *You* just have to pack in all the effort, while the Kupfers make none at all. He'll be sobering up by now. Putting his aristocratic head under the cold tap and shouting in that authentic Viennese drawl at whoever's picking up after him. You'd better, make it, I mean. Or you'll spend the rest of it in some defeated frontier town with debts. And more debts to look forward to as you go on. Probably the gout.
(*Pause.*) I just hope there isn't ever a war.
(*They smoke in silence. Slightly shy, tense.*
SICZYNSKI *leans against the vaulting horse.*)

REDL: You may underestimate Kupfer.

SICZYNSKI: Maybe. But then he overestimates himself. *You*'ve tremendous resources, reserves, energy. You won't let any old waters close over your head without a struggle first.

REDL: What about you?

SICZYNSKI: (*Smiles*) I'm easily disheartened.

REDL: He's destructive, *very* destructive.

SICZYNSKI: Who?

REDL: Kupfer.

SICZYNSKI: Yes, yes. And wilful. Coldly, not too cold, not disinterested.

REDL: That's why I think you underestimate him.

SICZYNSKI: But more vicious than most. You're right there. He's a killer all right.

REDL: Someone'll chalk him up . . . sometime.

SICZYNSKI: What about me?

REDL: That would be very good. Very good.

SICZYNSKI: Just not very likely . . .

REDL: Have you done this before?

SICZYNSKI: (*Smiles*) No, never. Have you?

REDL: Only as a bystander.

SICZYNSKI: Well, this time you're a participant. . . . I'd always expected to *be* challenged a hundred times. I never thought

89

I'd do it. Well, picked the right man. Only the wrong swordsman. May I?

(*He indicates Cognac.* REDL *nods.*)

Have you seen him?

REDL: Seen? Oh, with a sabre. No. Have you?

SICZYNSKI: No. Have you seen *me*?

REDL: Often.

SICZYNSKI: Well, there it is.

REDL: (*Softly*) More times than I can think of.

SICZYNSKI: They say only truly illiterate minds are obdurate. Well, that's me and Kupfer.

REDL: Why do you feel like this about him? He's not exactly untypical.

SICZYNSKI: Not by any means. For me, well, perhaps he just plays the part better. He makes me want to be sick. Over *him* preferably.

REDL: I don't understand you. You're more than a match for his sort.

SICZYNSKI: I just chose the wrong ground to prove it, here.

(*Pause.*)

REDL: Look, Siczynski, why don't I, I'm quite plausible and not half a bad actor, for one . . . reason and another, why don't you let me, sort of . . .

SICZYNSKI: Thank you, Redl. You can't do anything now.

REDL: Very well.

SICZYNSKI: Don't be offended.

REDL: Why should I?

SICZYNSKI: (*Wry*) Someone who looks as good as me ought to be able to handle himself a bit better, don't you agree?

REDL: Yes.

SICZYNSKI: At least – physically. . . . A *little* better don't you think? Why did you agree to be my second?

REDL: Why did you ask me?

SICZYNSKI: I thought you'd agree to. Did you get anyone else?

REDL: Steinbauer.

SICZYNSKI: As a favour to you? No, I didn't think you'd have to be persuaded.

REDL: No.

SICZYNSKI: Mine's gone out.
    (REDL *offers him a cigarette, from which he takes a light.*)
    I thought you always smoked those long Italian cigars.
    (REDL *nods.*)
    Expensive taste. What is it?
REDL: I was only going to ask you: *are* you a Jew?
SICZYNSKI: (*Smiles*) Grandmother. Maternal Grandmother.
    Quite enough though, don't you think? Oh, she became
    Catholic when she married my Grandfather. Not that she
    ever took it seriously, any more than him. She'd a good
    sense of fun, not like the rest of my family. You think it
    doesn't matter about Kupfer's insult, don't you? Well of
    course you're right. I don't think it would have mattered
    what he said. Oh, I quite enjoyed his jokes about calling
    me Rothschild. What *I* objected to, from him, – in the
    circumstances, was being called Fräulein Rothschild. . . .
REDL: You shouldn't gamble.
SICZYNSKI: I don't.
REDL: On people's goodwill.
SICZYNSKI: I don't. *You* do.
REDL: I do? No, I don't . . . I try not to.
    (*He is confused for a moment.* SICZYNSKI *watches him
    thoughtfully, through his cigarette smoke. It is getting lighter,
    colder.*)
SICZYNSKI: You smell of peppermints.
REDL: Nearly time. (*He stands.*)
SICZYNSKI: Kupfer's breath stinks.
REDL: I hadn't noticed.
SICZYNSKI: You mean you haven't got near enough? You don't
    need to. *He* should chew peppermints.
    (*Pause.*)
    Have some of your brandy.
REDL: Thanks.
SICZYNSKI: It's a cold time to be up, to be up at all.
REDL: I've hardly ever had warm feet. Not since I went to
    Cadet School.
SICZYNSKI: You work too hard.
REDL: What else can I do?

91

SICZYNSKI: Sorry. Of course, you're right. I'm just waiting. Can't think much any more.

(REDL *would like to help if there were some means. But he can't.*)

Go on. If you can, I mean. Don't if you can't . . . Won't be long, now . . .

REDL: We've never talked together much, have we? We must have both been here? What? Two years?

SICZYNSKI: Why couldn't you sleep?

REDL: Don't know. Oh yes, I had a dream . . .

SICZYNSKI: But then you're not what they call sociable, are you?

REDL: Aren't I?

SICZYNSKI: Well! Asking for extra duties, poring over all those manuals.

REDL: You don't make it sound very likeable.

SICZYNSKI: It isn't – much.

(REDL *takes out his watch.*)

REDL: I told Steinbauer two minutes before. He's pretty reliable.

SICZYNSKI: Anyway, you're taking a risk doing *this*. But I suppose Kupfer will draw the fire.

REDL: And you. You specially.

SICZYNSKI: The Galician Jew, you mean? Yes. But that's only if I win.

REDL: It needn't come to that.

SICZYNSKI: It will.

REDL: I'll see it doesn't.

SICZYNSKI: No, you won't. You can't . . . What, what does one, do you suppose, well, look for in anyone, anyone else, I mean?

REDL: For?

SICZYNSKI: Elsewhere.

REDL: I haven't tried. Or thought about it. At least . . .

SICZYNSKI: I mean: That isn't clearly, really, already in oneself?

REDL: Nothing, I expect.

(*Pause.*)

SICZYNSKI: Tell me about your dream.

REDL: Do you believe in dreams?

SICZYNSKI: Not specially. They're true while they last, I
suppose.

REDL: Well, it wasn't –

(*There is the sound of boots. Walking swiftly, confidently, this
time. The two men look at each other.*)

Steinbauer. On the dot.

(STEINBAUER *enters.*)

Morning, Steinbauer.

(STEINBAUER *nods, slightly embarrassed. Clicks his heels at*
SICZYNSKI.)

Cold.

STEINBAUER: Yes.

SICZYNSKI: Got the cutlery? Oh, yes I see.

STEINBAUER: All here.

SICZYNSKI: Redl was telling me his dream. Go on.

REDL: It's nothing.

SICZYNSKI: That hardly matters, does it?

REDL: Not really time.

SICZYNSKI: Please.

(STEINBAUER *takes out his watch.*)

REDL: Just, oh, I was, well later, I was, I won't tell you the
first –

SICZYNSKI: Why not?

REDL: It's too dull. So is *this* too. Anyway: I was attending a
court martial. Not mine. Someone else's. I don't quite
know whose. But a friend of some sort, someone I liked.
Someone upright, frank, respected, but upright. It was
quite clear from the start what the outcome would be, and
I was immediately worrying about having to go and visit
him in gaol. And it wasn't just because I knew I would be
arrested myself as soon as I got in there. It wasn't for that.
Anyhow, there I was, and I went and started to talk to him.
He didn't say anything. There was just the wire netting
between us . . . and then of course, they arrested *me*. I
couldn't tell whether he was pleased or not. Pleased that
I'd come to see him or that they'd got me too. They
touched me on the shoulder and told me to stand up,

93

which I did. And by that time he'd gone. Somehow.

(*Sound of several pairs of boots clattering on the unyielding floor into the Gymnasium.* REDL *frowns anxiously at* SICZYNSKI, *who smiles at him. As soon as* KUPFER *and his seconds arrive, they get to their feet. Both sides salute each other and prepare for the duel in silence. Sabres are selected. Tunics discarded, etc. All brisk. The duel begins. The four men watch almost indifferently at first. But the spectacle soon strips away this. Blood is drawn, sweat runs, breathing tightens. At one point* REDL *steps forward.* KUPFER *orders him back curtly. All settle down for the end. It comes fairly soon.*

SICZYNSKI *cries out and falls to the ground.* KUPFER *begins dressing almost immediately. He goes out with his companions, who are trying to be composed.*)

STEINBAUER: Shall I? Yes, I'd better get the doctor.

REDL: Yes, I suppose so.

(STEINBAUER *follows the others out.* REDL *wipes the blood from* SICZYNSKI's *mouth, cradling him in his arms. He is clearly dead.*)

(*Fade.*)

SCENE TWO

Office of the Commandant, Seventh Galician Infantry Regiment. The Commandant, LIEUTENANT-COLONEL VON MÖHL, *is seated at his desk. A sharp rap at the door.* VON MÖHL *grunts. The door is opened smartly by the* ADJUTANT.

ADJUTANT: Lieutenant Redl, sir.

(REDL *enters, salutes, etc.*)

MÖHL: Is Taussig there?

ADJUTANT: Yes, sir.

MÖHL: Good. All right.

(ADJUTANT *goes out.*)

Redl, Redl, Redl: yes. (*He looks up.*) Sit down, please.

(REDL *sits.* MÖHL *scrutinises him.*)

Well, Redl. You've quite a good deal of news to come it seems to me. Yes.

REDL: Yes, sir?

MÖHL: You may think that a young officer gets lost among all the others, that he isn't observed, constantly, critically and sympathetically. You might think that an officer with an unremarkable background, or without rather dazzling connections of one sort or another would go unnoticed. Do you think that, Redl?

REDL: Sir, my own experience is that genuine merit rarely goes unnoticed or unrewarded. Even, particularly in the Army.

MÖHL: Good. And quite correct, Redl, and for a very obvious reason. The future of the Empire depends on the Army, probably the future of Europe, on an alert, swift machine that can meet instant crisis from whatever quarter it may come. It's taken us a long time to learn our lesson, lessons like Solferino. Expensive, humiliating and inglorious, but worth it now. Only the very best kind of men can be entrusted in the modern army.

(*He waves at the map of pre-1914 Europe, with Austria-Hungary in the middle, behind him.*)

No one's going to be passed over, every man'll have his chance to prove himself, show what he could do, given half the chance. I don't say there still aren't short cuts for people who don't apparently deserve it, but that's not for you or me to argue. What we *can* do is make sure the way's made to virgin merit, someone with nothing else. What do you say?

REDL: I'm sure you're right, sir.

MÖHL: Oh?

REDL: It always seems quite clear to me, sir, the officers who complain about privilege are invariably inferior or mediocre.

(REDL *speaks coolly and carefully. He is anxious to be courteous and respectful without seeming unctuous, or sound a false, fawning note. He succeeds.*)

MÖHL: Exactly. The real good 'uns don't ever really get left out, that's why so much nonsense is talked, especially about the Army. You can't *afford* to ignore a good man. He's too valuable. A good soldier always knows another one. That's what comradeship is. It's not an empty thing, not an empty thing at all. It's knowing the *value* of other men. And cherishing it. Now: Redl. Two reasons I sent for you. I'll, yes, we'll, I think we'll deal with the best first.

(*He pauses.* REDL *waits.*)

As you know, as Commander, it's my duty to recommend officers for War College examination. This year I only felt able to recommend Von Taussig, Von Kupfer, and yourself. The result I can now tell you, after the final examination and interview, is that you have all three been granted admission, a very fine achievement for us all. Four hundred and eighteen candidates for thirty-nine places. Well, Von Taussig has been admitted number twenty-eight, yourself twenty-six and Von Kupfer seventeen. Congratulations.

REDL: Thank you, sir.

MÖHL: Well, I'm very pleased indeed myself, with the result. All three accepted. It's quite something for me too, you know, especially over you. I was pretty sure about the other two, well, of course. . . . But you, well, I knew you had the education, enough . . . There it is. Now you've done it.

REDL: I'm very grateful, sir.

MÖHL: By yourself. You. Number twenty-six! Please. Smoke, if you wish. Here – one of these.

(*Offers him a cigar. Takes one himself.* REDL *lights both of them.*)

So: How do you feel?

REDL: Very proud – and grateful, sir.

MÖHL: I don't think you realize, you've made quite an impression. Here, listen to this. Arithmetic, algebra, geometry, trigonometry – all excellent. Elementary engineering, construction, fortification, geography and international law, all eighty-five per cent, all first class. Riding – required standard. That's the only begrudging remark on any of your reports, required standard. Anyway, get that horse out in the school a bit. Yes?

REDL: Yes, sir.

MÖHL: Let's see now, what does it say, do you speak Russian?

REDL: No, sir.

MÖHL: No matter. You will. Native language?

REDL: Ruthenian.

MÖHL: German – excellent. Polish, French – fair. Punctilious knowledge military and international matters. Seems to know Franco-Prussian campaign better than anyone who actually took part. Learned. All the qualities of first-class field officer and an unmistakable flair for intelligence. No. Wait a minute, there's more yet. Upright, discreet, frank and open, painstaking, marked ability to anticipate, as well as initiate instructions, without being reckless, keen judgement, cool under pressure – *that*'s Erdmannsdorfer, so that's good, very good indeed – Yes, cool, fine interpreter of the finest modern military thinking. Personality: friendly but unassertive, dignified and strikes everyone as the type of a gentleman and distinguished officer of the Royal and Imperial Army. Well, what do you say?

REDL: I'm overwhelmed, sir.

MÖHL: Well, I like to see this sort of thing happen. Kupfer and Taussig are one thing, and I'm proud of them. But you're another. . . . Yours is effort, effort, concerted, sustained, intelligent effort. Which brings me to the Siczynski affair. Of course, you realize that if your part in that incident had been made properly known, it would almost certainly have prejudiced your application?

REDL: Yes, sir.

MÖHL: However, we chose to be discreet.

REDL: I'm more grateful than I can tell you, sir.

MÖHL: Well, of course, with Kupfer, it was more difficult. However, he has been in trouble of this kind before, and, let's be honest about it, he does have advantages. He is able to get away with incidents like Siczynski occasionally, though even he can't do it too often. Of course, he was a principal in this case and you weren't, but I must tell you it was a grave error on your part ever to have consented to become involved in an affair which ends in a brother officer's death. I'm saying this to you as a warning for the future. *Don't* get involved.

97

REDL: Yes, sir. May I ask where is Lieutenant Von Kupfer, sir?

MÖHL: Temporarily transferred to Wiener Neustadt. . . . Was Siczynski a friend of yours?

REDL: No, sir.

MÖHL: What was your opinion of him?

REDL: I hardly knew him, sir. (*Realizes quickly he needs to provide more than this.*) He struck me as being hyper-critical, over-sceptical about things.

MÖHL: What things?

REDL: Army life and traditions, esprit –

MÖHL: Religion?

REDL: We never discussed it. But – yes, I suspect so, I should think . . .

MÖHL: Jewish . . .?

REDL: Yes, sir. I believe.

MÖHL: Galician, like yourself.

REDL: Yes.

MÖHL: You're yes, Catholic, of course.

REDL: Yes, sir.

MÖHL: What about women?

REDL: Siczynski?

(*Nod from* MÖHL.)

As I say, I didn't know him well.

MÖHL: But?

REDL: I never thought of him, no one seemed to, as a ladies' man.

MÖHL: Precisely. Yet he was very attractive, physically, wouldn't you say?

REDL: That's a hard question for another man to answer –

MÖHL: Oh, come, Redl, you know what women are attracted –

REDL: Yes. Of course, I should say he was, quite certainly.

MÖHL: But you never heard of any particular girl or girls?

REDL: No. But then, we weren't exactly, and I don't –

MÖHL: You are a popular officer – Redl – Siczynski wasn't. He had debts, too. And quite hefty ones. Oh, one expects all young officers to have debts. It's always been so, and always will, till they pay soldiers properly. Every other week, a fund has to be raised for this one or that. Fine. But

98

this officer had, or so it seems, and frankly it doesn't surprise me, no friends, was in the hands of moneylenders, of his own race, naturally, and why? Women? Of course, one asks. But who? No one knows. No family. Who was worth nine thousand kronen in debts.

REDL: Nine . . .

MÖHL: Do you think I can find out? It *is* odd, after all. Young officer, apparently attractive in many ways, work excellent, intelligence exceptional, diligent, manly disposition and all the rest of it. Then: where are you?

REDL: Perhaps? – I don't think he was ever in his right element.

MÖHL: Well. There it is. Incident closed now, including your part in it.

REDL: Thank you, sir.

MÖHL: Only remember. Involvement. Debts – well, you'll be all right. Also, you have friends, and *will* have. As for women, I think you know what you're doing.

REDL: I hope so, sir.

MÖHL: What about marriage?

REDL: I'm not contemplating it, not for quite some time, that is.

MÖHL: Good. You've got ideals and courage and fortitude, and I'm proud and delighted you'll be going from this regiment to War College. You're on your way, Redl. Taussig!
(ADJUTANT *enters.*)
Send in Taussig.
(ADJUTANT *clicks heels. Enter* TAUSSIG *presently.*)
Ah, Taussig. Come in. You know Redl. You two should have something to celebrate together tonight.
(*Fade.*)

SCENE THREE

ANNA'S. *A private cubicle. In the background a gipsy orchestra, and flash young officers eating, drinking, swearing, singing, entertaining* ANNA'S *young ladies.* REDL *is alone in the cubicle. He leans forward, scoops a champagne bottle from its bucket to pour himself another*

99

glass. It is empty. He draws the curtain aside and bawls into the smoke and noise.

REDL: Anna! Anna! Hey! You! What's your name?!
    Max! Leo! Anna! Damn!
    (*He gives up. Looks in his tunic for his cigar case. Takes one out, a long black Italian cheroot.* A YOUNG WAITER *enters.*)
    Ah, there you are. Thank God. Another – please.
    Oh – you've got it. That's clever.

WAITER: I guessed you'd be wanting another, sir.

REDL: Good fellow. Open it, would you?

WAITER: At once, sir.

REDL: Which one are you then?

WAITER: Which one, sir?

REDL: You're not Leo or that other stumpy creature, what's his name –

WAITER: I am Albrecht, sir.

REDL: You're new then.

WAITER: Seven months, sir.

REDL: Oh. I didn't notice you.

WAITER: You don't often do us the honour, sir.

REDL: Light this for me.
    (WAITER *does so.*)
    I can't afford time for this sort of caper very often.

WAITER: What a magnificent cigar case, sir.

REDL: What? Oh. Yes. Present. From my uncle.

WAITER: Very fine indeed. Shall I pour it now?

REDL: Yes.

WAITER: Pol Roger eighty one, sir.

REDL: (*Shortly*) Fine.

WAITER: Would that be crocodile, sir?

REDL: Eh? Oh. Yes. Have you seen my guest anywhere among that mob?

WAITER: Lieutenant Taussig, sir?

REDL: Well, who else?

WAITER: He is talking with Madame Anna.
    (REDL *sips his champagne. The* WAITER *has increased his restless, uneasy mood. He can't bring himself to dismiss him yet.*)

REDL: Rowdy, roaring mob you've got in there.

WAITER: Yes, sir.

REDL: Why do they have to make such a damned show? Howling and vomiting and whoring.

(*They listen.*)

Drunk. . . . Why do they need to get so drunk?

WAITER: End of the summer manoeuvres they tell me, sir. Always the same then.

REDL: This place'll get put out of bounds one day. Someone should warn Anna.

WAITER: I think she just does her best to please the young officers, sir. Giving them what they ask for.

REDL: They'll get it too, and no mistake. What's that young officer's name?

WAITER: Which one, sir? Oh, with the red-haired girl, Hilde – yes, Lieutenant Steinbauer, sir.

REDL: So it is.

WAITER: Very beautiful girl, sir.

REDL: Yes.

WAITER: Very popular, that one.

REDL: Garbage often is.

WAITER: That's true too, of course, sir.

(*Pause.*)

REDL: Taussig! Where the hell is he?

WAITER: Shall I tell him you want him, sir?

REDL: No. Better not. I'm getting bored sitting here on my own.

WAITER: Can I do anything else, sir?

REDL: No. (*Detaining him.*) Do you remember Kupfer?

WAITER: Lieutenant Kupfer? Oh yes, he used to be in here nearly every night, sometimes when he shouldn't have been. We were sorry when he was re-posted.

REDL: And Lieutenant Siczynski? Do you remember him?

WAITER: No, sir, I don't.

REDL: You don't come from Lemberg?

WAITER: No, sir. From Vienna. Oh, you mean the one who was killed in the duel? He used to come in sometimes, usually on his own. But no one seemed to take much notice of him. He didn't exactly avail himself of the place. Like Lieutenant Kupfer. *He* used to have this cubicle regularly.

REDL: You must miss Vienna.

WAITER: I do, sir. There are always so many different things to do *there*. In Lemberg everybody knows who you are and everything about you. . . . Well, no doubt you'll be in Vienna yourself before long. May I congratulate you, sir?

REDL: Thank you.

WAITER: On the General Staff, I've no doubt, sir.

REDL: We'll see.

(*A roar and banging of tables.*)

What the devil's going on?

WAITER: Lieutenant Steinbauer has passed out, sir. They're passing him over their heads . . . One by one . . . Now he's being sick. I'd better go.

REDL: Well, he's better off: see someone takes him home, if you can.

WAITER: I'll do my best, sir. So, as I say, you'll soon be seeing for yourself.

REDL: What?

WAITER: Why, Vienna.

REDL: Oh. All I'll see is work. Maps, tactical field work, riding drill, Russian language, maps.

WAITER: Oh, of course.

REDL: That'll be enough for me.

WAITER: Yes, sir.

(*Pause. Enter* TAUSSIG.)

TAUSSIG: Well, I've fixed us up.

REDL: What?

TAUSSIG: Girls. One each. I've been arguing ten minutes with Anna, and she insisted she'd only got one spare, that lovely black gipsy with the mole on her cheek. There.

WAITER: Zoe.

TAUSSIG: That's the one. So I said to her, I know she's a big girl, but I know my friend Lieutenant Redl won't go much on sharing, especially on an occasion like this evening.

REDL: Please forget it. I'm bored with the place.

TAUSSIG: So am I. We'll take another, oh, you've got another,

we'll take some more champagne upstairs with us and be
entertained properly, me by big black Zoe, and you, you
my friend by Hilde. And very lucky you are, doubly lucky,
because she was tied up by young Steinbauer until a few
moments ago, but now he's safely on his face in the cellar,
he won't be capable of fulfilling his little engagement
tonight, he'll be lucky to stand up on parade in the
morning, and Hilde, red, pale, vacant and booked this
moment by me is all yours.

REDL: It doesn't matter.

TAUSSIG: Of course, it doesn't. It's all fixed. Fixed by me and
paid for.

REDL: Taussig, I can't allow it.

TAUSSIG: Nonsense. It's done.

(WAITER *pours champagne.* TAUSSIG *drinks.*)

You insisted on buying the dinner and champagne. And
now, *more* champagne. Now, *I* insist on treating you. Your
health.

(*He glances quickly at the* WAITER.)

To black Zoe and her gipsy mole. And Hilde and her red
whatever special she's got in there. Drink up.

(REDL *drinks.*)

(*To* WAITER.) WHAT ARE *you* standing about for?

REDL: He was opening the champagne.

TAUSSIG: Well, take another one up. On *my* bill.

REDL: Are you sure?

TAUSSIG: Of course I'm sure. We're going to need it. Come on,
I'm glad to see you smoking a cigar again. Can't stand the
smell of those peppermints. I've always wanted to tell you.
I say, that's a pretty classy case.

REDL: My uncle.

TAUSSIG: I didn't know you had rich relatives.

REDL: Only him.

TAUSSIG: Perhaps I should have let you pay for Hilde yourself.

REDL: Of course. Please.

TAUSSIG: Unless you *would* have preferred Zoe. Sharing, I
mean.

REDL: Hilde sounds just the thing.

TAUSSIG: I think she's more your type. Bit on the skinny side. No bottom, little tiny bottom, not a real roly-poly. And breasts made like our friend here. Go on, go and get that other bottle!

REDL: (*To* WAITER) Just a moment.

TAUSSIG: I'll round them up.

(*Pause.*)

Don't be all night then.

REDL: Just coming.

(*He goes to his wallet, trying not to be awkward. He hands a note to the* WAITER).

WAITER: Thank you, sir.

(*He lights a match for* REDL, *who looks up. Then notices his cigar is out.*)

REDL: Oh, yes.

WAITER: Shall I take this bottle up then, sir?

REDL: Yes. Wait a minute.

(WAITER *pauses.*)

Pour me another glass.

(*He does so. Picks up bucket.*)

WAITER: Good night, sir.

REDL: Good night.

(*The* WAITER *goes out.* REDL *stares into his glass, then drains it, fastens his tunic smartly and steps through the curtain into the tumult.*)

(*Fade.*)

SCENE FOUR

ANNA's. *An upstairs room. Bare save for a bed. Lying on it are* HILDE *and* REDL. *Only the outline of their bodies is visible. In the darkness* REDL's *cigar glows. Silence. Then there is an occasional noise from one of the other rooms.*

HILDE: (*Whispers*) Hullo. (*Pause.*) Hullo.

REDL: Yes.

HILDE: Alfred! Can't you sleep?

REDL: No. I'm not tired.

HILDE: You slept a little. Oh, not for long. Can I get you anything?

REDL: No thank you.

HILDE: You clench your teeth. Did you know that?

REDL: No.

HILDE: When you're asleep. It makes quite a noise. Scraping together.

REDL: I'm sorry.

HILDE: Oh, please. I didn't mean that. But it'll wear your teeth down. And you've got such nice teeth. You smell of peppermints. Can I put the light on?

REDL: It's your room.

HILDE: It's yours tonight.
 (*She lights the lamp.*)
 Some men's mouths are disgusting.

REDL: I'm sure.

HILDE: You look better. You almost fainted. Can't I get you anything? (*Pause.*) Is there any champagne left?
 (*He pours her some from beside the bed.*)
 Don't often get champagne bought me. Well, here's to Vienna. Wish I was going.

REDL: Why don't you?

HILDE: I shall, I'm saving up.

REDL: What will you do – the same thing – when you get there?

HILDE: I suppose so. Do you know, your eyes are like mine?

REDL: Are they?

HILDE: I've never seen a man faint before.

REDL: You should be in the army. Do you want to get married?

HILDE: (*Softly*) Yes. Of course. Why? Are you proposing?

REDL: I've seen what you've got on offer.

HILDE: Only just. I'm sorry.

REDL: What about?

HILDE: You don't like me.

REDL: What *are* you on about?

HILDE: Never mind. More warm champagne, please.
 (*He pours.*)

REDL: What do you mean? Eh?

HILDE: Nothing. Thank you. God bless. And I hope you'll, you'll be happy in Vienna.

REDL: I'm sorry. Those exams and things have taken it out of me. Perhaps I'll come back tomorrow.

HILDE: Was Lieutenant Siczynski a friend of yours?

REDL: No. Why, did you know him?

HILDE: I used to see him.

REDL: Did he –

HILDE: No. Not with anyone. He usually sat on his own in a corner, reading the foreign papers or just drinking. I used to look at his eyes. But he never looked at me.

(REDL *leans over the bed and kisses her lingeringly. She returns the embrace abstractedly. He looks down at her.*)

Peppermints!

REDL: Damn it! I apologized, didn't I?

(*She puts her finger to his mouth to calm him.*)

HILDE: *And* cigars. That's what you smell of, and horses and saddles. What could be nicer, and more manly?

REDL: You're very, very pretty, Hilde. I love your red hair.

HILDE: You don't have to make love to me, Alfred. I'm only a whore.

REDL: But I mean it.

HILDE: Hired by your friend.

REDL: Pretty little, brittle bones.

HILDE: Lieutenant Taussig.

REDL: Is that him, next door?

HILDE: (*Listens*) At this moment, I should say.

(*They listen.*)

Is he a good friend of yours?

REDL: I can't say I'd call anyone I know a good friend.

HILDE: Are you sure you can't sleep?

REDL: Yes . . . But why don't you?

HILDE: May I put my head on your arm?

REDL: If you wish . . .

HILDE: No, I'll finish my champagne. Do you like children?

REDL: Yes. Why?

HILDE: Would you like some of your own?

REDL: Very much. Wouldn't you?

HILDE: Yes, I would.

REDL: Then what's stopping you?

HILDE: One would like to be loved, if it's possible.

REDL: Love's hardly ever possible.

HILDE: Do you believe that?

REDL: Yes. Anyway, there are always too many babies being born. So –

HILDE: You may be right. Perhaps that's why you're in the army.

REDL: What's the matter with you? I'm in the army because it suits *me* and I'm suited to *it*. I can make my own future. I can style it my own way.

HILDE: What about Siczynski?

REDL: He wasn't suited to it. Who's in that other room, there?

HILDE: Albrecht . . . Would you like to go?

REDL: No. I just asked you a question, that's all. Albrecht who?

HILDE: The waiter you were talking to while I was with the young lieutenant.

(*Pause.*)

REDL: He's a noisy fellow.

HILDE: Or whoever's with him.

(*They listen. She watches* REDL's *face.*)

Your cigar's gone out. Here. He always gets the pick, Albrecht. Anything he wants. Anyone.

(*She moves over to the wall and pulls back a flap and looks through.*)

Come here.

REDL: What for?

(*But he joins her.*)

HILDE: Do you want to look?

(*He hesitates, then does so. She returns to the bed, empties the champagne into her glass, and watches him. Presently, he turns away and sits on the bed. She puts her arm round his shoulder. Offers him drink.*) Have some?

(*He shakes his head.*)

Sad?

REDL: No. Not sad. One always just wishes that a congenial evening had been – even more congenial.

HILDE: Think I'll go to bed. It's made me sleepy again.
  (REDL *listens.*)
  Shall I turn the light out?
  (*He nods. She does so. He goes to the window and looks out.*
  Presently –)
  Good night, Alfred.
REDL: Good night, Hilde.
HILDE: Sorry. I can't keep awake. But you don't mind . . .
  (*He looks across at her, puts on his tunic, takes out a bank note,*
  picks up his cap.)
REDL: Good night, Hilde. Thank you.
  (*He presses the note into her hand.*)
HILDE: I'll tell your friend you left in time for reveille.
  (*He turns.*)
  Alfred –
  (*She sits up and kisses him lightly.*)
  You have the most beautiful mouth that ever, ever kissed
  me. Good night, Lieutenant.
REDL: Good night.
HILDE: (*Sleepily*) You'll be a colonel one day. On the General
  Staff. Or even a general.
  (*He gazes down at her, re-lights his cigar. The noise from the*
  adjoining room has subsided. He slips out.)
  (*Fade.*)

SCENE FIVE

Warsaw. A darkened office. The light from a magic lantern shines
white on a blank screen which faces the audience. A figure is seen to
be operating it. Another, seated in front of it, is watching the screen.
The first figure is LIEUTENANT STANITSIN. *The second* COLONEL
OBLENSKY.
OBLENSKY: Next!
STANITSIN: Redl.
  (REDL*'s photograph in uniform on the screen.*)
  Alfred Von Redl. Captain. Seventh Galician Infantry
  Regiment. Lemberg. Born Lemberg March 4th, 1864.

Family background: parents Leopold and Marthe Redl. Eighth of eleven children. Father ex-horse trooper, now second-grade clerical worker Royal and Imperial Railway. Religion: Catholic. Education: Cadet School, passed out with honours. Equitation school.

OBLENSKY: Oh, do get to the meat, Stanitsin. I want my dinner.

STANITSIN: (*Flustered slightly*) Oh – just –

OBLENSKY: If there is any. They're not a very promising lot this time, are they?

STANITSIN: Passed out of War College May of last year, number twenty-three of his entry, recommended particularly, on pink paper, recommended.

OBLENSKY: (*Turns head*) So it is. Meticulous.

STANITSIN: For appointment on General Staff.

OBLENSKY: Yes.

STANITSIN: Health: periodic asthma while at Cadet School, twice almost leading to his discharge. However, in the past ten years, this complaint seems to have been almost completely overcome. Contracted syphilis two and a half years ago, underwent treatment and discharged Lemberg Military Hospital. One serious breach of discipline, involved in duel when fellow officer was killed. Acted as one of the officer's seconds. Affair hushed up and Redl reprimanded. Otherwise unblemished record sheet. Present duty: shortly returned from nine months on staff of Military Attaché in St. Petersburg, ostensibly learning Russian language.

OBLENSKY: Probably all he did do. That's all *ours* do in Vienna. Pick up German in that atrocious, affected accent. I don't know why either of us bothers to observe – just young officers going to diplomatic functions, learning the language painstakingly, like an English governess, and about as well, and not a secret in sight. Most of them just come back like Redl, with the clap at least, or someone else's crabs. Well?

STANITSIN: Waiting for new posting. Financial affairs: No source of income apart from army pay. Although he seems to have invented a fond uncle who occasionally gives him fancy presents or gratuities, of whom there is no trace. Debts, not exactly serious, are considerable. They include: tailor, the biggest trade debt, outstanding accounts at various cafés, restaurants, bootmakers, livery, wine merchants and cigar –

OBLENSKY: Oh, come along, friend. What else?

STANITSIN: Not much. Two moneylenders, small, Fink, Miklas also.

OBLENSKY: Oh – Miklas. I know him. How much?

STANITSIN: Together, some twenty-two hundred kronen.

OBLENSKY: Yes?

STANITSIN: He is also negotiating the lease of a third floor apartment in the Eighth District.

OBLENSKY: Yes?

STANITSIN: That's about it.

OBLENSKY: Personal?

STANITSIN: Studious. Popular with fellow officers.

OBLENSKY: Oh, come along: women?

STANITSIN: Occasionally. Nothing sustained.

OBLENSKY: Spare time?

STANITSIN: Work mostly. Otherwise cafés, reading foreign newspapers, drinking with friends.

OBLENSKY: All army?

STANITSIN: Mostly.

OBLENSKY: Languages?

STANITSIN: Ruthenian native. Polish, German, some French.

OBLENSKY: And Russian. Some. Yes?

STANITSIN: I'm sorry?

OBLENSKY: What else? If anything.

STANITSIN: That's all, sir.

OBLENSKY: All right. Clever, brilliant officer, unpromising background. Ambitious. Bit extravagant. Popular. Diligent. What do you want to do?

STANITSIN: Continue surveillance, sir?

OBLENSKY: Unpromising lot. Very well. Get me a drink. Ah – good. Redl. Yes. All right. Background: nil. Prospects of brilliant military career exceptional. What he needs now, at

this exact stage, is a good, advantageous marriage. An
heiress is the ideal. But a rich widow would do even better.
He probably needs someone specially adroit socially, a
good listener, sympathetic, a woman other men are pleased
to call a friend and mean it. Experienced. He knows what
he wants, I dare say. He just needs someone to
unobtrusively provide the right elements . . . Perhaps we
should think about it . . . Anyway, remind me – sometime
next week. Right. Come on then. Next!
STANITSIN: Kupfer.
  (REDL's photograph is switched abruptly from the screen and
  replaced by KUPFER's.)
  Kupfer. Ludwig Max Von Kupfer. Major.
  (Fade.)

SCENE SIX

A terrace in the Hofburg, the Emperor's residence in Vienna.
Through the french windows, naturally, is where the court ball is
going on, with the aristocracy, diplomatic corps, officers of the Royal
and Imperial Army, flunkeys, etc. Talking to VON MÖHL is Chief of
the General staff, General CONRAD VON HÖTZENDORF.
MÖHL: Haven't been here for years.
HÖTZENDORF: Oh?
MÖHL: It's good to be back.
HÖTZENDORF: I'm sure.
MÖHL: There's nowhere quite like it, really, is there?
HÖTZENDORF: No. There's not.
MÖHL: Not where I've been, anyway. What about you, General?
HÖTZENDORF: No, no I don't think so.
MÖHL: I haven't been here since, oh, well, when was it, well I
    was a young captain, and I was in the Railway Bureau.
HÖTZENDORF: Were you?
MÖHL: Wiry. I could bend, do anything. Like a willow. Where's
    your wife, General? Would you like me –
HÖTZENDORF: No. She's all right. She's somewhere . . . Paris,
    that's the nearest to it, I suppose.

MÖHL: Yes.

HÖTZENDORF: But really, altogether different.

MÖHL: Entirely.

HÖTZENDORF: In Vienna, well, everyone is bourgeois, or whatever it is, and a good thing too, everyone, the beggars in the street, kitchen maids, the aristocracy and, let's be honest, the Emperor.

MÖHL: Yes.

HÖTZENDORF: And they all of them enjoy themselves. In Paris, well, in my experience, they're all pretending to be bohemians, from top to bottom, and all the time, every one of them are tradesmen. Well, I don't think you're a real bohemian if you've one eye – or *both* eyes in the case of Paris – on the cash box.

MÖHL: Quite.

HÖTZENDORF: Yes. That's Paris. That's the French. Trouble with Vienna: seems to have old age built into it.

MÖHL: Still that's better than moving on to God knows what, *and* in such an ugly way, like Prussia, for instance.

HÖTZENDORF: Yes. Or England. Even more. They'll soon wreck it. Prussians *are* efficient. English wilful. There *is* a difference. Still, all *we* do is celebrate and congratulate ourselves on saving Europe from the infidel.

MÖHL: I know . . . There's little credit for it.

HÖTZENDORF: Still. It *was* a long time ago.

MÖHL: Redl!

(*He hails* REDL *from the ballroom, who appears.*)

Redl, my dear boy! What a pleasant surprise. General, may I? Captain Alfred Redl: General Von Hötzendorf.

(*They acknowledge.*)

Since I last saw you, Redl, I now have the honour of working on the General's staff.

REDL: Indeed, sir. Congratulations.

MÖHL: Redl was just about the finest young officer, all round, when I was commandant in Lemberg, for eleven years.

HÖTZENDORF: So you told me. Who was the very pretty young lady you were dancing with?

REDL: I'm sorry, sir, which one?

MÖHL: Hah! Which *one*!

HÖTZENDORF: Small-boned, dark, brown eyes.

REDL: Miss Ursula Kunz, sir.

HÖTZENDORF: Kunz?

MÖHL: Ah, Kunz. Miss Kunz, youngest daughter of Judge Advocate Jaroslaw Kunz.

HÖTZENDORF: Ah.

MÖHL: Good man. Very.

HÖTZENDORF: Is he?

MÖHL: Seems to be.

HÖTZENDORF: Would you agree, Redl?

REDL: I, sir? From the little I know, and have been able to observe reliably, he is very competent indeed.

HÖTZENDORF: No more?

MÖHL: Accomplished, too . . . Unpopular.

HÖTZENDORF: Why?

REDL: I don't know, sir.

HÖTZENDORF: I believe it. Something odd, don't know what.

MÖHL: Well – yes . . . But how useful.

HÖTZENDORF: Oh, yes. Useful. Remember what Radetsky said about General Haynau? He said about Haynau, let's see: 'He's my best general all right, but he's like a razor. When you've used him, put him back in his case'.

MÖHL: The General was talking about Vienna, Redl. Well – How are *you* enjoying it?

REDL: Very much, sir.

MÖHL: Better than St. Petersburg?

REDL: The Russians find it very difficult to enjoy life. Although they *do* manage occasionally.

HÖTZENDORF: Yes. Yes, but, you know, this is a great place to do *nothing*, sit in a café, and dream, listen to the city, *do nothing* and not even anticipate regretting it.

MÖHL: Ah, there's friend Kunz.

HÖTZENDORF: Who? Where?

MÖHL: With the Countess Delyanoff.

HÖTZENDORF: So he is.

MÖHL: You know her?

HÖTZENDORF: Just.

MÖHL: I think they're coming out here.

HÖTZENDORF: (*To* REDL) . . . Sort of woman, know her –?

(REDL *shakes his head.*)

Well, the sort of woman who looks at you for five minutes without a word and then says 'what do you think about Shakespeare?' Or, something like that. Unbelievable.

MÖHL: Ah, Kunz! Countess.

(*Enter* MAJOR JAROSLAW KUNZ *and the* COUNTESS SOPHIA DELYANOFF.)

We were just watching you.

(MÖHL *makes the introductions, leaving* REDL *till last.*)

COUNTESS: We've met before.

REDL: Forgive me –

COUNTESS: Oh, yes. Not once, but at least three times. You were on General Hauser's staff in St. Petersburg, and a short spell in Prague, were you not?

REDL: I'm sorry.

COUNTESS: Please. I'm sure you had no eye –

MÖHL: Oh, come, Countess, I can't think of anyone more likely to get his eye fixed on someone like you. You're being unfair.

COUNTESS: No. I think not. But I forgive him.

(*A* FLUNKEY *presents glasses of champagne.*)

MÖHL: The General and I were just talking about Vienna.

KUNZ: Yes.

MÖHL: We were just saying – there's nowhere quite like it.

KUNZ: No. You've been away some time, I believe, Colonel. Where was it?

MÖHL: Przemysl.

KUNZ: Przemysl. Ah yes, with all the fortifications.

MÖHL: Four twelve-inch howitzers, some nine- and some six-inch, forty battalions, four squadrons, forty-three artillery companies, eight sapper companies – oh, please forgive me.

KUNZ: Yes. Nowhere quite like Przemysl, in fact.

COUNTESS: I'm afraid I simply can't understand the army, or why any man is ever in it.

HÖTZENDORF: Nor should you. The army's like nothing else. It

goes beyond religion. It serves everyone and everyone
serves it, even Hungarians and Jews. It conscripts, but it
calls the best men out, men who'd never otherwise have
been called on.

KUNZ: I think perhaps it's a little like living in the eighteenth
century; the army. Apart from Przemysl, that is. Still that *is*
a Viennese speciality? Don't you think, General?

HÖTZENDORF: I see nothing about the eighteenth century that
makes me believe the nineteenth was any better. And what
makes *you* think that the twentieth will be an improvement?

KUNZ: But why do you assume *I* should think it would be?

COUNTESS: I don't think I could ever have been a soldier. I'd
want to be a stranger in a street, a key on a concierge's
board, inaccessible if I wanted.

MÖHL: But that's what a *soldier* is.

COUNTESS: Only at the cost of his identity. Wouldn't you say,
Captain? (*To* REDL.)

REDL: I think the General's right. The army creates an élite.

COUNTESS: No. I believe *it* is created. The army. It can't
change. And it is changed from outside.

MÖHL: Nothing else trains a man –

KUNZ: Aptitudes, aptitudes at the expense of character.

COUNTESS: But it can, in its own way, provide a context of
expression for people, who wouldn't otherwise have it.

KUNZ: I can only say, Countess, you have met very few
soldiers.

COUNTESS: You're quite wrong, Major. Why, look at me now.
Several hundred guests and who am I with? The Chief of
the General Staff himself, a distinguished Colonel from
Przemysl, a Judge Advocate Major from Vienna and a
splendid young Captain. And how different you all are,
each one of you. I must say: I can't think of anything more
admirable than not having to play a part.

KUNZ: I'm sorry, Countess, but nonsense! We all play parts, *are*
doing so now, *will* continue to do so, and as long as we are
playing at being Austrian, Viennese, or whatever we think
we are, cosmopolitan and nondescript, a position palmed
on us by history, by the accident of having held back the

Muslim horde at the gates of Europe. For which no one is grateful, after all, it was two centuries ago, and we resent it, feel ill-used and pretend we're something we're not, instead of recognizing that we're the provincial droppings of Europe. The Army, all of *us*, and the Church, sustain the Empire, which is what, a convenience to other nations, an international utility for the use of whoever, Russia, England or Francis Joseph, which again, is what? Crown Imperial of non-intellect. Which is why, for the moment, it survives. Like this evening, the Hofball, perspiring gaiety and pointlessness.

(*Pause.*)

HÖTZENDORF: Countess, please excuse me.

MÖHL: Plus a rather heavy odour of charm.

(HÖTZENDORF *clicks his heels and goes out.*)

COUNTESS: (*To* MÖHL) I'm sorry if I've offended the General.

KUNZ: *I* offended, not you, Countess.

MÖHL: Correct. He's not accustomed to your kind of young banter, Kunz.

KUNZ: I didn't expect him to take me so seriously.

COUNTESS: (*Smiles*) Of course you did.

MÖHL: He is still the finest officer in the Royal and Imperial Army.

KUNZ: Very probably.

MÖHL: He is an old friend. He may not be as clever as you, Major, but his heart is in the right place.

KUNZ: Where it can be seen by everyone.

MÖHL: And I will not stand by and allow him to be sneered at and insulted.

KUNZ: I quite agree. Please excuse me, Countess. Gentlemen.

COUNTESS: Well. What tempers you men do have! What about you, Captain, we've not heard much out of you yet? I've a feeling you're full of shocking things.

REDL: What about?

COUNTESS: Why, what we've been talking about.

REDL: Like the army, you mean? I'm afraid I don't agree with the Major.

COUNTESS: No?

116

REDL: No. I mean, for myself, I didn't want to be, or mean to be: rigid or fixed.

COUNTESS: But you're not.

REDL: No. At the same time, there must be bonds, some bonds that have more meaning than others.

COUNTESS: I don't follow.

MÖHL: Now you're baiting, Countess. Of course he's right. No officer should be allowed to speak in the way of Major Kunz.

COUNTESS: He offends against blood. He –

MÖHL: Against himself; it's like being a Pole or a Slovak or a Jew, I suppose. All these things have more meaning than being, say, a civil servant, or a watchmaker. And all these things are brought together in the army like nowhere else. It's the same experience as friendship or loving a woman, speaking the same tongue, that is a *proper* bond, it's *human*, you can see it and experience it, more than 'all men are brothers' or some such nonsense.

COUNTESS: And do *you* agree with that, Captain Redl?

REDL: I don't agree that all men are brothers, like Colonel Möhl. We are clearly not. Nor should be, or ever want to be.

COUNTESS: Spoken like a true aristocrat.

REDL: Which, as you must know, I am not –

COUNTESS: Oh, but I believe you are. Don't you, Colonel?

REDL: We're meant to clash. And often and violently. I am proud to be despised by some men, no perhaps most men. Others are to be tolerated or ignored. And if they do the same for me, I am gratified, or, at least, relieved.

MÖHL: I agree with the Countess about you, Redl. He has style, always had it, must have had it as a tiny boy.

COUNTESS: Your pride in the Captain is quite fierce, Colonel. It's quite touching.

MÖHL: I don't know about touching, as you call it . . . it's *real*, anyhow.

COUNTESS: But that's only too clear, and why not? It's quite obviously justified.

MÖHL: Some men have a style of living like bad skins. Coarse

grained, erupting, spotty. Let me put it this way: I don't
have to tell you that, even in this modern age of what they
call democracy, the army is still a place of privilege. Redl is
the rare type that redeems that privilege. And why?
Because he overpowers it, overpowers it by force, not mob-
trained force, but natural, disciplined character, ability and
honour. And that's all I've got to say on the subject.

COUNTESS: My dear Colonel, I don't know who is the most
embarrassed – you or Captain Redl.

REDL: Myself, Countess. A truly honest man is never
embarrassed.

COUNTESS: You mean: *you* are not honest?

MÖHL: The boy's an open book. He should be in Intelligence.
No one would believe him!

COUNTESS: But not tolerant.

REDL: I don't think so.

COUNTESS: Oh, indeed, I think you ignore what doesn't interest
you. Which is why you didn't remember me in spite of the
fact of our having met on three separate occasions.

REDL: Pardon me, Countess. I remembered immediately after.

COUNTESS: You think I am a snob because I accused you of
trumpeting like an aristocrat just now. *You* are the snob,
Captain Redl, not I. As Colonel Von Möhl here will tell
you, my husband was a petty landowner from Cracow and
I am the daughter of a veterinary surgeon.

MÖHL: (*Laughs*) Well, don't take that too seriously, Redl.

COUNTESS: Colonel: I appeal to you!

MÖHL: Well, let me say you would say there was only *some* truth
in it.

(*He chuckles again. A* FLUNKEY *approaches* REDL *with a
salver with a card on it.*)

FLUNKEY: Captain Redl, sir?

REDL: Please excuse me.

(*He takes the card out of the envelope, reads it, hands it to*
MÖHL.)

MÖHL: Archduke Ferdinand . . . Ah, well, you'd better get
along! Quickly. Here, you!

(*Grabs more champagne glasses from passing* FLUNKEY.)

Get this down you first. Very beautiful, if I may say so.
Redl! Countess, your health. The Archduke's the man
now. Ferdinand's the one to watch, and I think he's
probably all right. Knows what he's doing. Knows what's
going on in the Empire, Hungary, for instance, Serbia.
You see, the Belvedere, that's going to be the centre of
things, not the Hofburg any more. Pity that, about all that,
what do you call it, morganatic marriage business.

COUNTESS: Yes, indeed. Poor woman. Having to trail behind
countesses, a hundred yards behind him.

MÖHL: Why do you think he married her?

COUNTESS: Why does any man get married?

REDL: Children, property.

COUNTESS: But one sees all that, but it couldn't have operated
in this case. He could have had her as his mistress like his
uncle. But then, when you think of the men one knows
who *are* married, and who they're married *to*, and what
their real, snotty little longings are underneath their proud
watch and chains, their constant broken, sidelong glances.
Oh, I know all about it, even if it's difficult to understand
sometimes. Captain, you mustn't keep His Imperial
Highness waiting. Not while *I* lecture you on marriage.
(REDL *clicks his heels and leaves them.*)

MÖHL: Well!

COUNTESS: Yes, Colonel.

MÖHL: I was just thinking, what you were saying about
marriage then.

COUNTESS: And –?

MÖHL: It really is the most *lamentable* thing for most of us, isn't
it? I mean, as you say, it doesn't work really. Only the
appearances function. Eh? Everyone knows the *feelings*, but
what's the answer, what's the answer do you think?

COUNTESS: The only answer is not to be drawn into it, like the
Captain.

MÖHL: No, I think you're wrong there. Redl would make a
first-class husband.

COUNTESS: You think so?

MÖHL: Absolutely. He's steadfast, sober, industrious, orderly, he likes orderly things, hates chaos. That's why marriage would suit him so well. That's what marriage represents, I suppose. I say, I *am* enjoying talking to you.

COUNTESS: And I am enjoying talking to you. Do you think Captain Redl will come back to us?

MÖHL: Oh, I should think so. Order out of chaos. I know, we'll keep an eye out for him, learn what the Archduke had to say to him. You wouldn't care to dance with such an old man, would you?

COUNTESS: But, of course, delighted. Major Kunz is a very uninspired dancer.

MÖHL: That's because he doesn't like it. Now *I* love it. I'm so glad Redl got that invitation. Good boy! Oh, I say, I *am* having a good time.

(*He beams boyishly, offers his arm to her, and they leave the terrace to join the dancers in the ballroom.*)

(*Fade.*)

SCENE SEVEN

One drawing room of COUNTESS DELYANOFF*'s house. One oil lamp burns on a desk. On a chair are* REDL*'s tunic, sword, and cap and gloves. A sharp, clear, moaning cry is heard. Once, quickly. Then again, longer, more violent. Then silence. Fumbling footsteps outside the door.* REDL *enters in his breeches, putting on his vest, carrying his boots. He slumps into a chair, dropping the boots beside him. A voice outside calls softly: 'Alfred, Alfred!'*

The COUNTESS *enters swiftly, anxious, her hair down to her waist, very beautiful in her nightgown. She looks across at* REDL *as if this had happened before, goes to a decanter and pours a brandy. With it, she crosses to* REDL*'s armchair and looks down at him.*

REDL: Sophia?

COUNTESS: My dear?

REDL: Sorry I woke you.

COUNTESS: I should think you woke the entire street.

REDL: Sorry. So sorry.

COUNTESS: Don't be silly. Here.

(*She hands him the brandy. He takes some. Stares at his boots.*)

REDL: I think I'd better go.

COUNTESS: It's early yet. Why, it's only, I can't see, look, it's only half-past one.

REDL: Still . . .

COUNTESS: You left me *last* night at three. And when you're gone I can't sleep. I wake the moment you've gone. All I can do is think about you.

REDL: I know. Please forgive me . . . Better put these on. (*Takes one of the boots.*)

COUNTESS: Alfred. Please come back to bed . . . I know you hate me asking you, but I do beg you . . . Just for an hour. You *can't* go out now.

REDL: I need some air.

COUNTESS: (*Softly*) Darling –

REDL: Need my orderly on these occasions. Can't get my boots on. (*She grasps his knee and kneels.*)

COUNTESS: Why did you wake?

REDL: Oh: Usual.

COUNTESS: And you're crying again.

REDL: I know . . . (*His face is stony. His voice firm.*) Why do you always have to look at me?

COUNTESS: Because I love you.

REDL: You'd look away . . .

COUNTESS: That's why. What can I do, my darling?

REDL: Nothing . . . I must get these damned things . . . (*Struggles with boots.*) I'd love another brandy. (*She rises and gets it.*) It's like a disease.

COUNTESS: What is?

REDL: Oh, all this incessant, *silly* weeping. It only happens, it creeps up on me, when I'm asleep. No one else has ever noticed it . . . Why do you have to wake up?

COUNTESS: Here. Alfred: don't turn away from me.

REDL: My mouth tastes sour.

COUNTESS: I didn't mean that. Anyway, what if it is? Don't turn your head away.

(*She grasps his head and kisses him. He submits for a moment, then thrusts her away.*)

REDL: Please!

COUNTESS: What is it? Me?

REDL: No. You're – you're easily the most beautiful . . . desirable woman I've ever . . . There couldn't be . . .

COUNTESS: It's not easy to believe.

REDL: Sophia: it's *me*. It's like a disease.

COUNTESS: You must feel deeply. So do I. Why do you think you've got *me* crying as well. No one's done that to me for years!

REDL: It's like, I can't . . .

COUNTESS: (*Impatient*) But it *isn't* like the clap you got off some garrison whore. That's all over. You know it, you were cured, cured, you've got a paper to say so, and even if you weren't do you think I would care?

REDL: It isn't that.

COUNTESS: Then what is it? Why do you dream? Why do you sweat and cry out and *leave* me in the middle of the night? Oh, God!

(*She recovers.*)

REDL: Here, have some of this, I'll get some more.

COUNTESS: No, that's fine.

REDL: Why don't you commit yourself?

COUNTESS: Why don't *you*? My darling, try not to drink so much.

REDL: I've told you, I drink. I drink, heavily sometimes, I don't get *drunk*.

COUNTESS: Yes. So you say.

REDL: It's the truth.

COUNTESS: What are you saying? No, forget I asked. Don't take any of this as *true*, Alfred, I beg of you. It's early in the morning, everything's asleep and indifferent now – *threatening to us*, both of us, *you're* in tears, you wake up in a depression, in a panic, you're dangerous and frightened again and I'm in tears. Please, don't, please, stay, stay with me, I'll look after you, I'll make up . . . at least for something. I'll protect you, protect you . . . and love you.

REDL: I can protect myself.

COUNTESS: But you can't. Not *always*. Can you? What is it?

REDL: I must go. I can't sit here.

COUNTESS: Why can't you trust me?

REDL: I've told you . . . I *don't* mean to hurt you.

COUNTESS: And I believe you.

REDL: I just can't.

(*Pause.*)

COUNTESS: Have you never confided in anyone?

REDL: No.

COUNTESS: Hasn't there ever been anyone? (*Pause.*)
What about another man? I know friendship means a lot to
you . . . What about Taussig?

REDL: No. At least . . . Only a very, a very little. I did try one
evening. But he doesn't welcome confidences. He doesn't
know what to do with them . . . or where to put them.

COUNTESS: You mean nobody else, not *one*, your mother, your
grandfather, no one?

REDL: They might have been –

COUNTESS: Um?

REDL: But I never did.

COUNTESS: Why?

REDL: I suppose I . . . they, *I* waited too long, and then . . .
they were killed. An accident. You're shivering.

COUNTESS: Please try. Everyone owes something to someone.
You *are* in love with me, Alfred, I know you are, and
you've told me yourself. That must be something.

REDL: Put this on.

(*He places his tunic round her shoulders.*)

COUNTESS: What about you?

(*He shrugs.*)

You look better. *Are* you?

REDL: Yes. At least they go quickly. Just at a bad time. In the
night. Or when I'm having to force myself to do something
as an exercise, or a duty, like working late.

COUNTESS: I tell you: you work too hard.

REDL: Or sometimes I get caught in some relaxation. Sitting in
a café, listening to gossip, and I enjoy that after a long day,

and I'm curious. But if I listen to a conversation that's got serious, say, about politics, the Magyars or merging with Germany, or something like that, I feel myself, almost as if I were falling away and disappearing. I want to run. . . . But, I've felt I should take a serious, applied interest in this sort, in, ours is a complicated age, and I'm some small part of it, and I should devote as much attention and interest to it as I can muster. I should be giving up time –

COUNTESS: What time, for heaven's sake? You already –

REDL: Much more than I do, *much* more. I used not even to try.

COUNTESS: You mean *I* waste it?

REDL: But I can't relax or be at ease.

COUNTESS: Why are you so watchful? You always seem to be at the ready in some way, listening for something . . . some stray chance thing.

REDL: I don't know what that means.

(*He goes to the decanter.*)

COUNTESS: Please, Alfred. You've an early train in the morning . . .

REDL: Do you know: the only time I drink heavily is when I'm with you? No. I didn't mean that. But when you're badgering me and sitting on my head and, and I can't breathe.

COUNTESS: Why do you always have to make love to me with the –

REDL: There you go!

COUNTESS: Why? Why do you insist? Before we even begin?

REDL: I might ask why *you* insist on turning the light on.

COUNTESS: Because I want to look at your face. Is that so strange?

REDL: You must know, *you* must know, we're not all the same.

COUNTESS: Why do you never kiss me?

REDL: But I do.

COUNTESS: But never in bed.

REDL: Oh, let's go back. We're tired.

COUNTESS: And turn your head away?

REDL: Damn your eyes, I *won't* be catechized!

COUNTESS: Why do you never speak?

REDL: What do you want out of me? Well, I tell you, whatever it is, I *can't* give it. Can't and won't.
(*Pause.*)

COUNTESS: I thought it was only whores you didn't kiss or speak to.

REDL: You would know more about that.
(*She looks up at him miserably, shivering. He feels outmanoeuvred. Takes his tunic from her and puts it on.*)
Excuse me.

COUNTESS: If you leave me, you'll be alone.

REDL: That's what I want, to be left alone.

COUNTESS: You'll always be alone.

REDL: Good. Splendid.

COUNTESS: No it isn't. You know it isn't. That's why you're so frightened. You'll fall alone.

REDL: So does everyone. Even if they don't know it.

COUNTESS: You can't be *saved* alone.

REDL: I don't expect to be saved, as you put it. Not by you.

COUNTESS: Or any other woman?

REDL: Or anyone at all.
(*He picks up his cap and gloves.*)

COUNTESS: What have I done?

REDL: *I* am the guilty one. Not you. Please forgive me.

COUNTESS: Don't, don't go. (*Pause.*) One feels very old at this time of night.
(*She goes to the window. He watches her, distressed.*)
It's the time of night when people die. People give up.
(*He goes behind her, hesitates, puts his head against hers for comfort. Pause.*)
You can't have your kind of competitive success *and* seclusion.
(*He sighs, draws away and goes to the door.*)

REDL: Good night, Sophia.

COUNTESS: Good night.
(*Pause.*)

REDL: Would you like to have tea?

COUNTESS: When?

REDL: Tuesday?
COUNTESS: I can't.
REDL: Wednesday?
COUNTESS: Please.
    (*He turns.*)
    Yes, please.
    (*He goes out.*)
    (*Fade.*)

SCENE EIGHT

OBLENSKY*'s office. He is reading a letter to* STANITSIN.

OBLENSKY: 'In haste. Enroute for Prague. Wherever I am, my
    dearest, you will trouble my heart. I can say no more, I
    cannot think. The work here will do me good I expect. Try
    to do something yourself. This is a difficult time. I seem to:
    seem to – ' can't read it – 'speak . . . speak out of nowhere.
    You deserve only the best, not the worst. Forgive me:
    Alfred'. Where's hers? Ah: 'My dearest love, why are you
    writing to me like this? You seem to have forgotten
    everything. It was not all like those short times during the
    night. The rest *was* different' – underlined. 'Don't, I beg
    you, *don't* deceive yourself. Why don't you answer my
    letters? I wait for them. Give me a word, or something that
    will do. At least something I can go over. I can do nothing.
    Now *I* am helpless. Loved one, don't something this.
    Forever, your Sophia. P.S. Did you never intend coming
    that Wednesday? I can't believe it.' Hum. What do you
    suppose he means, where is it – 'this a difficult time'?
STANITSIN: Well, the moneylenders are pressing pretty hard.
    He's sold his gold cigarette case and fancy watch.
OBLENSKY: Has he? 'You deserve only the best, not the worst.'
    Odd sentiment for a distinguished officer, don't you think?
    He can't feel *that* sensitive about his extravagance, he's too
    reckless. Besides, as far as *he* knows, she's quite rich.
STANITSIN: Maybe he's just bored with her.
OBLENSKY: I don't think so, I'd say he's a passionate man, a bit

callous too, and selfish, very, but there's something *in* all this.

STANITSIN: Come to that, the Countess sounds pretty convincing.

OBLENSKY: I hope not. All right.

(*He nods to* STANITSIN, *who opens the office door, and admits the* COUNTESS.)

Sit down. You seem to have lost your man.

COUNTESS: For the moment.

OBLENSKY: You mean you think you can get him back?

COUNTESS: Possibly.

OBLENSKY: Do you want to?

COUNTESS: What do you mean? I do what you tell me.

OBLENSKY: What's your assessment of Redl?

COUNTESS: Ambitious. Secretive. Violent. Vain. Extravagant. I expect you know as much as I do. You don't have to sleep with him to find that out.

OBLENSKY: Precisely. It doesn't seem to have added much to our total knowledge. However, patience. We're in no hurry. Captain Redl will be with us for a long time yet. Years and years. He'll probably improve with keeping. What's he doing with himself?

STANITSIN: What he says, working. Of course, he's hard up for the moment, but he'll –

OBLENSKY: Have you offered him money?

COUNTESS: Twice. He refused.

OBLENSKY: Won't take money from a woman. And I suppose you told him it didn't count between lovers?

COUNTESS: Naturally.

OBLENSKY: And there's no woman in Prague, nowhere, anyone? No one-night stands or twopenny standups?

STANITSIN: Nothing. He leaves his office in the War Building every day at 4.15, goes down to the café, has a coffee or two, reads all the foreign newspapers, has an early dinner, then goes back to his office and works till about ten, even eleven or twelve sometimes.

OBLENSKY: He *is* telling the truth.

STANITSIN: Occasionally he'll drop in for a drink somewhere

on his way home or meet his friend Taussig for half an
hour. More often than not he just sits alone.

OBLENSKY: Doing nothing?

STANITSIN: Just sitting. Looking.

OBLENSKY: Looking at what?

STANITSIN: I don't know. What *can* you look at from a café
window? Other people, I suppose. Watch.

OBLENSKY: The Passing Show.

COUNTESS: Is there anything else?

OBLENSKY: No, my dear. Stanitsin will brief you.
(*She rises.*)

COUNTESS: Is it – may I have my letter?

OBLENSKY: I don't see why not.
(*Hands one to her.*)

COUNTESS: No, I meant his, to me.

OBLENSKY: I'm afraid that's for the File. Sorry. I can send you
a copy. I wonder if he *will* write again. Don't forget to
report, will you?
(STANITSIN *sees her out.* OBLENSKY *lights a cigarette.*)
(*Fade.*)

SCENE NINE

A café. REDL *sits alone at a table. Sitting a few tables away is a young
man.* REDL *reads a paper. Throws away his cigar butt. Enter* TAUSSIG

TAUSSIG: Ah, Redl, there you are. Sorry I'm late.

REDL: What will you have?

TAUSSIG: Don't think I'll bother. I promised to meet someone
in ten minutes.

REDL: The one in the chorus at the Opera House?

TAUSSIG: That's the one.

REDL: Where?

TAUSSIG: She's taking me to her lodgings.

REDL: Before the performance? I hope it doesn't affect her
voice. What's she like?

TAUSSIG: She rattles. Nice big girl.

REDL: They always are.

TAUSSIG: She's got a girl friend.

REDL: Thank you, no.

TAUSSIG: You seem awfully snobbish sometimes, Alfred.

REDL: Do I. I'm sorry. It's just that I'm not too keen on the
opera. Are you going – afterwards?

TAUSSIG: What?

REDL: To the performance?

TAUSSIG: Oh, yes, I suppose so. Your head must be hardened
by all those ciphers. *Löhengrin*, I think. What's it like?

REDL: Boring.

TAUSSIG: So I believe. Oh, well. Sure you won't have supper
after? She really is quite nice. They both are.

REDL: No, thank you, really.

TAUSSIG: Not going to Madame Heyse's do are you?

REDL: No. (*Pause.*)

TAUSSIG: Does that young man over there know you?

REDL: What young man?

TAUSSIG: Well, there's only one.

REDL: No. Why?

TAUSSIG: He's done nothing but stare at you. Oh, he's turned
away now. Knows we're talking about him.

REDL: Prague's as bad as Vienna.

TAUSSIG: Keeps giggling to himself, as far as I can see.

REDL: Probably a cretin. Or a Czech who hates Austrian Army
Officers. I can't face another of those evenings or dinners,
here or anywhere. They all talk about each other. They're
all clever and they're afraid of each other's cleverness.
They're like beautiful, schooled performing dogs.
Scrutinizing and listening for an unsteady foot. It's like
hunting without the pig. Everyone sweats and whoops and
rides together, and, at any time, any moment, the pig may
turn out to be *you*. Stick!

TAUSSIG: Well, if I can't tempt you . . . Can I have one of your
cigarettes? I say, the old case back, eh?

REDL: And the watch. Everything in fact.

TAUSSIG: Good for you. Make a killing?

REDL: I tipped my mare against Steinbauer's new gelding.
Want a loan?

TAUSSIG: No thanks. The Countess isn't bothering you, is she?

REDL: I told you – no. We never got on. She was prickly and we were always awkward together. It was like talking to my sister. Who died, last week incidentally, consumption, and I can't say I thought about it more than ten minutes.

TAUSSIG: What will you do?

REDL: Now? Oh, have a quiet dinner. Go for a walk.

TAUSSIG: A walk? I don't know – well, if I can't persuade you. 'Bye.

(REDL *nods.* TAUSSIG *strides off. He picks up a paper, lights a new cigar. Presently the* YOUNG MAN *comes up to him.*)

YOUNG MAN: Excuse me, sir.

REDL: Well?

YOUNG MAN: May I glance at your paper?

REDL: If you wish. (*Irritated.*) The waiter will bring you one if you ask.

YOUNG MAN: I only want to see what's on at the Opera.

REDL: *Löhengrin.*

YOUNG MAN: Oh, thank you. No. I don't think I like Wagner much. Do you?

REDL: No. Now please go away.

(*The* YOUNG MAN *grins at him, and leans across to him, saying softly.*)

YOUNG MAN: I know what *you're* looking for.

(REDL *looks stricken. The* YOUNG MAN *walks away. He is almost out of sight when* REDL *runs after him.*)

REDL: You!

(REDL *grabs him with ferocious power by the neck.*)

What do you mean?

YOUNG MAN: Nothing! Let me go!

REDL: You pig, you little upstart pig. What did you mean?

YOUNG MAN: (*Yells*) Let me go!

(*Heads turn.* REDL*'s anger subsides into embarrassment. The* YOUNG MAN *walks away.* REDL *returns to his seat, lights his cigar, orders a drink from the* WAITER. *A Gipsy Band strikes up.*)

(*Fade.*)

A bare, darkened room. In it is a bed. On it two figures, not yet identifiable. A light is struck. A cigar end glows.

REDL's VOICE: Why wouldn't you keep the light on?
>   (*A figure leaves the bed and goes to a wash basin. Sound of water.*)
>   Um? Oh! Why did I wait – so long.
>   (REDL *lights a lamp beside the bed. By the washstand is the handsome form of a young* PRIVATE SOLDIER.)
>   Paul?

PAUL: Yes?

REDL: Why?

PAUL: I don't know. I just prefer the dark.

REDL: But why? My darling. You're so exquisite to look on – You mean it's me?

PAUL: No. You look all right.

REDL: What is it, then? What are you dressing for?

PAUL: Got to get back to barracks, haven't I?

REDL: What's your unit?

PAUL: That'd be telling, wouldn't it?

REDL: Oh, come on, I can find out.

PAUL: Yes. General Staff and all that, isn't it?

REDL: Paul. What is it? What have I done? What are you opening the door for?
>   (PAUL *has opened the door. Four young* SOLDIERS *come in. They look at* REDL, *who knows instantly what will happen. He struggles violently at first, and for a while it looks as if they might have taken on too much. The young* SOLDIERS *in turn become amazed by* REDL's *vicious defence of himself, which is like an attack. All the while* PAUL *dresses, pockets* REDL's *gold cigarette case, cigar case, watch and chain, gold crucifix, notes and change.* REDL *becomes a kicked, bloody heap on the floor. The* SOLDIERS *leave.* PAUL, *having dressed fully by now, helps* REDL *sit up against the bed, looks down at his bloody face.*)

PAUL: Don't be too upset, love. You'll get used to it.
>   (*Exit.*)
>   (*Curtain.*)

ACT TWO

SCENE ONE

A Ballroom, Vienna. A winter evening in 1902. *In the background a small, eccentrically dressed* ORCHESTRA *plays. The light is not bright when the curtain goes up, except on the* SINGERS. *Concentrated silently, at first, anyway, are the* GUESTS, *among whom is* REDL, *one of the few not in fancy dress of some kind. However, he looks magnificent in his uniform and has put on his few decorations. He sprawls, listening thoughtfully to the* SINGER, *smoking one of his long black cigars. The* SINGER *is dressed in an eighteenth century dress which might allow the wearer to play Susanna in 'Figaro' or one of Mozart's ladies like* ZERLINA. *The* ORCHESTRA *plays very softly, the* SINGER *is restrained at this time, which is as well, because the voice is not adequate. However, it has enough sweetness in feeling to immediately invoke the pang of Mozart. Perhaps 'Vedrai Carino' or 'Batti, Batti' from 'Don Giovanni'. It ends quickly. Applause. Then a* MAN *dressed to play 'Figaro' appears, the lights become brighter, and the two go into the duet in the first scene of 'Figaro'. This should take no more than three minutes. It should be accepted at the beginning as the indifferent effort of a court opera house cast with amateurs, but not without charm and aplomb.*

The 'Figaro' in this case is a straight man. Presently, the 'Susanna' begins straight, then gradually cavorting, camping, and sending up the character, the audience, and Mozart as only someone in drag has the licence. The ballroom audience has been waiting for this, and is in ecstasy by the time it is over. Some call out 'do the Mad Scene'. Or 'Come Scoglio'. The 'Susanna', egged on, does a short parody of something like 'Come Scoglio', or 'Lucia' done in the headlong, take-it-on-the-chin manner.

This only takes a couple of minutes and should be quite funny. Anyhow, the ballroom audience apparently think so. Obviously, most of them have seen the performance before. There is a lot of giggling and even one scream during the ARIA, *which 'Susanna-Lucia' freezes with mock fury, and ends to great applause.*

'Susanna' curtsies graciously. The lights in the room come up, the ORCHESTRA strikes up and most of the guests dance. It is essential that it should only gradually be revealed to the audience that all the dancers and guests are men. The costumes, from all periods, should be in exquisite taste, both men's and women's, and those wearing them should look exotic and reasonably attractive, apart from an occasional grotesque. The music is gay, everyone chatters happily like a lot of birds and the atmosphere is generally relaxed and informal, in contrast to the somewhat stiff atmosphere at the ball in Act I. Among those dancing at present are KUPFER, dressed rather dashingly as SCARAMOUCHE. KUNZ, dancing one handed, with MARIE ANTOINETTE, looks rather good as LORD NELSON. The WAITER ALBRECHT from Scene 3, dressed as COLUMBINE with KUPFER. FIGARO dances with a LADY GODIVA in gold lamé jockstrap. DOWNSTAGE, holding court, is the host, BARON VON EPP. He is an imposing man with a rich flexible voice which he uses to effect. At present, he looks astonishingly striking with upswept hair, ospreys in pompadour feathers, a pearl and diamond dog collar at his neck, and a beautiful fan, as QUEEN ALEXANDRA. Again, it is essential that the costume should be in meticulous taste and worn elegantly and with natural confidence. Sitting beside him is someone dressed as a wimpled mediaeval lady, to be identified as STEINBAUER. Like REDL now, some years older. REDL is accompanied by LIEUTENANT STEFAN KOVACS, who is fixed in a mixture of amusement and embarrassment. REDL himself is quite cool, looking extremely dashing in his Colonel's uniform and decorations and close-cropped hair, staring very carefully around at all the guests, his eyes missing no one. He lights one of his long black cigars and joins the BARON's group, which includes STEINBAUER, SUSANNA and a ravishing TSARINA.

NOTE: At any drag ball as stylish and private as this one the guests can be seen to belong to entirely different and very distinct categories.

I. The paid bum boys whose annual occasion it is – they wait for it from one year to the next and spend between 3 and 6 months preparing an elaborate and possibly bizarre costume. This is the market place where in all probability they will manage to acquire a meal ticket for months ahead. They tend to

either tremendously careful, totally feminine clothes – or the
ultimate in revelation – e.g. Lady Godiva, except that he/she
might think, instead of a gold lamé jockstrap, that a gold
chastity belt with a large and obvious gold key on a chain round
her/his neck, be better.

2. The discreet drag queens. Like the Baron/Queen Alexandra,
and the Tsarina – their clothes, specially made for the occasion
by a trusted dressmaker, as the night becomes wilder are usually
found to have a removable skirt revealing stockings, suspenders,
jewelled garters and diamond buckles on their shoes. But even
despite this mild strip tease, they still remain in absolutely perfect
taste.

3. The more self-conscious rich queens, who, though in drag,
tend to masculine drag, and end up looking like lesbians.
Someone tells me they saw one once in marvellously cut black
riding habit – frilled white jabot and cuffs – long skirt and boots
– top hat with veil. Also in this category are the ones who go out
of their way to turn themselves into absolute grotesques, and
quite often arrive in a gaggle. They make a regal entry enjoying
having their disguise penetrated or not as the case may be. If, for
instance, the theme of the ball were theatrical they would
probably choose to come as the witches from Macbeth. But
marvellously theatrically thought out in every detail.

4. Another category of rich, discreet queens, who don't want to
offend their host by making no effort at all but who baulk at
dressing up; for them full and impeccable evening dress with
sash orders and neck decorations and elaborately over made-up
faces. They usually look more frightening than any of the others
– with middle-aged decadent faces, painted like whores.

5. There are the men who positively dislike women and only put
on drag in order to traduce them and make them appear as
odious, immoral and unattractive as possible.

6. Finally, the ones who don't even make that effort but wear,
like Redl, full-dress uniform and decorations – or evening dress.
It's not inconceivable that some of the bum boys would dress as
pampered children.

Remember when they dance you don't find the male ones only
dancing with the female ones – but possibly a hussar with a

man in evening dress – or two men in evening dress together – or
two shepherdesses together.
In category 4 you would also be likely to find the made-up face
– the impeccable tails and white tie plus ropes of pearls and
blazing diamonds.

BARON: Ah, Redl! How good to see you. Where have you been?
You're always so busy. Everyone says you're in Counter
Intelligence or something and you're frightfully grand now.
I hope you're not spying on anyone here, Colonel. You
know I won't have that sort of thing. I only give this ball
once a year, and everyone invited is under the obligation of
strictest confidence. No gossiping after. Otherwise you can
all do as you like. Who's this?

REDL: May I introduce Lieutenant Stefan Kovacs – Baron Von
Epp.

BARON: Very nice. Why are you both in mufti? You know my
rule.

REDL: I wouldn't call the dress uniform of the Royal Imperial
Army exactly mufti.

BARON: I'm surprised they let you in. I expect you know
everyone, or will do.

REDL: It's rather astonishing. Almost everyone.

BARON: It's not astonishing at all. Colonel Redl, this is Captain
Steinbauer – aren't you? Yes. She is.

REDL: (*To* STEINBAUER) Lemberg. Seventh Galician.

STEINBAUER: That's right. Siczynski.

REDL: Yes.

(*They look at each other. Sudden gratitude for the
remembrance. And weariness, sadness. The* BARON *quickly
dismisses the cloud.*)

BARON: And that's the Tsarina there. I don't know *who* she is
exactly. A Russian spy I should think. Watch yourself, my
dear, the Colonel eats a spy in bed every morning, don't
you, Alfred? That's what they all tell me. It's even in the
papers. And this is Ferdy.

(*He indicates* SUSANNA.)

Didn't you think he was divine?

REDL: Superb.

STEFAN: He really has a fine voice. I thought he was a real
soprano at first.
(*They all look at him with some suspicion.*)
SUSANNA: What do you mean? I *am* a real soprano?
(*They all laugh.* STEFAN *feels he has blundered more than he
has in fact.* REDL *chips in.*)
REDL: Isn't that Major Advocate Kunz?
BARON: Where? Oh, yes I see. Nelson, you mean. Doesn't he
look marvellous. One arm and all! Wonder where he keeps
it? He's my insurance.
REDL: What?
BARON: If there's ever any trouble, Kunz is my legal insurance.
Very influential that one! She'll deal with anything that ever
came up – Secret Police, anything, spies. No, spies is you,
isn't it, Alfred, *you're* the spy-catcher, we'll leave any lovely
little spies to you.
(*To* TSARINA.) Wait till he catches *you*. I daren't think *what*
he'll do to you!
(*The* TSARINA *giggles.*)
Eh. Alfred? What do you do to naughty little spies?
REDL: (*Bends down and grasps the* TSARINA*'s ear lobe*) I tie them
over the back of my mare, Kristina, on a leading rein, and
beat them with my crop at a slow canter.
BARON: How delicious! Now, her earring's fallen off, you've
excited her so!
(*The* TSARINA *retrieves her earring and smiles up in a sweet,
friendly curious way at* REDL, *who smiles back, touched by an
instant, simple, affectionate spirit. He turns to* STEFAN, *who
has looked away. Quickly noted by the* BARON.)
BARON: I haven't seen your Lieutenant Kovacs before, Alfred.
REDL: He's only just graduated from the War School.
BARON: All that studying and hardening the body and noontide
heat and sweating, and horses! You all look quite beautiful,
well, some of you, but I hate to think of you in a war. A
real war.
(*A* SHEPHERDESS *serves champagne.*)
Oh, come along, come along. No one's drinking half
enough yet. Alfred!

(REDL *downs a glass. He looks flushed and suddenly relaxed.*)
And another! You're behind the rest of us. And a good
place for you, said someone.
(REDL *takes another. Hands one to* STEFAN.)
And Ferdy, you have some more. Good for the voice. Bit
strained tonight, dear. I want you to do 'Una Donna A
Quindici Anni'.

FERDY: Don't think I can.

BARON: You can do *anything*. Practically. (*To* REDL.) He has
hair on his instep – like a goat. Show them. Oh, well . . .
Where have you two come from? The Lieutenant looks
rather glum.

REDL: We were at the Hofburg for an hour or two.

BARON: No wonder he looks glum. Come along! Drink up,
Lieutenant. I can't have anyone sober at my party. (*To*
REDL.) I suppose you *had* to go, being so powerful now
and impressive.

REDL: Oh, come along.

BARON: No, I hear it's quite true. (*To* STEINBAUER.) You
remember the Colonel then?

STEINBAUER: Years ago. I always knew he'd make a brilliant
officer. We all did. Congratulations, Colonel! (*Raises glass
– talks to* TSARINA.)

BARON: Mind your wimple. She gets drunk too easily, that one.
Which is probably why she's still only a humble captain in
number seventy-seven. (*Out of* STEFAN*'s hearing.*) Are you
sure your friend wouldn't rather be back at the Hofburg?

REDL: He'll be all right. Try and leave him alone.

BARON: I can't leave anyone *that* pretty alone. Do you want the
Tsarina? She's Kunz's really, but she's pretty available.
(*Pause.* REDL *considers.*) And Kunz isn't the kind who
makes scenes. He doesn't care . . . He's a bit cold too.
(STEFAN *hears the last of this.*)

STEFAN: Did you say Kunz? Isn't a man like that taking a bit of
a risk?

BARON: Aren't we all?

STEFAN: Yes. But for someone . . .

BARON: We are none of us safe. This –

(*He sweeps his fan round the ballroom.*)
is the celebration of the individual against the rest, the us's
and the them's, the free and the constricted, the gay and
the dreary, the lonely and the mob, the little Tsarina there
and the Emperor Francis Joseph.
(*They laugh.*)
Tell your friend it's so, Alfred.

REDL: Oh, I agree.

STEFAN: (*To* REDL) Forgive me, I feel I'm unwanted.

BARON: Nonsense. You're *wanted*. Tell him not to be a silly,
solemn boy, Alfred.
(REDL *squeezes the boy's arm and laughs. The* BARON *refills*
STEFAN's *glass.*)
Actually, Kunz is an odd one. He seems to take appalling
risks, but he knows the right people everywhere and
anywhere, and he'd sell anyone, and I know him. He's my
first cousin. He'd do it to me.

STEFAN: Blood not thicker than water?

BARON: His blood is thinner than anything, my dear.

FERDY: Darling! She wants to know –

BARON: What is it? I'm talking.

FERDY: Are you really a Baron?
(*The* TSARINA *giggles.*)

BARON: Tell her she'll find out if she's not careful.

TSARINA: (*To* FERDY) Are you the Baroness then?

FERDY: (*Nods*) Oh. I let him. He fancies himself chasing the
ladies, but he's just the same as I am. Nothing more at all.

TSARINA: What about the Lieutenant?

FERDY: Oh, I should think so. Either too stupid to know it, or
hasn't woken up to it yet.

TSARINA: Or doesn't want to wake up to it. Looks a bit dreary.

FERDY: Do you fancy him? You'll have the Colonel after you.
You'll be shot down.
(*While this duet has gone on, the* BARON, STEFAN *and* REDL
have drawn away from the GIRLS *into their own conversation.*
Some class division here too.)

BARON: Vienna is so dull! All that Spanish gloom at the
Hofburg gets in everywhere, like the moth.

FERDY: (*Calls out*) *You* need moth balls! (*Collapse.*)

BARON: The Viennese gull themselves they're gay, but
they're just stiff-jointed aristocrats like puppets,
grubbing little tradesmen or Jews and chambermaids
making a lot of one-two-three noises all the time.
Secretly, they're feeling utterly thwarted and empty.
The bourgeoisie daren't enjoy themselves except at
someone else's expense or misfortune. And all those
cavorting, clever Jews are even more depressing,
pretending to be generous – and *entirely* unspontaneous.
Hungarians, they're gay, perhaps that's because they're
quite selfish and pig-headed. Kovacs: oh, dear, are you
Hungarian? Well, never mind, that's me again I'm
afraid, speak first, think afterwards –

REDL: No, Baron, you're ahead of everyone.

BARON: Only wish I were. Poles are fairly gay. You're Polish or
something, aren't you, Alfred? And somehow they're less
common than Russians. Serbs are impossible, of course,
savage, untrustworthy, worse than Hungarians, infidels in
every sense. I think your friend despises me because I'm
such a snob. What is your father, Lieutenant?

STEFAN: A chef at the Volksgarten Restaurant.

BARON: And do you think I'm a snob?

STEFAN: You appear to be.

BARON: Well, of course, I am. Alfred will tell you how much.
However, I'm also a gentleman, which is preferable to
being one of our dear Burgomaster Lueger's mob. Taste, a
silk shirt, a perfumed hand, an ancient Greek ring are
things that come from a way not only of thinking but of
being. They can add up to a man. (*To* STEFAN.) Would
you like to walk on the terrace? The view is rather
remarkable on an evening like this.

STEFAN: Alfred?

BARON: We'll join you. Or come back soon. I want to ask the
Colonel's advice. About some espionage.
(STEFAN *bows and leaves through the high central glass doors.*)
Well, my dear friend. And how are you? You're prosperous
I hear.

REDL: I had a small legacy.

BARON: Good. A man like you knows what money's for. And you *look* so well. Forgive me for sending the boy away for a moment.

REDL: That's all right. He'll find something to amuse him.

BARON: Would it be impertinent to ask: you're not wasting your time there are you?

REDL: It would.

BARON: What? Oh, I see. Quite right. Only I admire you, Redl. So does everyone else. You're a credit to – everyone. I just want you to succeed in everything you undertake.

REDL: Thank you.

(KUNZ *comes over with his partner,* MARIE ANTOINETTE.)

BARON: Jaroslaw! Have some champagne.

KUNZ: Thank you.

BARON: And let me introduce Colonel Redl – Major Advocate Kunz.

(*They salute each other appropriately.*)

FERDY: Colonel! Would you come over here a minute. The Tsarina wants to give herself up.

(TSARINA *screams.*)

She says, she says she wants to confess!

(*The* TSARINA *pulls off* FERDY's *wig and smacks him with it.* REDL *smiles and excuses himself to* KUNZ.)

BARON: Ferdy! That's naughty! The Colonel was talking to Major Kunz.

FERDY: No, he wasn't. Here!

(*He places* REDL *beside him and the* TSARINA.)

We've been talking to you. (To BARON.) *You* don't listen! It's secret.

(*The* BARON *smiles happily.*)

BARON: Alfred *knows* all the secrets. It's his job.

(FERDY *and the* TSARINA *conduct a whispered conversation with* REDL *for a while. He is drinking freely now, and is excited and enjoying himself. The* BARON *turns to* KUNZ.)

Don't you think my little Ferdy's brilliant? He'd make an adorable 'Cherubino'.

KUNZ: I think he's prettier as 'Susanna'.

BARON: Perhaps. He made that costume himself. Up half the night.

KUNZ: Did you see who I came with?

BARON: No. Why?

KUNZ: Good. I thought I'd spice your party a bit this year.

BARON: What have you done?

KUNZ: I brought a woman.

(*The* BARON *looks astonished. Then yelps with laughter.*)

BARON: Oh, *what* a good idea! What a *stroke*! Where is she? (*He looks around.*)

KUNZ: That's the point. Later on, we'll all have to guess.

BARON: And find out! Marvellous! We'll unmask her. I'll offer a prize to the man who strips her.

KUNZ: And, I think, a punishment for anyone who is mistaken.

BARON: Exactly. What fun! I do enjoy these things. I wish we could have one every month. I'm so glad you liked Ferdy.

KUNZ: How long is it now?

BARON: Three years.

KUNZ: Long time.

BARON: For me. Let's be honest, for nearly all of us. *And* women. No, three years is a big bite out of a lifetime when you never know when it may come to an end, or what you may have missed. But he's very kind. He's still young. But his growing old gnaws at me a bit, you know. Not that he still doesn't look pretty good in the raw. Oh, he does. But about me, he doesn't mind at all.

KUNZ: Who's the little flower with Redl?

BARON: No idea. *Something's* made her wilt. They've both just come from the Hofball.

KUNZ: So have I.

BARON: Of course. Poor you. And with your lady escort. I wonder if I'll spot her.

(*He stares around.*)

That's her!

KUNZ: That is the doorman at the Klomser Hotel.

BARON: Oh! I see I'm not going to. What on earth made you go to the Hofball?

KUNZ: I thought it might be amusing to go there first.

(KUNZ *nods at* REDL, *who is being captivated by* FERDY, *and starting to get recurring fits of giggles.*)

Look at the Colonel.

BARON: (*Pleased*) He's enjoying himself.

KUNZ: I've never seen him like that before.

BARON: How many people have seen *you*? He's letting his hair down. What's left of it. It's starting to go. I noticed just now. He's a handsome devil.

KUNZ: Very.

BARON: And a brilliant officer, they say. Suppose you should be if you're at the top in counter espionage.

KUNZ: Preferably. He works morning and night.

BARON: He's only a railway clerk's son, did you know? So I suppose he's had to. Work, I mean. But he plays too. Look at him.

(REDL *and* FERDY *are swapping stories and giggling intermittently and furiously.* REDL *tries to light another cigar, but he can scarcely get it going. The* TSARINA *watches blankly and happily.*)

He told me once how hard he'd tried to change.

KUNZ: Hey, you! Little Shepherdess!

(*He takes a drink from a blushing* SHEPHERDESS.)

Beautiful. Yes?

BARON: Tried everything, apparently. Resolutions, vows, religion, medical advice, self-exhaustion. Used to flog a dozen horses into the ground in a day. And then gardening, if you please, fencing and all those studies they do, you do, of course – military history, ciphers, telegraphy, campaigns, he knows, hundreds of them, by heart. He knows his German literature, speaks superb French and Russian, Italian, Polish, Czech *and* Turkish if you please.

KUNZ: Not bad for a Ruthenian railway clerk.

BARON: As you say. Oh, take your eye off Redl. He's not after the Tsarina. Or Ferdy. Is he? No, I don't think so. He's just being himself for once. Don't you think we should all form an Empire of our own?

KUNZ: What's that?

BARON: Well, instead of all joining together, you know, one Empire of sixty million Germans, like they're always going on about. What about an Empire of *us*. Ex million queens.

KUNZ: Who would there be?

BARON: Well, you and me for a start. I'd be Minister of Culture, I think. Redl could catch any spies, *women* spies. And you could do what you liked.

KUNZ: And who else?

BARON: Not Jews I think. They're the least queer in my opinion. Their mothers won't let them. Germans, Prussians, they're *very* queer. All that duelling. Poles, not so much.

KUNZ: Italians?

BARON: No, they're like women, only better, women con brio. Hungarians are just goats, of course, but some are quite nice. French: too spry to let life play a trick on *them*.

KUNZ: What about the English?

BARON: Next, after the Germans.

KUNZ: I agree with that. Queen Victoria was quite clearly a man.

BARON: But *she* was a German, wasn't she?

KUNZ: Ah, yes. Still, you're right about the English.

BARON: I believe Redl has an Eton straw boater hanging over his bed as a trophy. They say it belongs to the younger son of the British Ambassador.
(*Pause.*)
How's that son of yours?
(KUNZ *looks immediately on guard.*)
I was only asking.

KUNZ: He's well.

BARON: I'm sorry. It must be difficult. If people *will* get married.

KUNZ: Well, *I* did.

BARON: The boy knows nothing?

KUNZ: Nothing.

BARON: His mother hasn't –

KUNZ: No. And she won't.

BARON: Why not? Doesn't she –

KUNZ: She pretends.

BARON: Ah! They *do*. And the boy?

KUNZ: *He's* all right, if that's what you mean.

BARON: You mean you're *not* all right?

KUNZ: Who knows? Is this Redl's flower?

(STEFAN *approaches.*)

BARON: Yes. My dear boy, you must meet the Major Advocate
Kunz. Lieutenant – I'm sorry –?

STEFAN: Kovacs.

(*They salute.*)

BARON: Hungarian. Did you enjoy the terrace? I knew you
would. Oh, thank heaven the music's stopped. Alfred's
been having the giggles with little Ferdy while you've been
away. Do have another glass, dear boy.

(REDL *and* FERDY *stand up, giggling helplessly. The others
listen.*)

FERDY: And the manager, said, he said to me: we don't allow
ladies in here, in here without male escorts.

(REDL *doubles up.*)

And, so I pointed at the Baron and said, what do you think
he is!

(REDL *falls on the* TSARINA *who squeals.*)

KUNZ: (*To* STEFAN) Is this your first visit to this kind of thing?

STEFAN: Yes, sir.

BARON: You don't call him sir. Just because he's dressed as
Nelson. He's only an old Army lawyer. I must say you look
very fine with that black patch. We must find a Lady
Hamilton for him before the evening's out, mustn't we? I
was saying, where do you keep your arm?

(KUNZ *leaves it out of his tunic, and stretches it.*)

Ah, there it is, you see?

KUNZ: That's better.

BARON: You danced very well, all the same.

KUNZ: (*To* STEFAN) Would you care to?

(STEFAN *is slightly confused for a moment.*)

STEFAN: Thank you, I'm a bit hot.

BARON: Must be cold on that terrace.

KUNZ: You see, this is a place for people to come together.

144

People who are very often in their everyday lives, rather lonely and even miserable and feel hunted. As if they had a spy catcher like the Colonel on their heels.

STEFAN: Of course. I understand that.

KUNZ: And, because of the Baron's panache and generosity – and, let's be frank, recklessness –

BARON: Look who's talking –

KUNZ: They come together and become something else. Like sinners in a church.

(FERDY *stands up.*)

LADY GODIVA: Two monks in the street.

TSARINA: I *like* monks.

LADY GODIVA: Two monks. Walking in the street. One's saying his rosary to himself. The other passes by as he's saying 'Hail Mary'. And the other stops and says: 'Hullo, Ursula.'

(REDL *collapses. So does* FERDY. *Then recovers professionally. The others watch, and some of the dancers too, including* KUPFER *and* ALBRECHT-COLUMBINE, *and* FIGARO *and* LADY GODIVA. *General laughter. The* BARON *is pleased.* FERDY *sits back next to* REDL *and they both drink and giggle together, mostly at nothing, until later in the scene when* REDL *takes in* KUPFER *and becomes hostile: to* KUPFER, *drunkenness and himself.*)

KUNZ: You're not enjoying yourself much. (*Small pause.*) Are you?

(STEFAN *blushes.*)

STEFAN: Not at all.

KUNZ: You mustn't judge the world at carnival time. There is such a thing, such a contract, such a bond as marriage –

BARON: You should know, poor soul.

KUNZ: And there is friendship, comradeship. In the midst of all this, I ask you not to sneer, or I will beat your sanctimonious head in –

BARON: Jaroslaw –

KUNZ: Aristotle, if you've heard of him.

STEFAN: I have –

BARON: Please; take no notice . . .

KUNZ: I'm glad to hear it. Says it can be either good, or

pleasant or useful. Which is true, but not always. But he also says it lasts in such men only, only as long as they keep their goodness. And goodness, unfortunately, Lieutenant, does not last.

STEFAN: No?

KUNZ: No. And don't be insolent.

STEFAN: Then don't be offensive.

BARON: Tempers, darlings, tempers!

KUNZ: It seldom lasts shall we say? But then such men are rare, anyway.

(*The other guests gather round, and listen, and begin to take part. During this sequence,* REDL *sobers up and stiffens.*)

KUPFER: Good evening, Colonel Redl.

REDL: I don't . . .

KUPFER: *Now* you do . . .

BARON: *Everyone!* Met *everyone* before. (*To* ALBRECHT.)

KUPFER: Kupfer. Major Kupfer, sir. General Staff. Ninth Corps. Prague.

REDL: Prague, Prague . . . This is Vienna. What are you doing here?

KUPFER: Same as you, sir. On leave.

REDL: *I'm* not on leave.

KUPFER: I didn't necessarily mean literally –

REDL: You'll remember Steinbauer then?

KUPFER: Of course.

(*He greets the wimpled* STEINBAUER *casually.*)

It was a blow about Siczynski. (*Pause.*) Wasn't it?

REDL: Was it?

KUPFER: Wasn't he a particular friend of yours?

REDL: I scarcely knew him. We neither of us did . . .

KUPFER: Why did you agree to be his second? It wasn't a very correct thing for such a correct officer as you to be doing.

REDL: I thought he should have support . . . No one liked him.

KUPFER: But *you've* always been popular, Colonel.

REDL: Are you being . . . because if so . . .

KUPFER: You only have my admiration, Colonel. With all the advantages I was born with, I only wish I – could – ever go

– so far. You seemed to be having an entertaining time just there, Colonel. Please don't let me –

FERDY: Don't you think he's beautiful? I adore it when he screws his monocle in his eye.

(REDL *doesn't think this at all funny, though the* BARON *and* KUNZ *are pleased, and, of course,* KUPFER. REDL *stands more erect than ever, and lights up a fresh cigar, grabbing a glass from the passing* SHEPHERDESS.)

REDL: Hey, you! Fräulein!

FERDY: Have you heard about the extraordinary Dr. Schoepfer?

KUPFER: No. Who is he?

FERDY: Don't you know? My dear, he sounds divine! The Tsarina went there last night.

STEINBAUER: What does he do?

FERDY: Just talks, my dear, for *hours*. Not a smile. Medical do's and all that, but, if you say you're a student, you can get in.

KUPFER: What's he talk about?

FERDY: Why, *us*. He sounds an absolute scream. Can't stop talking about it.

REDL: Us? Speak for yourself.

BARON: What's he say then, Ferdy?

FERDY: Oh, that we're all demented something, something cox on the end, darling.

(*Laughter.*)

LADY GODIVA: Well, he's right, of course.

FERDY: That we're all potential criminals, and some of us should even be castrated.

(*Screams.*)

And that we're a warning symptom of the crisis in, oh, civilization, and the decline in Christian whatnots.

BARON: Oh, and he goes on about marriage and the family being the basis of the Empire, and *we* must be rooted out. *She* says he's a scream.

(*They look at the* TSARINA, *who nods, giggles and goes crimson.*)

MARIE ANTOINETTE: Is he a Jew?

FERDY: But, of course, darling! She says he looks like Shylock's mother.

KUPFER: But who is he?

KUNZ: A neurologist, I believe. Nerves.

BARON: Well, I'm sure he'd get on mine.

KUNZ: I think he's one of those people who insist they can penetrate the inner secrets of your own nature.

BARON: I understand the inner secrets of my nature perfectly well. I don't admire them, but I do know them, anyway better than this Dr. Schoepfer.

FERDY: Silly mare!

BARON: And I'm quite happy as I am, I'm no criminal, thank you, and I don't corrupt anything that isn't already quite clearly corrupt, like this ghastly city. On the contrary, I bring style, wit, pleasure, energy and good humour to it that it wouldn't otherwise have.

KUPFER: Well said, Baron.

BARON: More drinks, everyone! And music? (*To* MUSICIANS.)

ALBRECHT: I went to a doctor once, and he just said 'pull your socks up'. Do you know what he told me to do? Go into the Army! (*Shrieks.*) And find yourself a nice girl. Get married. So: naturally, I went into the Army. Artillery. In the second week I'd been seduced by the Corporal of Horse *and* a sub-lieutenant.

BARON: Oh, I went to a doctor like a silly thing when I was a student. He just looked very agitated and told me there was nothing he could do and go away. A few years later I heard he'd cut his throat . . .

MARIE ANTOINETTE: I plucked up courage to tell *our* family doctor, and I said I'd like to be sent away to some special clinic in Vienna . . . Well, I thought he was going to go raving mad. Vienna, he said, Vienna, *you* want to go to Vienna. I'll send you to hell. You'll find all you want *there*, you quivering, scheming little sissy!

ALBRECHT: When I first came to Vienna, it seemed like paradise, but now I do get a bit bored. Not here, of course, Baron. But you know what I mean. Same tired old exhibits. Nothing new ever seems to come in.

TSARINA: (*Now sitting on the* BARON's *knee shyly*) I remember the first time a man tickled the palm of my hand with his middle finger, when we shook hands, and then later he told me what he was. I was very religious then, and I thought he was wicked. I really did at the time.

KUNZ: Perhaps you were right.

LADY GODIVA: *I* went to our priest. He quoted Aquinas and said anything that was against nature was against God . . . He always kept an eye on me afterwards, always pulling me up and asking me questions.

STEINBAUER: *My* priest said: you *can't* be like that. You're a soldier, a man of courage and honour and virtue. Your uniform itself embodies the glory of the Empire and the Church. I worshipped Radetzky at the time, and he knew it. So he said do you think someone like Radetzky could have ever been like that? I didn't know about Julius Caesar and Alexander then.

FIGARO: (*To* REDL, *who is like a frozen ox*) I hate these screamers, don't you?

I used to go to the priest after I'd confessed I was in love with Fritz. Then I used to lie like crazy about it, and say nothing was happening, although we were having sex regularly. And he'd give me absolution and say, 'It may not take on immediately –'

(*Laughter.*)

If Fritz just moved his little finger at me, I'd go back. Then he went with a girl suddenly and got married. When she was pregnant, we had beers together, and he pinched my arm and kissed me. Then he laughed and said: You know what you are, find someone else the same . . . but he laughed . . .

FERDY: I should think so, you soppy little thing.

(FERDY *is bored with all this and wants attention.*)

I only went to a doctor once and he just said take more exercise, dear. So I did.

(*He executes a skilful entrechat to general amusement till* REDL *strikes him hard across the face, knocking him down right into the other guests. The boy is stunned by the force of it. Silence.*)

REDL: Baron – forgive me.

(*He clicks his heels and goes, followed presently by* STEFAN *in silence. Then the* BARON *booms out over a few 'Wells!', etc.*)

BARON: Someone pick up poor Ferdy. You silly boy! I knew you shouldn't have flirted with Colonel Redl. He's a dangerous man. Are you better? There now! Come along, everybody, that's quite enough melodrama. On with the ball – I suppose –

(*They reassemble. Lights lower. And they hear the spirit of Mozart as* FERDY *sings, not without some sweetness, 'Vedrai Carino' or 'Batti, Batti'. Or something similar which is tolerably within his range.*)

SCENE TWO

Lecture Room. Rostrum. A glass of water. DR. SCHOEPFER *is speaking.*

SCHOEPFER: The *evasion*, naturally, of responsibility . . . For instance in enjoying the physical sensations of the body without any reference to the responsibilities involved in the relationship. Or, indeed, to society or any beliefs, such as a belief in God. They can never, in their ignorance, some men say folly, in their infirmity, never attain that complete love, the love that only is possible between men and women, whose shared interests . . .

(*There is a suppressed giggle.*)

. . . whose shared interests include the blessed gift of children and grandchildren which alone, I think, most people would agree even today, which alone gives a grand and enduring purpose to sexual congress.

(*He drinks from the glass of water.*)

Now, gentlemen: these traits are caused by regression to the phallic stage of libido development, and can be traced to what is in fact a flight from incest . . .

(*Fade.*)

A hill clearing outside Dresden, surrounded by fir trees. Cold winter.
OBLENSKY *is warmly wrapped up in his greatcoat, sitting on a tree*
trunk smoking a cigarette. STANITSIN *stands beside him.*

STANITSIN: Here he comes.

OBLENSKY: To the minute. As you'd expect. You'd better give
me the file. Oh, just a minute, have you got the parcel I
asked for?

(STANITSIN *nods.*)

It wasn't easy this week getting in. The boy Kovacs is
staying there while he's commanding this exercise.

(REDL *enters, smoking a cigar. He looks cool and sure of*
himself.)

REDL: Mr. Smith?

OBLENSKY: Yes, indeed. Rather *this* is Mr. Smith.

REDL: Look, I haven't time to waste fooling about –

OBLENSKY: Quite. You got our message, and, blessedly, you
are here, Colonel Redl.

REDL: And who the devil are you?

OBLENSKY: Colonel Oblensky.

REDL: Oblensky . . .

(OBLENSKY *waits for the effect to take, and goes on.*)

OBLENSKY: It won't take you long, Colonel. I know your
regiment is waiting for you . . . loosely speaking. I have a
file here, which I would like to acquaint you with briefly.
Would you care to sit down?

(REDL *doesn't move.*)

Just a matter of minutes. I have no anxiety about you
reaching for your revolver to shoot either of us. I know you
will realize that all this file is duplicated both in Warsaw
and St. Petersburg. What I do beg of you is to pause before
you think of turning it on yourself. I think we can find a
satisfactory, and probably long-term arrangement which
will work out quite well for all of us, and no trouble.

REDL: (*Recovering, coldly*) May I see?

OBLENSKY: Naturally, oh, this is Lieutenant Stanitsin.

(STANITSIN *bows.*)

REDL: Mr. Smith?

STANITSIN: My pen name, sir.

(REDL *puts out his hand impatiently for the file.*
OBLENSKY *hands him the contents in batches. They watch*
REDL *flip through, stone faced.*)

REDL: Mess bills in Lemberg! Eighteen eighty-nine! Tailors'
bills, jeweller's, stables, coachbuilders, tobacconists. What
is all this? They're just bills.

OBLENSKY: Rather unusual bills for a young officer of no
independent means.

REDL: I have an uncle –

OBLENSKY: You have no uncle, Colonel. Two brothers only.
Both happily married – and penniless.

(*Hands him another bill.*)

Cartiers. One gold cigarette case inscribed 'to dearest
Stefan with love, Alfred'.

REDL: My nephew.

(OBLENSKY *hasn't the heart to smile at this.* REDL*'s immediate
humiliation is so evident.*)

OBLENSKY: Your bank statements from the Austro-Hungarian
Bank in both Vienna and Prague for the month of
February.

(REDL *hardly looks at them. Pause.*)

REDL: Well?

OBLENSKY: I'm sorry, Colonel. We'll soon get this over. One
letter, date, February 17th 1901. 'My darling, don't be
angry. When I make no sign, you know or should know,
that I love you. Please see me again. All I long for is to lie
beside you, nothing else. I don't know what to do to kill
the time before I see you again, and watch you, how I can
do something to pass the time.'

REDL: It is no crime to write a love letter, Colonel, even if it
isn't in the style of Pushkin.

OBLENSKY: The style's tolerable enough for a man in love . . .
But this letter is not addressed to a woman.

REDL: There's no name on it.

OBLENSKY: There is on the envelope.

REDL: *Not* very convincing, Colonel.

OBLENSKY: Very well. Those – if you'd just glance through them quickly – are signed affidavits from –

(REDL *won't look at them. He has mustered himself wonderfully. He feels the chance of a small hope.*)

(*Politely, casually.*) The page at the Grand Hotel, a musician at the Volksgarten – this is only the last six weeks, you understand – a waiter at Sacher's, a Corporal in the Seventh Corps in Prague, a boatman in Vienna, a pastry cook, a compositor on the 'Deutsches Volksblatt' and a *reporter* on the 'Neue Freie Press'. (*Pause.*) One right-wing paper, one liberal, eh?

(REDL *puffs on his cigar.*)

REDL: (*Slowly*) Whores. Bribed, perjuring whores.

OBLENSKY: Yes. Against the word of a distinguished officer in the Royal Imperial Army . . . Oh, dear . . . Stanitsin. Photographs . . .

(STANITSIN *hands a bundle of large photographs to* REDL *who looks at the first four or five. Then he hands them back. Pause. He sits on another trunk and slowly puts his face in his hands.*) Offer the Colonel some brandy.

(STANITSIN *offers him a flask, which he drinks from.*) I think *I'll* have some, Stanitsin. Now that's all over, let us all have some. Forgive me, Colonel. Now: time is short for us. What you decide to do is up to you. There are three courses open to you. One we have mentioned. The second is to leave the Army. The third is to remain in the Army and continue with your brilliant career. Do you know what Russia spent on espionage last year. Colonel? Nine million roubles. Nine. This year it will be even more. What do your people spend? Half? No, I've watched you for more than ten years, and you'd be surprised probably, or perhaps I'm wrong, about how much I know about the kind of man you are. What can you do? Change your way of life? It's getting desperate already, isn't it? You don't know which way to turn, you're up to your eye-balls in debts. What could you do? Get thrown out, exposed for everything you are, or what the world would say you are. Would you, do you think, *could* you change your way of

life, what else do you want after all these years, what would
you do at your age, go back to base and become a waiter or
a washer up, sit all alone in cafés again constantly *watching*?
What are you fit for?
(*His tone relaxes.*)
The same as me, my dear friend, the same as me, and very
good indeed you are at it, soldiering, war and treachery, or
the treachery that leads to wars. The game. It's a fine one.
And no one's better at it in Europe than me – at the
moment. (*Smiles.*) Heavy turnover sometimes. Tell me, do
none of your brother officers know or suspect?

REDL: Kovacs, Kupfer, Steinbauer . . . No.

OBLENSKY: And Kunz? Kunz's only real indiscretion is the
Baron's annual ball, and he could always say he went as a
relation or even as a tourist even though it's hardly
respectable. We've never caught him out in all these years,
have we, Stanitsin? He does . . . doesn't he . . .?

REDL: I assume so.

OBLENSKY: The other two, Steinbauer and Kupfer, well, they
seem to have left wormcasts all over Europe, so they're no
threat to you. And Kovacs, he's only – been – with *you*,
hasn't he?

REDL: Yes.

OBLENSKY: Sure?

REDL: (*Wryly*) Colonel Oblensky, I may find myself here before
you, in this position, but I remind you that I *am* an officer
in the Austrian Chief of Staff's Counter Espionage
Department. *I* know how to interrogate myself. The
answer's yes.
(OBLENSKY *smiles.*)

OBLENSKY: Oh, I'm the last to under-estimate you, Colonel.
Last report from General Staff Headquarters January 5th:
'supremely capable, learned, intuitive and precise in
command, tactful, excellent manners.' And now your
handling of the corps exercise on Monday: 'He is
uncommonly striking. Both as a battalion and regimental
commander.' And there's your Regiment, the 77th
Infantry. Didn't the Emperor call it 'my beautiful Seventy

Seventh'. Oh, you certainly chose the right career, Colonel. Cigarette? I think the really interesting thing about you, Redl, is that you yourself are really properly aware of your own distinction – as you should be. If you ever do feel any shame for what you are, you don't accept it like a simpleton, you heave it off, like a horse that's fallen on you. And the result is, I suppose what they mean by that splendid Viennese style. Ah, the time, yes, we must be going. Give the Colonel his package.

(STANITSIN *does so.*)

REDL: Is that all?

OBLENSKY: You must be returning to the regiment, Colonel.

REDL: What's this?

OBLENSKY: Mr. Smith will contact you when you've had a few days to rest and recover generally. The package contains seven thousand kronen in notes . . . Far more than *you* pay, Colonel.

(REDL *puts it in his pocket slowly, collects himself, and bows.*)

Goodbye, Colonel. I don't suppose we shall meet again for a long time – if ever . . . It *is* a little risky, even for you, isn't it?

(*He laughs, full of good humour.*)

Oh, Stanitsin, the parcel.

(*He hands a paper bag to* REDL, *who, puzzled, takes from it an Etonian straw boater.*)

Perhaps you should return it to the British Ambassador.

(*He laughs heartily.*)

Forgive me, Colonel, but I do have a very clumsy, clumsy sense of humour sometimes. No, always!

(STANITSIN *smiles and goes out. The two men watch him. Presently they hear his laughter floating back through the woods.*)

ACT THREE

SCENE ONE

REDL's *apartment in Vienna. Baroque, luxurious. It is late afternoon, the curtains are drawn, the light comes through them and two figures can just be seen in bed. One is* REDL *who appears to be asleep. The other, the figure of a* YOUNG MAN, *is getting up very quietly, almost stealthily, and dressing. There is a rattle of coins and jewellery.*

REDL: Don't take my cigarette case, will you? *Or* my watch.

(*The boy hesitates.*)

There's plenty of change. Take that. Go on. Now you'd better . . . hurry back.

(*The boy slips out quickly, expertly.* REDL *sits up and lights a cigar. He gets up and puts on a beautiful dressing gown. Presently* KUPFER *comes in.*)

Who's that? Oh, you? Why don't you knock?

KUPFER: I knew you were alone.

REDL: What's the time?

KUPFER: Four. Shall I open the shutters?

(*He does so.* REDL *shrinks a little.*)

REDL: That's enough.

KUPFER: The sun's quite hot.

(*He sits in an armchair by the window.*)

I waited. Till your little friend left.

REDL: Very courteous. Well?

KUPFER: I've news.

REDL: Bad, no doubt.

KUPFER: Afraid so.

REDL: Out with it.

KUPFER: Stefan was married secretly this morning.

(*Pause.*) To the Countess Delyanoff.

(*Pause.*)

REDL: Naturally. The bitch . . . Does she want to see me?

KUPFER: Why, yes – she's waiting.

156

REDL: Well, go and get her. And then go away.

(KUPFER *turns*.)

No. Wait outside.

(KUPFER *goes and* REDL *smokes his cigar, looking out of the window. Soon the* COUNTESS *enters*.)

COUNTESS: Alfred?

REDL: So: you pulled it off.

COUNTESS: Alfred. We've endured all of that. Can't we –

REDL: No. What's he doing, marrying *you*?

COUNTESS: He loves me. No more . . .

REDL: I suppose you're calving.

COUNTESS: I'm having his child, Alfred.

REDL: I knew it! Knew it!

COUNTESS: He *would* have married me. He was disgusted by your behaviour.

REDL: Oh?

COUNTESS: You must admit, Alfred, telling him I was Jewish wasn't very subtle – for *you*.

REDL: Well, you are, aren't you? And I don't believe you'd told him.

COUNTESS: No, I hadn't. But my *not* telling him was cowardly, not vulgar, like yours *was*. You surprise me, Alfred.

REDL: And he'll have to resign his commission as he's no means?

COUNTESS: He wants to go into journalism.

REDL: And become a politician.

COUNTESS: Alfred, we had such feeling for each other once.

REDL: I didn't, you Jewish prig, you whited sepulchre, does he know what you really are, apart from a whore, a whoring spy?

COUNTESS: No. He doesn't. No one knows. Except you. It's extraordinary you should have kept it a secret, but I don't expect you to behave differently now.

REDL: Don't count on it . . . You little Jewish spy –

COUNTESS: I'm not, not now, Alfred, you know . . . it was my husband, when he was alive –

REDL: Don't snivel. You took *me* in.

COUNTESS: I didn't. I loved you . . .

REDL: Well, I didn't love you. I love Stefan. *We* just fooled one
another. Oh, I tried to hoax myself too, but not really
often. So: tonight's your wedding night. (*Pause.*) I tell you
this: you'll never know that body like I know it. The lines
beneath his eyes. Do you know how many there are, do
you know one has less than the other? And the scar behind
his ear, and the hairs in his nostrils, which has the most,
what colour they are in what light? The mole on where?
Where, Sophia? I know the place here, between the eyes,
the dark patches like slate – like blue when he's tired, really
tired, the place for a blow or a kiss or a bullet. You'll never
know like I know, you can't. The backs of his knees, the
pattern on the soles of his feet. Which trouble him, and so
I used to wash them and bathe them for hours. His thick
waist, and how long are his thighs, compared to his calves,
you've not looked at him, you never will.

COUNTESS: Stop it!

(*Pause.*)

REDL: You don't know what to do with that. And now *you've*
got it.

COUNTESS: God, I'm weary of your self-righteousness and all
your superior railing and your glib cant about friendship
and the Army and the way you all roll out your little
parade: Michelangelo and Socrates, and Alexander and
Leonardo. God, you're like a guild of housewives pointing
out Catherine the Great.

REDL: So: you'll turn Stefan into another portly middle-aged
father with – what did you say once – snotty little longings
under their watch chains and glances at big, unruptured
bottoms.

COUNTESS: Alfred: every one of *you* ends up, as you well know,
with a bottom quite different, much plumper and far wider
than any ordinary man.

REDL: You think, people like you, you've got a formula for me.
You think I'm hobbled, as you say. But I'm free of you,
anyway. You, what about you, I can resist you!

COUNTESS: Do you know, remember, what you once said to
me: I can never blame you. You are in my heart.

REDL: I do blame you. I was lying. And Stefan is my heart.
(*Pause.*)
COUNTESS: He said you told him I was Jewish. And what I
looked like, what I *would* look like, drooping hairy skin and
flab, and so on –
REDL: And now you're going to be a mother. You think you're
a river or something, I suppose.
COUNTESS: That's right, Alfred. A sewer. Your old temple built
over a sewer.
REDL: Sophia, why don't we . . .?
COUNTESS: No, Alfred. I'm in your grip. But I'll make no
bargains. Do as you wish.
REDL: I bought him a beautiful new gelding last week.
COUNTESS: It should be back in your stables by now. And your
groom's got all the other –
REDL: Get out.
COUNTESS: I'm going, Alfred. Do as you wish. You may think a
trick was played on you once, but you've repaid and re-
played it a thousand times over. I pity you; really –
REDL: Don't then. I'm really doing quite well.
(*She goes out.* KUPFER *comes in.*)
KUPFER: Well?
REDL: Well? Nothing . . . I suppose you think you're moving in?
KUPFER: Do you want me to draw up a full report on your file
on the Countess?
REDL: That file is *my* property. And *you'll* do as you're told. I'm
going to sleep. Close the shutters.
(KUPFER *does so.* REDL *falls asleep almost immediately on the
bed. Soon little moaning noises are heard from him.* KUPFER
smokes a cigarette in the early evening light.)
(*Fade.*)

SCENE TWO

*The Red Lounge of the Sacher Hotel, Vienna. A string orchestra
plays.* REDL *and* KUPFER *are drinking together.* KUPFER *is in a
sour, watching mood.* REDL *is even cooler than usual and is smoking*

159

and appraising the other occupants of the lounge. He hails a
WAITER.

REDL: (*To* KUPFER) Another?

KUPFER: No. I'm going.

REDL: (*To the* WAITER) Just one then. So soon?
  (*Pause.*)

KUPFER: Why St. Petersburg, for heaven's sake?

REDL: Because I've signed the order, and General Staff is not
  equipped to countermand orders. It works on the sweet
  Viennese roundabout method. Anyway, there's no one
  else.

KUPFER: But a whole year. I don't even speak Russian. It's
  nonsense.

REDL: Not to the Bureau. And now you *can* learn Russian, as I
  did. You should pick it up in half that time. It's the vowels
  that'll bring *you* down.

KUPFER: Thank you.

REDL: I'll get you back before the year's out. Don't worry.

KUPFER: You *are* sure of yourself, aren't you?

REDL: I have to be, don't I? And why not?
  (*He takes his drink from* WAITER.)
  No one is interested in doubts. This is an age of iron
  certainties, that's what they want to know about, run by
  money makers, large armies, munitions men, money
  makers for money makers. *You* were born with a silver
  sabre up your whatnot.
  (*Lifts his glass.*)
  St. Petersburg! I'll give you some names and addresses.

KUPFER: If only you'd at least admit it's because of Mischa.
  Why can't you be honest?

REDL: Because honesty is no use to you. People who don't
  want it are always yelling the place down for it like some
  grizzling kid. When they get it they're always miserable . . .
  Besides, Mischa is getting married, as you know.

KUPFER: I thought you'd put the stopper on that.

REDL: I didn't think we should tie him to a girl in a
  confectionery shop, a broad-faced, big-hipped little
  housefrau who can hardly read and write, and, what's

more, doesn't care, all chocolates and childbirth. Still, if he wants that, he shall have it. It's a poor reward. Sad, too . . .

KUPFER: You do pick them, don't you?

REDL: Yes . . . But that is the nature of it. Marriage has never occurred to *you* for instance, has it?
(*Pause.*)
Since Stefan I've let them go their own ways. If that's all, if that's the sum of it, if that's what they want . . .

KUPFER: At least be honest with *yourself*. The girl came round again last night.

REDL: Did she then? I told Max to throw her out. Next time he'll throw her down the stairs.

KUPFER: Then *she'll* end up in hospital as well.

REDL: Damn it, he's only got a nervous breakdown, or whatever they call it nowadays.

KUPFER: She says he's off his head.

REDL: Nonsense. He's always been over-strung. Maybe a bit unbalanced. He'll recover. And then he can marry her.

KUPFER: And he calls *me* cruel?

REDL: *You* were born like it. All your sort of people are. It's expected of you.

KUPFER: And what about *your* sort of people then?

REDL: Sometimes it's inescapable. I'm still nicer than you, Kupfer.

KUPFER: Why do you hate me, Alfred?
(*Pause.*)
Why then?

REDL: I've said often enough no one, and not you, is to call me Alfred in public . . . (*Hesitates.*)

KUPFER: Then why do you let me live with you?

REDL: You don't. I allow you a room in my apartment.

KUPFER: Exactly. You know, better than anyone, about jealousy.

REDL: It's a discipline, like Russian. You master it, or you don't. It's up to you, isn't it. Ah, here's Hötzendorf and Möhl.

KUPFER: Who's the boy?

REDL: Try and restrain your curiosity a little.

(*They rise and greet* GENERAL HÖTZENDORF, GENERAL
MÖHL *and* SUB-LIEUTENANT VIKTOR JERZABEK. *All salute
stiffly, aware of their own presence in the lounge.*)

HÖTZENDORF: Ah, Colonel, the Lieutenant tells me that great
automobile and chauffeur outside belong to you.

REDL: Yes, sir. New toy, I'm afraid.

HÖTZENDORF: Expensive toy. Don't see many like that.
Thought it must belong to some fat Jew.

(REDL *is discomfited.*)

Oh, don't misunderstand me, the vehicle itself is in
impeccable taste, Redl, like everything to do with you.

REDL: Will you join us, sir?

HÖTZENDORF: Just having a quick dinner. Brought some work
with us, then back to the office.

MÖHL: The lieutenant is the only one who seems able to take
down the General's notes fast enough.

HÖTZENDORF: Well, quickly then. I wanted a word with you.

REDL: Waiter! I was just celebrating some good fortune. My
uncle in Galicia has just left me a legacy.

(*Chairs are feverishly placed round the table for the arrivals.
Everyone sits and orders.*)

HÖTZENDORF: Well done. Good. Yes, very good taste. Though
I still prefer a good pair of horses, can't run an army with
automobiles. No, but you know it's not that the Jews
themselves are specially rotten. It's what they represent.
For instance, no belief in service, and how can the Empire
survive without the idea of service? Look at the Jews in
Galicia, you must know, Redl, getting them into the army
– quite impossible.

REDL: Indeed. *And* the high percentage of desertion.

MÖHL: Really? I didn't know that.

REDL: Nineteen per cent.

HÖTZENDORF: There you are. They're outsiders, they feel
outsiders, so their whole creed of life must be based on
duplicity – by necessity.

REDL: I agree, sir. Even their religion seems to be little more
than a series of rather pious fads.

HÖTZENDORF: Quite. We're all Germans, all of us, and that's the way of it. At least: Jews when they get on, remind us of it.

REDL: Which I suppose is a useful function.

HÖTZENDORF: Talking of that, Redl, I want to congratulate you on your handling of that Cracow spy affair. Everyone, absolutely everyone's most impressed and highly delighted, including the Emperor himself.

REDL: I'm deeply honoured, sir.

HÖTZENDORF: Well. You do honour to us. I see you already have the order of the Iron Crown Second Class. Möhl here is recommending you for the Military Service Medal.

REDL: I don't know what –

HÖTZENDORF: You know your stuff, Redl. You've an extraordinary understanding and intuition as far as the criminal intelligence is concerned. And, there it is, spies are criminals like any other. We all just use them like any thief or murderer.

MÖHL: That's right, he's right.

HÖTZENDORF: Cracow is our first bastion against Russia. If war breaks out, it's imperative those fortresses don't crack. They'll go for them first. If that little ring you rounded up had succeeded, we could have lost a war the day it started. From April I am proposing that you take over the Prague Bureau. Rumpler will direct Vienna.

REDL: I'm overwhelmed, sir.

MÖHL: To be confirmed of course.

REDL: Of course.

(HÖTZENDORF *raises his glass.*)

HÖTZENDORF: Congratulations, Colonel. To your continued success in Prague.

(*They drink the toast. The three arrivals rise at a signal.*)
Well, gentlemen. Goodbye, Redl. Oh, this young man tells me he's your nephew.

REDL: That's right, sir.

HÖTZENDORF: Good. Well, the General Staff can do with all the Redls there are around.

(*Salute. They pass through the lounge.* REDL *sits.* KUPFER *is dumbfounded.*)

REDL: Rumpler *would* stay in Vienna, naturally, with his coat of
arms. Still, Prague . . .

KUPFER: Nephew!

REDL: Not yet. But I can't let an unknown Lieutenant from
nowhere ride about Vienna in my new Austro-Daimler
Phaeton. And I promised him faithfully the other day he
could drive it himself sometime. He's quite clever
mechanically.

(KUPFER *turns on his heel, and goes out.* REDL *lights a cigar
and nods to the* HEAD WAITER.)

Send me the waiter over. I want the bill.

WAITER: Yes, sir.

REDL: No, not him. The young one.

(*Fade.*)

SCENE THREE

*Hospital Ward. High, bare and chill. In an iron bed, sitting up, is a
young man,* MISCHA LIPSCHUTZ. *Beside him is a young girl,*
MITZI HEIGEL. *The sound of boots striking smartly on the cold floor
of a hospital corridor.* REDL *enters briskly. In greatcoat, gloves,
carrying cane. An* ORDERLY *comes up to him respectfully.*

ORDERLY: Colonel, sir.

REDL: Colonel von Redl. To see Mischa Lipschutz.

ORDERLY: At once, Colonel, sir.

(*He leads him to* MISCHA's *bed.* MISCHA *hardly takes him in.*
MITZI *looks up, then down again, as if she has become numbed
by sitting in the same cold position so long.*)

ORDERLY: Shall I tell the young lady to go?

REDL: No. Mischa. How are you? I've brought you a hamper.
(*No response. He hands it to the* ORDERLY.)
See that he gets all of it. Are you feeling any better? When
do you think you'll be out then, eh? You look quite well, you
know . . . Perhaps you're still not rested enough . . . Mischa
. . . (*To* ORDERLY.) Can't he hear me? He looks all right.

ORDERLY: Perhaps your voice sounds strange, just a fraction
sir? Mischa: Colonel Redl is here.

MISCHA: Mischa.

ORDERLY: How are you, the Colonel's asking?

MISCHA: I've been here quite a long time. I don't quite know how long, because we're absorbed into the air at night, and then, of course they can do anything they like with you at will. But that's why I keep rather quiet.

REDL: Who, Mischa?

MISCHA: They do it with rays, I believe, and atoms and they can send them from anywhere, right across the world, and fill you up with them and germs and all sorts of things.

REDL: Mischa, do you know where you are?

MISCHA: On a star, sir, on a star. Just like you. I expect you were sent to Vienna too, sir, because you are the same kind of element as me. The same dual body functioning.
(REDL *stands back. The* ORDERLY *shrugs, the* GIRL *doesn't look up.* REDL *walks out quickly.*)
(*Fade.*)

SCENE FOUR

An hotel room near the Polish border in Galicia. It is cheap, filled with smoke but quite cosy. OBLENSKY *is sprawled on a low sofa, his tunic open, relaxed, hot with much vodka.* REDL *is slightly drunk too, though less cheerful.*

OBLENSKY: Come here, over here, have some more. Where are you, Redl, you're always disappearing? Why are you so restless always? All the time limping home with scars, and now you've got a bitten lip, I see. Tell me now, about this new boy, what's it – Viktor –

REDL: He's not new.

OBLENSKY: I thought it was last February.

REDL: December.

OBLENSKY: Five months! Oh, I suppose that is a long time for you.

REDL: How often are you unfaithful to your wife?

OBLENSKY: When I'm not working too hard, and if I can arrange it, daily.

REDL: You seem to arrange most things.

OBLENSKY: Don't say it in that tone of voice. I was looking it up the other day. You've had eighty thousand kronen out of me over the years.

REDL: Out of Mother Russia.

OBLENSKY: Quite so. And she can ill afford your way of life.

REDL: She's had her money's worth.

OBLENSKY: Not over Cracow.

REDL: Oh, not again.

OBLENSKY: Well, later. Tell me about what's it, Viktor? Is he handsome?

REDL: Extremely.

OBLENSKY: Yes, but how handsome, in what way?

REDL: Tall, fair, eyes pale . . .

OBLENSKY: Is that what you like? Watery?

REDL: Tell me what *you* like.

OBLENSKY: My dear friend, ha!
(*He roars with laughter.*)
Nothing has the enduring, unremitting crudity of what I like. And *no* interest. I like nothing exotic. Now, the Countess, you know, Delyanoff, you used to write those strained love letters to, I could have had her at any time, naturally. But, nothing, no interest, here, whatsoever.
(*He crosses himself.*)
Too exotic. And I suppose intelligent. I can understand *you* trying her out very well. All I want is a lump, a rump, a big, jolly roaring and boring, let us have no illusion, heaving lovely, wet and friendly, large and breasty lump!
(*He roars, jumps up laughing, and fills their glasses.*)
What I wouldn't do for one now! Yes, with you here too, Redl! Would that disgust you?

REDL: No.

OBLENSKY: Flicker of interest?

REDL: Very little I *have* watched.

OBLENSKY: Oh, dear. You make me feel cruder than ever.
Tears of Christ! I'd make her jump and giggle and give her fun. All girls like fun. Even if they're educated. Do you give fun? Much?

REDL: Some, I imagine. Perhaps not too much. If I liked anyone it was because they were beautiful, to me, anyway.

OBLENSKY: Yes, I see. That's quite different. I don't see very much beauty. I mean I don't need it. You're a romantic. You lust after the indescribable, describe it, to yourself at least, and it becomes unspeakable.

REDL: You sound like a drunken Russian Oscar Wilde.

OBLENSKY: Me? Oscar Wilde!
(*He splutters with pleasure, and pours them out more vodka.*)
Perhaps there's a cosy chambermaid here, if they have such a thing in this hole. I'll ask Stanitsin. Do you get afraid very often?

REDL: Yes.

OBLENSKY: (*Switching*) I'll tell you some things that stick in my throat about you people. Do you mind?

REDL: If you wish.

OBLENSKY: Well, one: you all assume you're the only ones who can understand anything about yourselves.

REDL: (*Politely*) Yes?

OBLENSKY: Well, two: frankly you go on about beauty and lyricize away about naked bodies as if we were all gods.

REDL: Some of us.

OBLENSKY: Or else you carry on like – rutting pigs.
(*They both address each other in a friendly away across the barrier they both recognize immediately.*)
It isn't any fun having no clear idea of the future, is it? And you can't re-make your past. And then when one of you writes a book about yourselves, you pretend it's something else, that it's about married people and not two men together . . . That is not honest, Alfred.

REDL: Don't be maudlin, Colonel.

OBLENSKY: Redl; you are one of those depressing people whom you always know you are bound to disappoint. And yet one tries. (*He looks quite jolly all the same.*) Well, you must be used to dancing at two weddings by this time. You've been doing it long enough.

REDL: You do enjoy despising me, don't you? Can we finish now?

OBLENSKY: Not till Cracow is settled. I don't despise you at all. Why should I? I don't care. I'm only curious.

REDL: My confessions are almost as entertaining as the Cracow fortifications.

OBLENSKY: You're quite wrong, quite, quite . . . I listen to you. I enjoy your company, see how much vodka we've drunk together, I don't drink with many people, Alfred. May I? I don't know anyone quite like you. It's taken a long time, hasn't it? You're giving nothing away this time.

REDL: What about Cracow?

OBLENSKY: Well, my dear friend, it was most embarrassing. Suddenly, my whole organization pounced on – *poum*! And who did it! You!

REDL: It was unavoidable. I felt there were suspicions . . .

OBLENSKY: But no warnings . . .

REDL: I tried, but it had to be.

OBLENSKY: Hauser was about my best agent.

REDL: I'm sorry. But you might have lost *me* otherwise.

OBLENSKY: Maybe. But if *I* don't turn up with something, something *now*, I'll be roasted. You've got to *give* me someone. And someone significant I can parade at a big trial, like your affair. Well?
(*Pause.*)

REDL: Very well. I have someone.

OBLENSKY: Who?

REDL: Kupfer.

OBLENSKY: Isn't he on your staff? St. Petersburg?

REDL: Yes.

OBLENSKY: Governments don't usually pounce on the diplomatic or military missions of other governments.

REDL: If it were outrageous enough.

OBLENSKY: Well, if you can fix it, and it's really scandalous.

REDL: I can.

OBLENSKY: Very well then, fix it, Redl.
(*He hurls his glass into the fireplace where it smashes.*)
Fix it. Now: We've hardly started yet.
(*Fade.*)

REDL *'s apartment in Prague. A beautiful baroque room, dominated by a huge porcelain fireplace and double Central European windows.* VIKTOR *is in bed, naked from the waist up.* REDL *is staring out of the window angrily. Pause.*

VIKTOR: I think *I'll* get up. . . .

REDL: Why do you make such disgusting scenes with me? If you had the insight to imagine what you look like.

VIKTOR: Oh, don't. (*He flings his blond head across the pillow.*)

REDL: Oh, stop screaming, you stupid little queen! You don't want to get married, you whore, you urchin! You just want to bleed me to death. You want more. Dear God, if ever there was a ludicrous threat, you don't want the girl or any girl, you couldn't. I've seen her too, remember. *I* could, mark you, and *have*. But not you. When I think . . . How do you imagine you would ever have got a commission in a cavalry regiment, you, who would have bought you three full-blooded horses, and paid your groom and mess bills, *and* taught you to shoot like a gentleman, to behave properly as a Fire leader and be a damned piss-elegant horseman in the field? You couldn't open your mouth and make an acceptable noise of any sort at all.

(VIKTOR *weeps softly.*)

You're so stupid you thought you could catch me with a shoddy ruse like that. You'll get no bills paid, nor your automobile, that's the bottom of it, you're so avaricious, you'll get nothing. You're so worthless you can't even recognise the shred of petty virtues in others, some of which I have still. Which is why you have nothing but contempt for anyone, like me, who admires you, or loves you, or wants and misses you and has to beg for you at least one day a fortnight. Yesterday, yesterday, I spent two excruciating hours at the most boring party at Möhl's I've ever been to, talking to endless people, couldn't see or hear, hoping you – God knows where you were – that you'd possibly, if I was lucky, might turn up. Just hoping you might look in, so I could light your cigarette, and watch you talking and even touch your hand briefly out of sight.

VIKTOR: I *do* love you.

REDL: In your way, yes. Like a squalling, ravenous, raging child. You want my style, my box at the opera instead of standing with the other officers. You're incapable of initiating anything yourself. If the world depended on the Viktors, on people like you, there would be no first moves made, no inexpedient overtures, no serving, no invention, no spontaneity, no stirring whatsoever in you that doesn't come from elsewhere . . . Dear Mother of God, you're like a woman!

(VIKTOR *howls.* REDL *pulls him out of bed by the leg and he falls heavily to the ground with a thump.*)

You've no memory, no grace, you keep nothing.

(REDL *bends over him.*)

You are thick, thick, a sponge, soaking up. No recall, no fear. You're a few blots . . . All you are is young. There's no soft fat up here in the shoulder and belly and buttocks yet. But it will. Nobody loves an old, squeezed, wrinkled pip of a boy who was gay once. Least of all people like me or yourself. You'll be a vulgar fake, someone even toothless housewives in the market place can bait.

(*Grabs his hair and drags him.*)

You little painted toy, you puppet, you poor duffer, you'll be, with your disease and paunch and silliness and curlers and dyed wispy hair and long legs and varicose veins like bunches of grapes and prostate and thick waist and rolling thighs and big bottom, that's where we all go.

(*Slaps his own.*)

In the bottom, that's where we all go and you can't mistake it. Everyone'll see it!

(*He pauses, exhausted. His dressing gown has flown open.* VIKTOR *is sobbing very softly and genuinely.* REDL *stands breathless, then takes the boy's head in his arms. He rocks him. And whispers:*)

It's not true. Not true. You *are* beautiful . . . You always

will be . . . There, baby, there . . . Baby . . . It won't last
. . . All over, baby . . .
(*Fade.*)

SCENE SIX

Office of GENERAL VON MÖHL, TAUSSIG *is handing papers to the*
dazed GENERAL.

TAUSSIG: This is the envelope, sir. As you see, it's addressed to
Nicolai Strach, c/o General Postal Delivery, Vienna. It lay
there for several weeks before it was opened by the Secret
Police, who found it contained five thousand kronen and
the names of two well-known espionage cut-outs, one in
Dresden and another in Paris. The letter was re-sealed.
Rumpler was informed immediately and we waited.

MÖHL: And?

TAUSSIG: Redl took three days' leave and motored in his
automobile to Vienna where he picked up the letter. On
Thursday evening.
(*Pause.*)

MÖHL: Redl?
(*He might almost have burst into tears.*)

TAUSSIG: Sir. Then. His account at the Austro-Hungarian
Bank, unpaid bills for stabling, furniture, tailoring, *objets*
d'art and so on. Automobile maintenance, totalling some
fifty thousand crowns. Assets: a little over five, plus
valuable personal properties as yet unvalued. Some
securities worth perhaps eight thousand kronen. His
servant Max is owed a year's wages, but doesn't seem to
mind. A trunk full of photographs, women's clothes,
underwear, etc., love letters to various identified and
unidentified men, a signed oath from Lieutenant Jerzabek,
swearing not to marry during Redl's lifetime and only
afterwards by way of certain complicated financial losses in
Redl's will. Redl's will . . .

MÖHL: All right. General Von Hötzendorf must be informed at
once. No: I must do it. He'll go out of his mind. Redl!

How people will enjoy this, they'll enjoy this. The *élite*
caught out! Right at the centre of the Empire. You know
what they'll say, of course? About the *élite*.

TAUSSIG: Perhaps it can be kept a secret, sir. Do you think? It's
still possible.

MÖHL: Yes. We must do it now. Where is Redl?

TAUSSIG: The Hotel Klomser.

MÖHL: We'll see Hötzendorf, get his permission, and then we'll
go there, together, you and I. We'll need a legal officer,
Kunz I'd say. But he *must* be sworn to outright secrecy.
Those damned newspapers . . .

TAUSSIG: Kunz is the man for that, sir.

MÖHL: Very well. Let's break the news to General Hötzendorf.
(*Fade.*)

SCENE SEVEN

REDL*'s bedroom at the Hotel Klomser. Above his bed the black,
double-headed eagle of Austria and a portrait of Francis Joseph.*
REDL *is seated at a bureau. In front of him stand* MÖHL, TAUSSIG
and KUNZ. REDL *signs a document, gives it to* KUNZ, *who examines
it, then puts it into his briefcase which he straps up briskly.*

KUNZ: That's all, General Möhl . . .

REDL: You know, General, I know you'll be offended if I say
this because I know you're a deeply religious man, and I
. . . well, I've always felt there was a nasty, bad smell about
the Church. Worse than the Jews, certainly. As you know,
I'm a Catholic myself . . . Who isn't? Born, I mean.
(*He takes the champagne bottle out of the bucket and pours a
glass.*)
Born. But I think I hate the Spaniards most of all.
Perhaps that's the flaw . . . of my character . . . they *are*
Catholics. Those damned Spaniards were the worst
marriage bargain the Habsburgs ever made. Inventing
bridal lace to line coffins with. They really are the worst.
They stink of death, I mean. It's in their clothes and their
armpits, quite stained with it, and the worst is they're so

proud of it, insufferably. Like people with stinking breath always puff and blow and bellow an inch away from your face. No, the Spaniards are, you must admit, a musty lot, the entire nation from top to bottom smells of old clothes in the bottom of trunks.

(MÖHL *motions to* TAUSSIG, *who hands him a revolver.* MÖHL *places it on the bureau in front of* REDL. *Pause.*)

TAUSSIG: Are you acquainted with the Browning pistol, Redl?

REDL: No. I am not.

(TAUSSIG *takes out the Browning Manual and hands it to* REDL.)

Thank you, Taussig. Gentlemen . . .

(*They salute and go out.* REDL *pours another glass of champagne and settles down to read the manual.*)

SCENE EIGHT

A street outside the Klomser Hotel. Early morning. MÖHL, TAUSSIG *and* KUNZ *wait in the cold.* REDL'*s light is visible.*

TAUSSIG: (*Looks at watch*) Five hours, General. Should we go up?

MÖHL: No.

KUNZ: Forgive me, gentlemen. I'm going home. My wife is waiting for me. My work seems to be done.

MÖHL: Of course.

KUNZ: Good night.

(*A shot rings out. They stare.* KUNZ *moves off.*)

MÖHL: Well . . .

(*They light a cigarette.*)

(*Fade.*)

SCENE NINE

A Chamber of Deputies. Vienna. Deputies. In the background blow-ups of The Times *for May 30th 1913, headed* 'SUICIDE OF AN AUSTRIAN OFFICER (FROM A CORRESPONDENT) VIENNA. MAY

(*Facsimiles available from British Museum Newspaper Library.*)

DEPUTY: The autopsy showed the bullet had penetrated the oral cavity, passing obliquely through the brain from left to right. Death must have been practically instantaneous due to haemorrhage. The question is, not who gave this officer the manual, but who allowed him to be given a revolver for this purpose at all?

MINISTER: There will be no concealment of any irregularities.

DEPUTY: Is it not true that this officer was exposed by reason of his official contacts with certain confidential elements in the military-political sphere for a period of some years, with special duties in connection with the frontier protection and the order of armament?

DEPUTY: Was not this same officer in the confidence of Von Moltke, the Chief of the Imperial German High Command?

DEPUTY: Surely someone must have been around with the wit or perception to have suspected something . . .

DEPUTY: Are we all asleep or what!
(*Roar.*)

DEPUTY: *What's become of us?*
(*Roars.*)

DEPUTY: Is it not true that he was, in fact, the son of one Marthe Stein, a Galician Jewess?
(*Uproar.*)
Why was this fact not taken note of?

MINISTER: The high treason which General Staff Colonel Redl was able to practise with impunity for a period of many years is an occasion of the gravest possible public disquiet, which is far from being allayed, if not actually increasing. This is due not only to the abominable crime committed by this officer – but more by the way in which the case has been managed by the authorities of the Royal and Imperial Army.

DEPUTY: Yes, but what do you *do* about it? What do you *do*?

MINISTER: We must not alarm the public more than is necessary. It is true that the crime committed by Colonel

Redl against his country and the uniform he wore is felt in the most sensitive way by the whole population. However, the only adequate protection of the honour of officers lies in rigid standards, and if individuals act against the honour of that class, the only helpful thing is the expulsion from it of these individuals by all the forms prescribed by law . . .

SCENE TEN

OBLENSKY's *office. Lights dimmed. Stanitsin working the magic lantern.*
OBLENSKY: Next!
   (*A photograph is snapped on to the screen.*)
STANITSIN: Schoepfer. Julius Gerhard. M.D., Ph.D., F.R.C.S., Member Institute Neuro Pathology, Vienna. Member Vienna Institute. Hon. Fellow of the Royal Society of London. Born Prague March 25th 1871. Family Jewish. Distinguished patients. List follows. Political and Military. In 1897, at the age of twenty-five he delivered a brilliant lecture on the origins of nervous diseases . . .
   (*Fade.*)

When *A Patriot for Me* was written it was not licensed for public performance by the Lord Chamberlain. A list of the cuts and alterations requested by the Lord Chamberlain – and to which Mr Osborne refused to agree – appears below.

Act I–I 'His spine cracked in between those thighs. Snapped . . . All the way up.'

I–4 This scene must not be played with the couple both in bed.

I–4 From: Stage direction – She moves over to the wall. . . .
To: . . . Presently, he turns away and sits on the bed.

I–5 Reference to 'clap' and 'crabs'.

I–7 Reference to 'clap'.

I–10 Omit the whole of this scene.

II–I Omit the whole of this scene.

III–I The two men must not be in bed together.

III–I From: 'You'll never know that body like I know it. . . .'
To? '. . . you've not looked at him, you never will.'

III–I From: 'So: you'll turn Stefan . . .'
To: '. . . than any ordinary man.'

III–2 'You were born with a silver sabre up your whatnot.'

III–4 'Tears of Christ!'

III–5 Omit the whole of this scene.

INADMISSIBLE EVIDENCE

CHARACTERS

BILL MAITLAND
HUDSON
JONES
SHIRLEY
JOY
MRS GARNSEY
JANE MAITLAND
LIZ

The first performance of *Inadmissible Evidence* was given at the Royal Court Theatre, Sloane Square, London, on 9th September 1964, by the English Stage Company. It was directed by Antony Page, and the décor was by Jocelyn Herbert. The part of Bill Maitland was played by Nicol Williamson.

The play was revived by the Royal National Theatre at the Lyttelton Theatre, London, on 17th June 1993. The cast was as follows:

JONES	Jason Watkins
BILL MAITLAND	Trevor Eve
HUDSON	Roger Sloman
SHIRLEY	Helen Schlesinger
JOY	Matilda Ziegler
MRS GARNSEY	Lynn Farleigh
JANE MAITLAND	Juliette Gruber
LIZ	Amelia Bullmore
Director	Di Trevis
Designer	Stephen Brimson Lewis
Lighting	Heather Carson
Music	Dominic Muldowney

ACT ONE

The location where a dream takes place. A site of helplessness, of oppression and polemic. The structure of this particular dream is the bones and dead objects of a Solicitor's Office. It has a desk, files, papers, dust, books, leather armchair, a large, Victorian coat stand, and the skeleton of an outer office with clerks, girls and a telephonist. Downstage is a dock in which stands the prisoner of this dream, BILL MAITLAND. *At back, high above the outer office, hangs the Royal Coat of Arms. In front of this are the green benches of one of the High Courts of Justice, in which sits one of* HER MAJESTY'S JUDGES. *From centre a* CLERK *of the court reads the indictment. Before this there has been an air of floating inertia before the three actors come to some sort of life out of the blur of dream.*

CLERK: William Henry Maitland, you are accused of having unlawfully and wickedly published and made known, and caused to be procured and made known, a wicked, bawdy and scandalous object. Intending –

BILL: Object?

JUDGE: Proceed, proceed.

CLERK: Object. Intending to vitiate and corrupt the morals of the liege subjects of our Lady the Queen, to debauch and poison the minds of divers of the liege subjects of our Lady and to raise and create in them lustful desires, and to bring the liege subjects into a state of wickedness, lewdness and debauchery. How do you plead? Guilty or Not Guilty?

BILL: Not guilty.

(*Pause.*)

CLERK: Place your right hand on the book and repeat after me: I swear by Almighty God –

BILL: I swear . . . My Lord, I wish to affirm.

JUDGE: Very well.

CLERK: Do you swear and affirm?

BILL: I swear and affirm (*Pause. Then a hoarse rattle. Clearing his throat at intervals.*) I hereby swear and affirm. Affirm. On my . . . Honour? By my belief. My belief in . . . in . . . the

181

technological revolution, the pressing, growing, pressing, urgent need for more and more scientists, and more scientists, for more and more schools and universities and universities and schools, the theme of change, realistic decisions based on a highly developed and professional study of society by people who really know their subject, the overdue need for us to adapt ourselves to different conditions, the theme and challenge of such rapid change, change, rapid change.

(*Flails. The* JUDGE *looks at him reassuringly and he picks up again.*)

In the ninety seven per cent, ninety seven, of all the scientists who have ever lived in the history of the world since the days of Euclid, Pythagoras and Archimedes. Who, who are alive and at work today, today, now, at this time, in the inevitability of automation and the ever increasing need, need, oh, need for, the stable ties of modern family life, rethinking, reliving, making way for the motor car, forty million by nineteen; in a forward-looking, outward-looking, programme-controlled machine-tool-line reassessment. With, yes, with faculties of memory and judgement far beyond the capacity of any human grief, being. Or any group of human who has ever lived.

(*Pause.*)

JUDGE: Yes?

BILL: In the facts, above all the facts, inescapable. Anna, my wife, Hudson, I mean my managing clerk. Hudson, Joy, the telephonist, the enrichment of our standard of living, I've lost my prescription, Jane, my father's too old to be here, thank God, the National Research, Research Development Council, the Taylor Report, the Nayler Report, failure report, and a projected budget of five hundred thousand million, millions for this purpose, the practical dangers of premarital in the commanding heights of our declining objects.

JUDGE: Objects?

BILL: I think so, my lord. I think that's what I meant to be saying. (*Continuing.*) Facing up realistically, the issues that are important, really, central, social change, basic, burning issues.

JUDGE: I think that is evident.

BILL: I wish I could see more clearly.

JUDGE: Very well.

(*Pause.*)

CLERK: My lord, I have been retained by the defendant. However, after long discussion with myself, and my learned colleagues, he has expressed his intention of conducting his own case.

JUDGE: I see. You have tried to dissuade him from this course?

CLERK: We have, my lord. He is quite adamant.

JUDGE: Mr Maitland, you must be fully aware of the implication of your decision?

BILL: Yes.

JUDGE: It is my duty to warn you of the difficulties that may be involved in discarding the services of learned counsel.

BILL: I see that. Except I wish I *could.*

JUDGE: And to warn you against taking an irrevocable decision which will almost certainly . . .

BILL: But I'm incapable of making decisions.

JUDGE: Involve you in onerous difficulties, in view of the complexities we are faced with here. Even though, as a practising solicitor of, I believe, some standard and experience, you are no doubt better equipped to conduct yourself than would ordinarily be the case.

(BILL *smiles.*)

I put it to you now, once and for all: do you persist in this decision?

BILL: (*Looks at* CLERK) I do, my lord.

JUDGE: Very well.

(*Pause.*)

Proceed.

BILL: I beg your pardon?

JUDGE: Carry on, Mr Maitland.

BILL: Me, my lord?

JUDGE: Yes. You, Mr Maitland.

BILL: But what about them?

JUDGE: Are you – or are you not conducting your own case?

BILL: But them? What about them?

JUDGE: Mr Jones, will, I believe, lead for the prosecution.

CLERK: This is correct, my lord.

JUDGE: Come then. Do let us get on.

BILL: He was supposed to be defending me.

JUDGE: Mr Maitland. Have we not, just a few moments ago, established that you had dismissed Mr Jones?

BILL: Yes.

JUDGE: And that you have elected to conduct your own defence?

BILL: Well, it is. I did. But then it shouldn't be me.

JUDGE: Shouldn't be you?

BILL: No.

JUDGE: What shouldn't be you?

BILL: Well, if it is. Why isn't he starting off then?

JUDGE: Starting off?

BILL: Yes.

(*Pause.*)

JUDGE: You have already started off.

(BILL *ponders.*)

BILL: But – I seem to have made some sort of absurd . . . Isn't it? I mean, he should have started off first. In the very first place.

(*Pause.*)

JUDGE: That is true. However . . . *You* have done so instead.

BILL: But what about the . . .

JUDGE: That is my ruling. It is possible that it may be reversed or reinterpreted at another time elsewhere.

BILL: What about the last word?

JUDGE: I suggest you begin.

BILL: I shouldn't be the one to have to start off.

JUDGE: Possibly not, but you have, and the ruling is quite clear.

BILL: (*Bafflement. Tries to focus*) I ought to have the last word.

JUDGE: No doubt, we shall see in the event.

BILL: What event? I'm here, aren't I?

JUDGE: You must be aware, with your training and background, that the law can often be very flexible in these matters.

BILL: As your lordship pleases. As you say, it probably makes very little difference.

JUDGE: Demonstrably.

BILL: Before I –

JUDGE: Yes?

BILL: May I have a glass of water?

(*The* JUDGE *motions to the* CLERK, *who obliges.* BILL *tries to study his face.*)

My Lord – which one is Mr Jones?

JUDGE: There. (*He indicates the* CLERK *a little impatiently. The* CLERK *hands him the glass of water.*)

BILL: Please forgive me. I have rather a headache. Perhaps that's why I'm here now. I had too much to drink last night, that's just the simple truth of it. Well, when I say that, I mean not much more than I usually have. Most nights. But that's well, I do drink quite a lot. Quite a lot? Oh, anyway, I'm what you'd call a serious drinker. That's to say, I just don't mess about once I get going – when I do. When I do? I nearly always do. I can drink a whole bottle of whisky. Can't be any good for the heart, can it? It must be a strain, pumping all that fire and damned rigour and everything all out again? Still, I'm pretty strong. I must be. Otherwise, I couldn't take it. That is, if I *can* take it. I can't, I'm sorry, I can't find my pills. I always have three or so in my ticket pocket. So sorry.

(*Pause.*)

If you knew me, if you knew me, you'd know I wouldn't come out without them. I'm so sorry. Just a moment. The glands or whatever these lumps are in my neck feel as if they were trying to batter their way out. Just here, trying to force their way out. Like broken marbles, real big gob-stoppers. With chipped edges. I must have left them in my overcoat pocket. Do you think the constable could get my overcoat or look in the left-hand pocket? Or the inside? It shouldn't take a moment. Only. It's a bit like a gimlet too. Right up behind the eyeballs. All that and the marbles too.

(*Pause.*)

I know that none of this is very interesting to you, but the fact is I could do a lot better, a lot better, that is acquit myself, acquit myself better. Yes. Well, they don't seem to be there, my pills. Or tablets or whatever you call them. What's the difference? Only, I really do need three of them at least. And nothing else will do the job properly. Then, if I keep my head upright and don't move it about too much, and talk fairly slowly, if you can bear with me, with your lordship's indulgence, I can make a start. Some sort of start, anyway.

JUDGE: Do you think you can proceed now?

BILL: I have a feeling there is very little choice involved. And so, I will do my best, your lordship. I don't want you to think that because of these minor difficulties – and – that I have come here unprepared. I have always expected this, and, consequently, I have done my best to prepare myself as well as I can.

JUDGE: Yes?

BILL: In. With. Your lordship's indulgence, I will . . . make some sort of a start.

JUDGE: Please.

BILL: And see what comes to me. In the event. Now, I wish I could open my eyes. My eyelids. They're like oysters. However, this is my concern and not yours. I'll think of something. (*He presses his eyeballs*). My name is William Henry Maitland. I am thirty-nine years old, practising solicitor and commissioner for oaths at 34, Fleet Chambers, EC3. I have worked in service of the law – if you can call being a solicitor working in the service of the law – for nearly twenty-five years. In fact I started work in this very office, this court, since I was at least fifteen. Perhaps earlier. That (*points to Judge's seat*) is my old boss's chair. You see, I took his position over from him. My managing clerk, old Hudson, he was working for the old man even then. Not that he was much older than me. He just always seemed older. Anyway, he works for me now. I don't even know why I took up the law. I don't think there was any reason at all much. I can't think of any now, and I couldn't think of any then. Perhaps I did think I might

land up on the bench even. Or with learned counsel. Mr
Jones. No, but I never seriously thought of myself being
brilliant enough to sit in that company, with those men,
among any of them with their fresh complexions from their
playing fields and all that, with their ringing, effortless
voice production and their quiet chambers, and tailors and
mess bills and Oxford Colleges and going to the opera God
knows where and the 400, whatever I used to think that
was. I can't remember at the time. I have always been
tolerably bright.

JUDGE: Always been?

BILL: Bright. *Only* tolerably bright, my lord. But, to start with,
and potentially and finally, that is to say, irredeemably
mediocre. Even at fifteen, when I started out in my
profession. Oh no, before that. Before that. Mark. I have
never had any but fugitive reasons – recurrent for all that –
that this simple, uncomplicated, well, simple, assumption
was correct. I knew that in order to become even a small
market-place solicitor, as distinct even from a first-rate
managing clerk with a big, substantial firm, I should have
to study very hard indeed for my, oh for my Law Society
examinations all the while I was picking up probate and
conveyancing, running out for jugs of tea, packets of fags
for the other clerks or calling in the chemist for the
telephonist.

JUDGE: Telephonist?

BILL: I'm afraid there's always one like that, my lord. Mine is
called Joy. The one who works for me now, that is. This
one was called Jill.

JUDGE: Is anything the matter?

BILL: I seem to have lost my drift, my lord. What's my wife
doing here? Well, she would be here, of course. No, it's
Sheila, it's my ex-wife. I didn't even know where she was.
How did she know? They all seem to *find out* about these
things. They find out. I'm sure my old man's there, but I
can't see him. I hope not. He'll hate this. I seem to have
lost my drift, my lord.

JUDGE: (*Kindly*) Mediocrity?

BILL: Well, it might perhaps be misleading to you and everyone to dwell on it too much. I merely wanted to draw your attention.

JUDGE: There is time enough, Mr Maitland.

BILL: I have always had a certain facility, it's true. But little else. A fairly quick mind, not profound, a bit flashy I should say, indeed, *you* would say, not even that, a little more than perky. They said I had a quick mind, for getting fags and remembering things for a while, long enough to get my exams, for instance. A quick mind they said was useful, not that I had it, but helpful, as your lordship will know, in a profession where time doesn't mean a thing to anyone except some poor bloody agonized client who wants to know whether he's going to get the house he wants, an overdraft, or a divorce, eighteen months or a fine. However, however, my lord. I seem to retain very little. Very little indeed, hardly anything at all, in fact. Which is disturbing. Because I don't see how I can carry on my work even, well I am carrying on with it, but I must be getting less and less any good at it. *Even* my work, that's almost the least of it, which is probably, no doubt, one of the reasons I find myself here, in the dark dock arraigned before you. But both my clients and my colleagues seem to think, at least they used to think, I had a sort of dashing flair for making decisions, which might have been true to some extent. This can't hide the fact from me, and never has done, that I am by nature indecisive. Nor will it escape you, my lord. I am almost forty years old, and I know I have never made a decision which I didn't either regret, or suspect was just plain commonplace or shifty or scamped and indulgent or mildly stupid or undistinguished. As you must see. As for why I am here, I have to confess this – I have to confess that – that I have depended almost entirely on other people's efforts. Anything else would have been impossible for me, and I always knew in my own heart that only that it was that kept me alive and functioning at all, let alone making decisions or being quick minded and all that nonsense about me . . . That I have never really been able

to tell the difference between a friend and an enemy, and I
have always made what seemed to me at the time to make
the most exhausting efforts to find out. The difference. But
it has never been clear to me, and there it is, the
distinction, and as I have got older, and as I have worked
my way up – up – to my present position. I find it even
more, quite impossible. And out of the question. And
then, then I have always been afraid of being found out.

JUDGE: Found out?

BILL: Yes.

JUDGE: Found out about what?

BILL: I'm sorry, my lord. I don't understand. I have always
been quite certain that this is where I should end up, here,
I've seen it too many times, with you there and counsel
over there. There. And there. Down to the cells. Off to the
Scrubs, hand over your watch and your money, take all
your clothes off, have a bath, get examined, take all your
clothes off in the cold, and the door shut behind you. I
should like to stand down if I may. I am not feeling very
well. I never hoped or wished for anything more than to
have the good fortune of friendship and the excitement and
comfort of love and the love of women in particular. I
made a set at both of them in my own way. With the first
with friendship, I hardly succeeded at all. Not really. No.
Not at all. With the second, with love, I succeeded, I
succeeded in inflicting, quite certainly inflicting, more pain
than pleasure. I am not equal to any of it. But I can't
escape it, I can't forget it. And I can't begin again. You
see?

(A torpid moan escapes him. Fade. The light remains on BILL.
The JUDGE *and the* CLERK *leisurely take off their wigs and
robes, coming into the office area, hanging them on the upstage
end of the coat stand. The* JUDGE, *who is* HUDSON, *the*
MANAGING CLERK, *speaks to the* CLERK, *who is called*
JONES. *During this,* BILL *remains still. The actor has to
indicate the painful struggle into consciousness, without, at the
same time, making the physical metaphor too explicit: the
difficulty of breathing, the violent inner effort to throw off the*

burden, the fishy, palpitating struggle of the heart being landed into wakefulness. The gasping will takes over. The dream, the prison of embryonic helplessness for the moment, recedes, but not altogether. The focus fades on BILL, *who emerges slowly out of it. Presently, he makes his way out of it, into the outer office, then through into the office itself.*)

HUDSON: (*To* JONES) Parky this morning.

JONES: Yes.

HUDSON: What's the matter then? Late night?

JONES: No, not specially.

HUDSON: How's that girl of yours?

JONES: OK.

HUDSON: Still getting married?

JONES: Suppose so. Got to get these finals out of the way first. Hardly see her except on Sundays.

(SHIRLEY, *the secretary, comes in with post and hands it to* HUDSON.)

SHIRLEY: There's yours.

HUDSON: Thank you, Shirley. And how are you today?

SHIRLEY: Looking forward to Friday night, thank you.

JONES: Is mine there?

SHIRLEY: Why don't you try looking for it? (*Goes out.*)

HUDSON: What's up with her?

JONES: Dunno. Packing it in, she says.

HUDSON: What, again?

JONES: I think she means it this time.

(BILL *comes into* OUTER CIRCLE *fairly briskly.*)

BILL: Morning all!

JONES: Better start getting it sorted out myself then.

BILL: (*Coming in*) Sorry I'm late.

HUDSON: You're the boss.

BILL: I couldn't get a taxi. That's the first time I've never got one. All got their bloody lights on and all going home. I don't know what they're doing. (*Goes to desk. He has a plaster by his ear.*)

HUDSON: Cut yourself?

BILL: Yes.

HUDSON: I don't know why –

BILL: Why I don't use an electric razor. There's quite enough almighty racket going on in the world without tuning it into my chin the minute I wake up.

HUDSON: But it's so simple.

BILL: Not for me it isn't. Two bathrooms in my house and my wife has to use mine while I'm having a quiet little shave to myself. She has to talk.

HUDSON: Not your morning.

BILL: Can't be worse than the evening.

HUDSON: What, have a skinful, did you?

BILL: More than that, one way and another.

(SHIRLEY *brings in Bill's post and puts it in front of him*.)

BILL: Hullo, sexy. Is that all?

HUDSON: Don't worry – there's enough here.

BILL: What – no make up this morning?

SHIRLEY: You *do* remember Mrs Garnsey's coming at 9.30?

BILL: Of course, I forgot you girls don't really wear make-up nowadays, do you? All leaking eyeshadow and red noses. Go and put on some lipstick, dear. What's the matter? Isn't he giving it to you?

SHIRLEY: Finished?

BILL: Don't tell me you're getting too much. I don't believe it.

SHIRLEY: Oh, knock it off.

BILL: Well, something's made you bad-tempered this morning, and I don't believe that languid pipe-cleaner of an accountant you're engaged to has got *that* much lead in his pencil.

SHIRLEY: Do you ever think of anything else?

BILL: Not so much. Probably less than you do though.

SHIRLEY: Me?

BILL: I just talk about it at great boring length mostly to boring, bad-tempered, and silly girls. Without make-up.

SHIRLEY: You know what you can do! And quick.

BILL: (*To* HUDSON) Do you hear that, Wally? Do you think I should let her talk to me like that?

HUDSON: I think she'd better get back to her work. I'll see you in a minute, Shirley.

(*She nods and goes out*.)

BILL: And put some lipstick on!

HUDSON: Thought she was going to let you have it there for a minute.

BILL: What's the matter with her?

HUDSON: Jones here says she's giving in her notice.

BILL: But she does that every other month.

JONES: I think she means it this time.

BILL: Oh, why?

(BILL's *manner to* JONES *is slightly hostile, more polite than he is to most people.*)

JONES: Oh, just says she's fed up with the place.

BILL: And?

JONES: Oh, well just that really.

BILL: What else?

HUDSON: Well, out with it.

JONES: Well, this is just what she said to me –

BILL: He'd make a great witness wouldn't he? I wouldn't like to see you in the box up against someone like old Winters.

JONES: (*Dimly nettled*) She just said last night while we were locking up that she was sick of the sight of Mr Maitland and couldn't even bear to be in the same room with him.

BILL: She said what!

HUDSON: (*To* JONES) It's all right, you needn't repeat it.

JONES: Well, you asked me what she said.

HUDSON: You know what these girls are. They get a bit, you know. And Shirley's an independent sort of a –

BILL: What a funny thing to say. Do you think she meant it?

JONES: Dunno. Wasn't listening properly.

BILL: (*Irritated*) I'll talk to her later. When she's calmed down a bit. (*To* HUDSON.) Remind me.

(HUDSON *looks amused.*)

What are you smirking about? Oh? Keep it outside of the office and all that? Look, I haven't touched that girl for months, not for about six or seven months at least. *I've* done no harm to her. If she's unhappy it's not my fault. Besides, she's engaged.

HUDSON: That wouldn't stop you.

BILL: No, it wouldn't, but I didn't. It's probably that droopy young book-keeper making her miserable. Giving her dinner-dances on the Kingston Bypass. The morning she came back from that she had red eyes for a week.

HUDSON: He seemed a nice, quiet, serious . . . fellow, I thought.

BILL: Nice, quiet, serious fellow, I thought. That just about sounds like every supine, cautious, young husband all about six degrees under proper consciousness in the land. The whole bloody island's blocked with those flatulent, purblind, mating weasels. You know who they are? Her fiancé? They're the ones who go out on Bank Holidays in the car! And have mascots in the rear window.

HUDSON: Well, it's their lives.

BILL: Yes, and if we only had enough Bank Holidays they'd kill each other on every coast road from Blackpool to Brighton.

HUDSON: You're not suggesting they should all be killed off just because they don't please you?

BILL: I'm just suggesting we might hope they'll do it themselves for us.

HUDSON: You'll be getting one of your headaches in a minute.

BILL: Don't worry. I have. Do you know who they are?

HUDSON: No. Only don't forget Mrs Garnsey.

BILL: Damn Mrs Garnsey. She's probably one too. They are the people who go up every year like it was holy communion to have a look at the Christmas decorations in Regent Street. They're the ones who drive the family fifty miles into the countryside and then park their cars beside the main road with a few dozen others, get out their thermos flasks, camp stools and primuses, and do you know what they do? They sit and watch the long-distance lorry drivers rattling past, and old people's coaches and all the other idiots like themselves about to do the same thing.

HUDSON: Sometimes I'd like to see you and old Winters have a go at each other – in court. I think you'd enjoy that.

BILL: Don't think I couldn't, either. He's not all that good. Just because he wears a wig and I don't.

HUDSON: Well, then –

BILL: This place'd be a lot different if you were running it, wouldn't it, Wally?

HUDSON: Everyone has their own methods. You've got yours.

BILL: Yes, but mine just aren't different. They're not respectable for a solicitor. But then I don't feel like you do about the law. I don't think the law is respectable at all. It's there to be exploited. Just as *it* exploits us.

HUDSON: You'll be putting young Jones here off the job.

BILL: I don't think there's much danger of that.

HUDSON: Well, we all have our different methods, as I say. Different ways of looking at things.

BILL: Wally, do me a favour, will you? You'll be saying 'with all due respect', or 'be that as it may' in a minute. I'd thought I'd broken you of that stinking habit. No, I don't think young Jones here is the type to end up goosing telephonists and knocking off secretaries, to say nothing of cooking up evidence on occasion or risking collusive agreements. Do you have it off with that girl of yours?

(JONES *is discomfited.*)

I'm sorry. That's an impertinent question. Isn't it? Forget it.

JONES: Well –

BILL: No, don't bother. But I was right about what I said?

JONES: Yes. Yes. I think so.

BILL: Why?

JONES: I just don't think it –

BILL: What?

JONES: Any of those things are really worth the candle.

BILL: Not really worth the candle. No you're quite right. It's not. Well, now we've disposed of the candle, you'd better take it with you into Shirley. She's probably in need of it. Have you got plenty to do?

(JONES *nods.*)

Got to keep you busy. Busy, busy, busy. That's what you want isn't it? That's why you came to me isn't it, for no other reason. See what's in, what business there is, any money in, any problems, anything else. Right?

JONES: Yes, Mr Maitland. (*Goes.*)

HUDSON: What's the matter then?

BILL: What do you mean what's the matter then?

(*Calls.*) Shirley!

HUDSON: You seem to have it in a bit for him.

BILL: He's a tent peg. Made in England. To be knocked into the ground.

(SHIRLEY *appears*.)

SHIRLEY: Yes?

BILL: What? Oh, get me a glass of water, Shirley.

SHIRLEY: (*Pause*) Helpless?

(*Goes out.* HUDSON *and* BILL *look at each other. More satisfaction for* HUDSON.)

HUDSON: I think you're wrong there. He's got quite a good brain. Bit slow for your taste, but you shouldn't underestimate him.

BILL: I don't. He's got all the makings of a good, happy, democratic underdog like that bitch's boyfriend who won't even get me a glass of water when I ask her. He irritates me. He doesn't like me any more than I like him. Why does he work for me?

HUDSON: Why don't you sack him?

BILL: What for? He does his work well enough. Doesn't he?

HUDSON: Fine.

BILL: Well then. Joy! He even laughs at my rotten jokes. Or anyway, his little filleted spine rattles about a bit. Otherwise – no sound . . .

(JOY *appears*.)

Joy, get me a glass of water, will you?

JOY: OK.

BILL: And ask Shirley – no, you'd better get it. See if you can bring in Mrs Garnsey's file.

(*She goes out.*)

One thing I'll say for you, Wally, you've never pretended to laugh. Not even at my good ones.

HUDSON: We don't all have your sense of humour.

BILL: Well, don't sound so pleased about it. Anyway, I haven't got a sense of humour. I haven't had a good laugh for years. Not only that, Mr Jones may find his finals and working for me won't do him a damn bit of good in the long run. Or you, for that matter.

HUDSON: What's that?

BILL: I say, soon we'll all be out of a job. If anyone's riddled with the idea that being busy is the same thing as being alive it's our young Jones.

HUDSON: What are you talking about?

BILL: Jones.

HUDSON: You're sure you're all right?

BILL: Sure, fine. Now what about Mrs Garnsey, why are you shoving her on to me? No. I don't, I don't think I do. Things seem a bit odd. I still can't understand why I couldn't get a taxi. They all had their lights on – for hire.

HUDSON: Well, you know what they are.

BILL: Yes, but I've never known it to happen to me before. Not in the morning.

HUDSON: You look all right. But if you'd like to . . .

BILL: And the caretaker turned his back on me. I was walking up the stairs and I was going to ask him – you know, quite politely – why the lift wasn't working. And he turned his back on me.

HUDSON: Didn't notice you, I expect.

BILL: No, he looked straight at me. And turned his back on me.

HUDSON: Well, he's a contrary old devil.

BILL: Not with me, he hasn't been.

HUDSON: I gave him a quid at Christmas, and he didn't even give me a thank you.

BILL: I gave him five. (*Self-consciously.*) Well, I know it's too much, but we had a drink together over at The Feathers.

HUDSON: Too much is right.

(*Slight pause.*)

BILL: They won't need us much longer. They'll need no more lawyers. Have you seen the papers this morning? Some mathematical clerk will feed all our petitions and depositions and statements and evidence into some clattering brute of a computer and the answer will come out Guilty or Not Guilty in as much time as it takes to say it. There'll be no more laws' delays, just the insolence of somebody's office. They'll need no more lawyers. I don't understand who will be needed.

HUDSON: I shouldn't think it'll quite come to that.

BILL: How do you know what we'll come to? Or when? Sometimes I wish I were older so I had less chance of finding out. (*Bangs newspaper.*) Look at this dozy bastard: Britain's position in the world. Screw that. What about my position? Vote wheedling catchfart, just waiting to get us into his bag and turn us out into a lot of little technological dogs turning his wheel spit of endless bloody consumption and production. Why doesn't he stick his scientific rod – into the Red Sea or where he likes and take everyone he likes with him – including Jones. The sooner the sea closes up behind them the better. With Jones entering the Promised Land in his Mini.

HUDSON: Oh, leave the boy alone. What's he done to you? Anyway, he's got a motorbike.

BILL: Even better. I can't think of a better way to emerge – in an emergent country. Why don't they all go and emerge? Emerge.

HUDSON: Why don't *you* do it a bit of emerging yourself?

BILL: I'm never likely to do that.

(*Pause.*)

HUDSON: Well, we should make a start. (*Joke.*) Before they move in the computers.

(BILL *doesn't respond.*)

BILL: Joy! What are you doing?

JOY: (*Off*) Coming.

HUDSON: Seen that Betty lately?

BILL: Where's my glass of water? Which Betty?

HUDSON: Oh, were there more?

BILL: I know three girls called Betty. No. Four.

HUDSON: What a life. I don't know.

BILL: She married some corpulent financier.

HUDSON: Who?

BILL: Betty.

(JOY *comes in with glass of water and a file.*)

I'm always seeing his name on building sites. Spends his time pulling down Regency squares – you know – and putting up slabs of concrete technological nougat. Like old, pumped-up air-raid shelters. Or municipal lavatories.

She's a nice kid. Don't see much of her now, Seen her at
some of those theatre first nights he's so fond of. Hemmed
in by all his thrusting sycophants – I think she can hardly
see him through her mink. Jones now.

JOY: Sorry. Shirley wouldn't tell me where to find it.

BILL: Jones should work for him. Britain's future. Betty's old
man is certainly one of the architects. What's that, my
love?

JOY: Your glass of water.

BILL: Oh, thank you. At last, a friend.

JOY: Mrs Garnsey's file. Shirley –

BILL: Yes, I'm sure. And how are you?

JOY: I'm all right thank you. Is that all?

BILL: Not enough for me. She looks pretty today, don't you
think, Wally.

HUDSON: Yes. She does.

BILL: When are we going to have an orgy together?

JOY: You can't have an orgy with two.

BILL: No, but you can make a start.
  (*She smiles and goes out.*)
  Look at that beautiful bottom. Don't go much on her face.
  But the way her skirt stretched over that little bum. You
  could stick a bus ticket in there. Joy. What do you think,
  Wally?

HUDSON: Yes, it's quite nice, I suppose.

BILL: It's a beauty. Wonder what's she like?

HUDSON: No doubt you'll find out.

BILL: Don't know. Maybe not. Like who was it. You know, Dr
Johnson said whatsit, 'Paradise Lost'; more of a beauty
than a pleasure. Still she looks as though she could do with
a bit. She's got the galloping cutes all right. Joy. *She's* had
more joy sticks than hot dinners.

HUDSON: I was only waiting for that. What about Mrs Garnsey?

BILL: I have an extraordinary thing about blondes. They're like
plague carriers for me. Even dyed blondes. My first wife
was blonde. *Really* blonde. Blonde, blonde, *blonde!* It was
beautiful. I've never known hair nicer. Right, Mrs Garnsey.

HUDSON: Well, try and let her settle down a bit, will you? Joy, I

mean. She's only just mastered that simple little
switchboard. If *you* get started on her, we'll get nowhere.
BILL: Right. No Joy. For the moment, anyway. Goes against
the Rules. Which is the best thing. Right – work, work.
Mrs Garnsey. Where are my pills? There should be some
in here. Anyway, I always keep three in reserve in my ticket
pocket. Where the hell are they? Joy! Wish I didn't drink so
much. And I keep wanting to sleep. I finally took a pill at
four this morning, went off at five, then I couldn't get up. I
couldn't even move at first.
(JOY *appears*.)
I was all trussed up. My darling, have you seen my pills,
my headache pills?
JOY: No, sorry.
BILL: Never mind, here they are. I might just do a bit better
with Mrs Garnsey when she comes. Ask her to wait five
minutes when she comes. Give her a cup of that stinking
tea you and young Jones brew up together.
JOY: OK. (*Goes out*.)
BILL: I don't know whether I really like that blonde bat or not.
She's rather a tuneful little thing, if you know what I mean.
Wally, try not to let me have anything to drink at
lunchtime. OK?
HUDSON: I'll do my best.
BILL: 'And if I drink oblivion of a day, so shorten I the stature
of my soul.' Who said that now? Some poor crazy bastard –
Blake, I think. Just bitter lemon, all right?
HUDSON: Right.
(JOY *reappears*.)
JOY: Oh, and your wife rang just before you got in. I said you'd
ring back.
BILL: Right, thanks.
JOY: Shall I get her for you?
BILL: No, not just for the moment. But remind me.
(*She goes out*.)
She knows how long it takes me to get here.
HUDSON: But you couldn't get a taxi. Remember?
BILL: I've always managed to keep everything in place, in

place enough to get on with it, do my work, enjoy things,
enjoy other people, take an interest in all kinds of things.
I've tried to read, not just my own subject. I keep trying
and the circle just seems to get smaller. If Anna rings will
you speak to her, say I'm with Mrs Garnsey?

(HUDSON *nods*.)

It's only about next weekend.

HUDSON: I thought you were going to Blackpool. On a business
trip.

BILL: Yes, with Liz. We'd planned it before Christmas. We
haven't really had a long weekend together since last
summer when Anna took the kids with her down to north
Devon.

HUDSON: So what's happening?

BILL: I don't know. Anna's fixed some crazy do for the entire
weekend for the girl's birthday.

HUDSON: How old is she?

BILL: I don't know. Seventeen. Eighteen. Anyway, too old and
too sophisticated and too unhampered by anything in
particular to need my presence at her birthday for two
whole days.

HUDSON: Does your wife know about Blackpool?

BILL: Cancel it, she says. Business doesn't mean all that to *you*.
Give your daughter a good time.

HUDSON: She knows you were going with Liz?

BILL: Why else should she arrange this daft junket? She doesn't
like the kids' chums any more than I do. It'll be all jazz and
noise and black leather and sour teenage squalor and
necking, and oh –

HUDSON: You've always been pretty fond of necking and –

BILL: Squalor! I may have helped to knock it together often
enough but I haven't enjoyed it, and I haven't ever been
made to feel sharp or with it or representative of any
damned thing. I was never, at any time, like that bunch of
kids my daughter runs around with, so don't compare me
to them.

HUDSON: Sorry.

BILL: And as for necking, I never went in for it, never would,

and pray God I am never so old, servile or fumbling that I
ever have to wriggle through that dingy assault course. Do
you like it, do you want it, those are the only questions I
have ever thought worth while going into. You think I'm
not telling the truth? Well, it's as near the truth as I can
find at this moment – for one thing I have never had very
strong fingers, which is why I had to give up learning the
piano.

HUDSON: What are you going to do then?

BILL: Do?

HUDSON: About the weekend?

BILL: I've no idea. I don't know which is worse, which prospect
frightens me more. I keep seeing their faces. Anna's. Liz.
And some of the others. It's even worse when they ring up.
Not that Liz rings very often. She has an immaculate idea
of a mistress's rights. I want to feel tender, I want to be
comforting and encouraging and full of fun and future
things and things like that. But all I feel is as if my head
were bigger and bigger, spiked and falling off, like a mace,
it gets in my way, or keeps getting too close. It's not worth
the candle is it?

HUDSON: Certainly doesn't seem like it, does it?

BILL: No. But then I've never discovered what is. That blessed
candle of yours and Jones, the Holy Grail of the people
who hold back.

HUDSON: No, it's just that some people seem to use things like
sex, for instance, as a, a place of, of escape, instead of
objects, well – in themselves.

BILL: Yes, I know what you mean. I've thought of that. But
what about work? I know we're not doing any at the
moment, but we're going to, we both work pretty hard,
Wally. *You* certainly do, and you don't get a great deal for
it. And I think even you'll admit I work harder than most
when I'm actually at it.

HUDSON: Oh, sure.

BILL: But what sort of object is that? Is it an enjoyment, a duty,
an obligation, a necessity or just the effort of fighting, of
fighting off the end, whatever is to come to you.

HUDSON: I don't know. I don't think it matters all that much. So long as you're reasonably interested in what you do. You mustn't ask for too much.

BILL: Then you don't get disappointed. Mrs Garnsey'll be disappointed if we don't get her her divorce all right. You're quite right, Wally, as usual. Anyway, why have you foisted Mrs Garnsey on to me? I thought you and Jones had been dealing with her up till now. There's nothing specially difficult is there?

HUDSON: No, nothing special.

BILL: Well?

HUDSON: We've both got rather a lot on at the moment.

BILL: Well, so have I. I'm supposed to be at the Scrubs by 11.30 to see that Bennet kid.

HUDSON: What that? The indecent assault?

BILL: Yes. We didn't get very far. He was too upset. Clothes off, possessions signed for, bath, medical inspection in the whistling cold, keys jangling. He wasn't in any state for anything. I don't know why we do any criminal work.

HUDSON: I couldn't agree more.

BILL: I thought if I did Mrs Garnsey, you'd go down to see Bennet. I suppose it's not your line?

HUDSON: Not really.

BILL: But does it depress you?

HUDSON: No. I just don't go for it, you might say.

BILL: You'd rather not do divorce either.

HUDSON: I don't feel that strongly. I get a bit fed up listening to it, trying to find out what really did happen all the time. But I don't actually mind it. I just wouldn't go out of my way to choose it, that's all.

BILL: What would you choose? Straightforward bit of complicated conveyancing.

HUDSON: I'd say divorce was *your* line. Living other people's lives.

BILL: What do you mean by that?

HUDSON: I thought you enjoyed it.

BILL: Enjoyed what?

HUDSON: Oh, you know. Probing, taking a part.

BILL: You mean I'm not detached enough.

HUDSON: No, I didn't say that.

BILL: I don't want to live anyone's life, not anyone's. I dread those clients, clients like Mrs Garnsey. I've got all the lumber I can carry. Are you sure you can't get along to see Bennet?

HUDSON: Don't see how I can.

BILL: Does he disgust you that much?

HUDSON: Nothing disgusts me. Any longer. I am simply not very interested or aroused by contemplating such people or such things. Apart from that, I've got to take Mrs Rose down to counsel at eleven. That'll take till lunch time for certain. I've tried to piece it all together, but she never says the same thing twice in the same breath.

BILL: What is it? She lying about her husband?

HUDSON: Oh yes, I think so.

BILL: What's he supposed to have done?

HUDSON: Kicked her up the bottom with his heavy gardening boots on, locked her out of the house all night, and she had to sleep in the car in her nightdress.

BILL: What else?

HUDSON: Not much. Something about hot tablespoons. But nothing really admissible.

BILL: Was it a cold night?

HUDSON: What? Oh, in the car. Right in the middle of the big freeze-up. She says she got flu as a result and nearly got pneumonia.

BILL: Nearly?

HUDSON: And pleurisy.

BILL: Nearly. Why didn't she go for a drive with the heater on?

HUDSON: What, in her nightie at two o'clock in the morning?

BILL: Sounds a very romantic thing to do to me. She could have taken a turn up the Great West Road in her old man's car and ended up at some pull-in with a bacon sandwich and a cup of tea. I should think she'd have been made very welcome.

HUDSON: Well, her husband had the keys of the car.
(*Pause.*)

203

I can see you don't like her.

BILL: Me? Haven't met her have I? I'm just listening to you.

HUDSON: No. But I don't think you'd go much on her. That's why I've done it.

BILL: Good old Wally. She'll get a good run out of you. And you'll get your revenge watching her withering in front of Winters. I – as you'd expect – feel sorry for her husband. Old heavy garden boots. What's he sound like?

HUDSON: Difficult to say. Excessive sexual demands. All that.

BILL: Oh yes. King Kong, according to her, I suppose.

HUDSON: Perversions.

BILL: Spectacular?

HUDSON: Oh, usual sort of thing.

BILL: And what's she got? A wall eye and varicose veins, I'll bet. He sounds fairly ordinary.

HUDSON: No, I don't think he's such a bad chap. Still –

BILL: Any adultery?

HUDSON: She says so, but there doesn't seem to be much evidence. Winters has seen the papers. He didn't seem to think much of it. I'm afraid he won't touch it under 300. Still, if he can get her to stick to her story, we should get him on cruelty.

BILL: You've applied for alimony and maintenance?

HUDSON: You bet.

BILL: Poor bastard. Well, what about Jones?

HUDSON: What about him?

BILL: Well, couldn't he go along to the Scrubs for me?

HUDSON: I suppose he could. If you really want him to.

BILL: No. You're right. I'd best do that myself. I don't think Jones would exactly inspire poor old Bennet with the confidence to go through with his appeal at all.

HUDSON: Anyway, I think he's pretty busy this morning.

BILL: Perhaps I should ring Anna now – and get it over before Mrs Garnsey. Get it *over* – what am I thinking of?

HUDSON: He's got that Pole in again this morning. Third time in a week.

BILL: Pole?

HUDSON: You know – Zubuski, or whatever his name is.

BILL: Joy, get me Mrs Maitland will you? What's up with him?

HUDSON: Well, he wants a divorce.

BILL: Grounds?

HUDSON: Adultery.

BILL: Well?

HUDSON: Well, the thing is this, sufficient evidence all right, I don't think there's any doubt of that, but he wants it on his own terms.

BILL: What do you mean 'his own terms'?

HUDSON: Quite simple. He insists on having sexual relations with his wife three times a week until the case comes up.

BILL: And the wife?

HUDSON: Oh, she agrees.

BILL: Well – good for them. (*Laughs.*)

HUDSON: Extraordinary, isn't it?

BILL: Yes.

HUDSON: We've both tried speaking to him. He just gets furious and won't listen.

BILL: What's he going to do? Report us to the Law Society? What's really extraordinary is you and Jones.

HUDSON: Well, I suppose it's funny.

BILL: Yes. I think it is.
(*His laugh is interrupted by buzz and* JOY*'s voice from his desk*.)

JOY: Mrs Eaves is on the line.

BILL: (*Pause*) I'll – no, tell her I'll ring her back as soon as I can.

HUDSON: (*Pleased*) Well, there's number two bringing up the rear already. Busy morning.

BILL: Come on. Be fair. It isn't often Liz rings up. Not like Anna now.

HUDSON: Well, there is –

BILL: I know, Anna's my wife. There's never any doubt which side you're on.

HUDSON: I'm not on any side.

BILL: Yes you are. Wives and angels. Me, mistresses and devils. No. I'm not the one who's on any side. I don't have any idea of where I am. I have tried not to cause pain, I really

205

have, you think I haven't, but I do try, I ought to be able to give a better account of myself. But I don't seem to be functioning properly. I don't seem to retain anything, at least not for very long. I wish I could go back to the beginning, except I wouldn't do any better. They used to say I had a quick brain.

HUDSON: Well, you have that.

BILL: No, I haven't. I have a very small, sluggish, slow moving brain. I just run it through quickly, at the wrong speed like a piece of film, and it darts and flickers, but it perceives little, and it retains nothing. What do you think I should do, Wally

HUDSON: About the weekend? Tell Liz the truth.

(*Pause.*)

BILL: I'm always trying to do that. I'd like to cheer her up for once, to go in free and uncluttered and tell her we'd got three whole days together.

HUDSON: Well, do that then.

BILL: Thanks for the advice. I can see what put you in this business. What's your problem, Mrs Garnsey? Well, legally you can do this. Or that. I would advise this. However, you may prefer to do that. Morally – or emotionally – do as you like.

HUDSON: I don't know.

BILL: What? How she puts up with me.

(HUDSON *nods*.)

Which? Anna or Liz?

HUDSON: Either of them.

BILL: But especially Anna.

HUDSON: There must be some compensations. You've got two nice kids.

BILL: They're all right. I don't think they think we're as nice as we assume *they* are. Do you know that boy actually *wanted* to go away to boarding school. I told him he was crazy. But he couldn't wait. Couldn't *wait*. And he writes dull, beady little letters all about house matches and photographic societies and getting up at God knows what hour every morning to go *swimming* – in February. It's like having a priest in the family.

HUDSON: How old is he?

BILL: Eleven! At his age I was thinking about girls. Madeleine Caroll.

HUDSON: (*Doing his irony*) Perhaps he's just a late developer.

BILL: Seems to me he's in the right place to stay that way.

HUDSON: Still, he's happy.

BILL: Blissful. I don't understand. I think I'd rather be in the Scrubs. Same thing really. Chaplains, lousy food, hard work, lights out, no birds.

HUDSON: Well, he's growing up.

BILL: Yes. That's what Anna says. Perhaps she should have married *you*. You have so many points of agreement.

HUDSON: I'm all right, thank you.

BILL: Yes. You are. But I don't think Anna is quite as absorbed in her children as yours. I mean, she hasn't turned their growing up into some protracted act of holy communion that'll end up with an empty chalice and hot flushes when she's fifty.

(HUDSON *looks uncomfortable. Pause.*)

I've asked you this before, do you think I should leave her?

HUDSON: I've told you before. I don't think it makes any difference. To you.

(JOY's *voice from desk.*)

JOY: Your wife, Mr Maitland.

BILL: Right. (*Motions to* HUDSON *to stay.*) Shan't be a minute. (*On phone.*) Hullo. Hullo, love. Sorry, I was late. I couldn't get a cab. It was strange. Yes. First time I've never managed it. Even the old famous whistle didn't work . . . Do I? . . . No, I don't think so . . . Only old Wally. Trying to get sorted out . . . Well, my darling, I'm sorry if I do happen to sound like that. I didn't sleep as you know, or not much, and . . . well, perhaps I am feeling a bit odd and you can just hear it that's all. I've got a client coming in any minute . . .

(WALLY *goes out in spite of* BILL's *signals.*)

No, of course, it's all right. That's why I rang you back. I just haven't got started, and nothing seems to be working very well . . . What's that? Yes . . . Well, I know. Well. I'm

sorry, . . . I wish I could. What's that? . . . I don't seem to
be able to hear . . . I said I'm sorry. It's a rotten line . . . I
can't *hear* you very well . . . Yes, that's a bit better . . .
Look, why don't I ring you back, . . . what about lunchtime . . . No, I can't have lunch . . . Well, I've got to go
down to the Scrubs . . . Well, I can't get anyone else to go,
then I'm seeing counsel, and I'm in court the rest of the
day, then I'm . . . Yes, Bennet . . . Well, I think I'm the
best judge of that . . . Well, a lot of people would agree
with you, especially on the Bench . . . I'll probably be late
. . . I'm not sure yet . . . You know it's no good asking
me at this time of day . . . Eight or nine. I don't know. It
might even be later . . . If that's what you think . . . well,
if that's what you know, why bother to ask me the
question . . . Look, please don't, why don't I ring you? I
may get away, we'll see . . . You know I haven't decided
. . . That's how I cut myself – at half past eight, remember
. . . I've told you, I don't know yet . . . I simply don't
know . . . I don't know now, all I know is I probably am
. . . Well, it won't be the greatest disappointment of her
life as you well know and I know, and *she* knows. Look
love, I've got Wally waiting to go down to Winters . . .
Why don't you go out and . . . all right . . . well, I'm sorry
you're feeling like that . . . oh, headache, . . . yes, the
usual only a bit worse . . . and just odd things . . . well
. . . all right . . . look after yourself . . . I'm sorry, love . . .
I promised not to say that any more . . . (*He puts the phone
down. Stares. Looks at the file in front of him. Drinks some
more water. Presses eyeballs.*)

JOY: (*Voice*) When do you want me to get Mrs Eaves?
BILL: When I ask you to. No. Er, remind me will you, love?
Perhaps after Mrs Garnsey . . .
JOY: She's not turned up yet.
BILL: Well, ask Mr Hudson if he'll come back in, will you? And
– get me another glass of water.
JOY: OK. Oh. And I think Shirley wants to see you when you've
a minute.
BILL: All right, when I've time. How's your sex life out there?

208

JOY: Thrilling. How's yours?

BILL: Oh – fairly quiet. Come in and see me.

JOY: When?

BILL: Oh – before you leave work.

JOY: OK.

BILL: And – oh, I've asked you, haven't I?

JOY: Have you?

BILL: I don't know.

(HUDSON *appears.* JOY *swishes out.*)

HUDSON: D'you want me?

BILL: Yes. Yes, was there anything else?

HUDSON: No, no I don't think so.

BILL: Nothing to sign?

HUDSON: No.

BILL: Right.

HUDSON: Well, I'd –

BILL: You'd better get on.

(HUDSON *turns to go.*)

Wally, Wally, there's just one thing I'd like to bring up.

HUDSON: Will it take long?

BILL: No, but I'd like to have a chat about it. Why? Aren't you interested or something?

HUDSON: I've just got rather –

BILL: OK, OK.

HUDSON: And I think Shirley's a bit keen to see you.

BILL: Shirley? Yes, I just thought this seemed like a good time to bring it up.

(*Pause.*)

HUDSON: Well, I'll drop in later then.

(SHIRLEY *comes in with glass of water.*)

BILL: Wally! Wally, try and pop in before you go down to Winters. I'll try and get through Mrs Garnsey quickly. After all, Jones can take a lot of the stuff down from her . . .

HUDSON: Just as you like.

(*Goes out.* BILL *looks more than deserted. He looks at* SHIRLEY *gratefully. She hands him the water.*)

BILL: Thank you love, that's very kind of you.

(*He drinks. She watches.*)
Anything the matter?

SHIRLEY: Not with me there isn't.

BILL: Sure? You all right?

SHIRLEY: Fine, thank you.

BILL: Then what is it? We're friends aren't we? Why are you like this?

SHIRLEY: I'm not like anything.

BILL: Then?

SHIRLEY: I just want you to know I'm giving in my notice, that's all. You owe me a week's holiday but I'll give you a week, anyway.

BILL: But what for?

SHIRLEY: I've just made up my mind I'm going, that's all. Do you mind?

BILL: Of course I mind –

SHIRLEY: Well, that's bad luck for you, isn't it?

BILL: I don't know, love. Perhaps it's bad luck for both of us.

SHIRLEY: Not for me it isn't. I don't know why I didn't clear out before.

BILL: You've always gone on about it –

SHIRLEY: And who talked me out of it?

BILL: What have I done?

SHIRLEY: Nothing. I'm just giving you notice. OK?

BILL: But – you must have a reason.

SHIRLEY: Sure, I've got reasons. Do I have to tell them to you?

BILL: No.

SHIRLEY: I've had enough.

BILL: What of?

SHIRLEY: Do you think I mean you?

BILL: I don't know. I don't know. I honestly don't know. If you wouldn't be in such a rush, perhaps I could –

SHIRLEY: Oh, well if you must know what for, for one thing, I'm pregnant.

BILL: You're what?

SHIRLEY: Mit child, dear. You've had two haven't you? At least.

BILL: I'm sorry. (*Trying to focus.*) I thought you were on the pills.

210

SHIRLEY: I was. I got fed up with them.

BILL: But you've only just got engaged.

SHIRLEY: So?

BILL: You mean you're going to get married?

SHIRLEY: That had always been the idea.

BILL: And you still want to?

SHIRLEY: Do I have to ask for your blessing or something?

BILL: I'm just a bit taken aback.

SHIRLEY: These things do happen, you know.

BILL: Are you really in love with him?

SHIRLEY: I thought you didn't go much on being in love.

BILL: Does he know?

SHIRLEY: I told him last night.

BILL: (*Irritated*) Well?

SHIRLEY: He said he'd rather have waited a bit, he's quite
pleased. What's the matter? Seen something?

BILL: Naturally, I see you a little differently . . . I mean
physically . . . I feel . . .

SHIRLEY: Poor you! You should feel like I do.

BILL: Is this the right thing?

SHIRLEY: Why? Should I ask advice from you? Father?

BILL: No, Shirley, no, don't do all that, I'm concerned –

SHIRLEY: Look – you can stick your long farewell. I just want
you to know now: I'm pregnant.
(*Even Shirley's flush of relish is abated by Bill's dismay. Pause.
Quieter.*)
I'm getting married. And I'm giving in my notice. A week
Friday. OK?

BILL: OK, love.
(*She waits.*)
When is it?

SHIRLEY: Fortnight.

BILL: No. The baby.

SHIRLEY: Oh. September.

BILL: September! But that's, that's about nine months away.

SHIRLEY: Seven.

BILL: You could go on working for ages yet. Everybody does.

SHIRLEY: Well, *I've* decided not to.

BILL: What about the money? You'll need that more than ever now.

SHIRLEY: We'll manage.

BILL: But think how useful it'd be. What'll you do all day, sitting round the house, waiting like some silly bomb to go off?

SHIRLEY: Ted's doing all right.

BILL: But with two of you working – you'll need all sorts of things –

SHIRLEY: He doesn't want me to go on.

BILL: He doesn't want me to go on! Who is he? Godfrey Winn? He'll do what you *want*. Do you want more money? You know you can have it. Of course you can. You're worth it. You're worth it to anybody.

SHIRLEY: Perhaps I might go to anybody.

BILL: No, stay here. You're wanted here.

SHIRLEY: What's all this, are you bribing everyone now?

BILL: Shirley, I'm very fond of you. What you've told me –

SHIRLEY: Don't tell me you're short of it.

BILL: No, I'm *not*!

SHIRLEY: Anyway, that's out.

BILL: I haven't touched you –

SHIRLEY: Oh. (*Pause.*) Forget it.

BILL: I haven't touched you. You're accusing me. But I haven't touched you. Not for three months. At least.

SHIRLEY: Thanks so much.

BILL: Oh, for God's sake, throw off that half-baked, cheap, show-girl act and listen to me.

SHIRLEY: Why? What have you ever done for me?

BILL: Nothing. I suppose. But I do know we had some affection for one another, beneath all the arguing and banter and waste of breath. I know I liked you. And when we were in bed together you dropped all your pretences and deceits, after a while anyway. Perhaps I did even. I don't think I let you think it was an enduring love affair – in the sense of well of endless, wheedling obligations and summonses and things. But, if you think back on it, detail by detail, I don't think you can say it was fraudulent. Can you?

212

SHIRLEY: No.

BILL: You can't *disown* it. If you do that, you are helping, you are conspiring to kill me.

(*Pause.*)

SHIRLEY: One weekend in Leicester on client's business. Two weekends in Southend on client's business. Moss Mansions – remember them? Four days in Hamburg on clients business. One crummy client's crummy flat in Chiswick, and three times on *this* floor. (*She moves to go.*) And another thing, just don't push any more of Joy's work on to me. I don't intend doing it. Any more than I like you, any more than I like your promising me for your clients when you're too busy with your wife or that Mrs Eaves or – I think you'd better forget about my notice. I'm going now.

(*She goes out.*

Presently JOY *buzzes.*)

JOY: (*Voice*) Mrs Garnsey is downstairs.

(*Pause.*)

I said Mrs Garnsey is downstairs.

BILL: (*Croaks*) Would you? Ask her to wait! Could you, could you send in Mr Hudson?

JOY: He's just on his way out.

BILL: Well, stop him.

JOY: I think he's gone.

BILL: I need him. Get him.

JOY: Well, I'll do my best.

BILL: And then I want to speak to Mrs Eaves.

(*Silence.* BILL *tries to look through Mrs Garnsey's file.*

HUDSON *enters, wearing his overcoat.*)

HUDSON: You want me?

BILL: Oh, yes. Wally

HUDSON: Only I'm just off. You know what old Winters is like. Can't keep him waiting two minutes.

BILL: Won't take a minute.

(HUDSON *looks at his watch.*)

What would you say to becoming a partner?

(*Pause.*)

Eh?

(HUDSON *seems to react rather pleasurably*.)

HUDSON: I don't know. Really.

BILL: Well?

HUDSON: Are you asking me?

BILL: Yes. Yes. I am.

HUDSON: I see. Well . . .

BILL: I realise it's a bit . . .

HUDSON: Yes. Well. Needs a bit of thinking about, doesn't it?

BILL: Sure. Sure. Why don't we talk about it later? Chew it over.

HUDSON: Yes. Right. OK. I will. Well thanks then. It'd . . .

BILL: You're not thinking of leaving?

HUDSON: No. Not exactly.

BILL: You mean you *are* thinking of leaving?

HUDSON: I wouldn't say that exactly.

BILL: What would you say exactly?

HUDSON: I have had an offer, as a matter of fact.

BILL: Who from?

HUDSON: Several actually.

BILL: Who?

HUDSON: Well . . .

BILL: Oh come on Wally, for God's sake.

HUDSON: Well, Piffards –

BILL: Piffards! Those crooks!

HUDSON: Very high-class crooks. *If* that's what you think they are.

BILL: Well, as you know, I think they're crooks, so do you
really. Still, if you want to wear striped trousers and work
for Cabinet ministers' wives.
(*Pause.*)
As you would say, we all have our ways of looking at these
things. OK, then. Well, perhaps you'll have a think about
it?

HUDSON: (*Smiles, then slowly*) Yes. I will. Better get Mrs Rose
down to the inquisition then. Cheerio. (*Goes out.*)

BILL: Joy. Did you get my call to Mrs Eaves!

JOY: She's engaged.

BILL: Well, keep trying. Tell the exchange to break in. Where's
Shirley?

JOY: She's gone.

BILL: Gone where?

JOY: I don't know.

BILL: I mean do you think she's coming back?

JOY: No idea. Shouldn't think so somehow.

BILL: Really?

JOY: She took her soap and towel.

BILL: What'd she say?

JOY: She was just crying. Shall I send in Mrs Garnsey?

BILL: No. I must speak to Mrs Eaves.

JOY: Oh, wait a minute, I think they've got it. Hold on . . .
You're through.

BILL: (*On phone*) Liz? My darling, I've been trying to get hold
of you . . . Are you all right? . . . Well, no . . . Everything's
. . . I said everything's . . . What? Oh, I couldn't get a taxi
for a start, well, not a start . . . Well, you know, if I keep
my head upright and don't move it about too much, and
talk fairly slowly . . . Look, try and bear with me a minute
. . . What was what like? Oh, last night . . . Well, yes there
was an Anna situation . . . Oh, before we went out and
afterwards . . . Yes, that was bad enough, but the whole
thing was very strange . . . It's difficult to explain . . . No, I
can't quite . . . I'm sorry. I just don't seem to retain very
much of anything, of anything that happened . . . I just felt
everyone was cutting me . . . cutting me . . . I know, I
should care! I like them as much as they like me . . . I
don't know whether they're more afraid than I am . . . I
think they really *want* to be liked . . . in that sort of way
. . . I don't exactly do my best do I. No, well then . . . No,
Anna quite enjoyed herself while she was there . . . Oh, the
usual shower . . . They all seem to adore her . . . I know,
but more than ever . . . it's only all right when I'm with her
. . . Yes . . . But it seemed at my expense this time, it
seemed to be out of me . . . as if they were disowning me
. . . it's wonderful to hear your voice . . . Well, I don't
know yet . . . something this evening . . . Look, please
don't *you* press me . . . Yes. It'll be all right . . . I may not
sound like it, but it will be . . . you don't think I want to go

215

to her silly birthday junket, do you? . . . Do you think I don't know that? Of course it's Anna . . . Well, I'll probably talk to the kid myself . . . Look, love, I've got to go . . . Can I ring you back? I've got this client and she's been waiting about . . . Let me ring you . . . You *will* be in, won't you . . . Yes, but you will *be* there . . . Promise? Don't go out till I ring you back . . . I need to talk to you . . . It'll be all right. Don't worry. (*To* JOY.) I'll see Mrs Garnsey now.

(JOY *shows* MRS GARNSEY *in.* BILL *rises to greet her.*)

Mrs Garnsey, I'm sorry I've kept you waiting.

(MRS GARNSEY *nods.*)

Have you had a cup of tea? Joy?

(JOY *nods. Goes out.*)

Right. I had a client on. I'm afraid I couldn't get her off. Now, you've already had several little sessions with Mr Hudson haven't you?

MRS GARNSEY: That's right.

BILL: Yes. Well, I haven't been into it in great detail. As you know, Mr Hudson has had to pass it on to me . . . for the moment . . .

(MRS GARNSEY *looks slightly alarmed.*)

Well, he had to see counsel this morning and he also thought it might be a good idea if you were to see me some time.

MRS GARNSEY: I see.

BILL: The adultery seems quite clearly established. There are these three women, apart from all the others, there, there seems to be more than enough there. You *have* made a claim for maintenance and alimony. Two children, that's right isn't it?

MRS GARNSEY: Do you think I should?

BILL: Mr Hudson's already advised you, hasn't he?

MRS GARNSEY: Yes.

(*Pause.*)

BILL: Mrs Garnsey. I can tell you what the law is, and on the basis of what you tell me, and on the assumption that what you tell me – is the truth – as best you know it, I can

advise you what the legal possibilities are. The rest is up
to you.

MRS GARNSEY: Yes. That's what Mr Hudson said to me. It's
the law. And –
(*Pause.*)

BILL: Perhaps Mr Hudson hasn't . . . Would you like to tell me
how you feel? About the whole question. I mean –
(*She nods dumbly.*)
The first question is always, why doesn't the marriage
work?
(*Silence.*)
Is it the women? Only? When I say *only*, as far as the law is
concerned, that's quite enough.

MRS GARNSEY: I don't know. I still don't know what to do. You
see, he's a good man really. He's kind, he's very sensitive
indeed, he seems to be one step ahead of me all the time in
everything, everything. He always has been. He loves me. I
know that . . . I think we . . . Well, I . . . disappoint him.
But no more than he disappoints himself . . . You've got
all that stuff that Mr Hudson took down?
(BILL *nods.*)
He *is* clever, he does his job well. He works hard. He's
good looking. He has a lot of charm, in his own way, he
really has, he can make you laugh like almost no one else.
But what, what kills me is that he is being hurt so much.

BILL: How do you mean?

MRS GARNSEY: By everyone. He comes home to me, and I
know that nothing really works for him. Not at the office,
not his friends, not even his girls. I wish they would. God
knows, he tries hard enough. I wish I could help him. But I
can't, and everyone, everyone, wherever, we go together,
whether it's a night out, or an evening at our club, or an
outing with the children, everyone's, I know, everyone's
drawing away from him. And the more people have been
good and kind and thoughtful to me, the worse it's been
for him. I know. And now. Now *I'm* doing the same thing.
The children hardly notice him. And now it's *me*. I can't
bear to see him rejected and laughed at and scorned

217

behind his back and ignored –
(*All this last is scarcely audible.*)
And now it's *me*. I've got to leave him.
(*Nothing more meaningful comes from her.*
BILL *gets up to comfort her but is paralysed.*)
BILL: Joy!
(*Silence but for* MRS GARNSEY.)
Joy! Joy!
(JOY *appears, surprised.*)
Mrs Garnsey isn't feeling very well. Would you take her
and give her a brandy? There's some in Mr Hudson's
cabinet.
(JOY *supports* MRS GARNSEY *and takes her out.*) And get me
Mrs Eaves.
JOY: OK.
BILL: The minute you can.
(*They go out.* BILL *takes three more pills.*)
Joy!
JOY: (*Voice*) Yes?
BILL: Where's that call?
JOY: No reply.
BILL: What, engaged or no reply?
JOY: No reply.
BILL: Try again. Now! (*He waits.*)
JOY: (*Presently*) Still no reply.
BILL: Oh. How's Mrs Garnsey?
JOY: I gave her a whisky. There wasn't any brandy. She's
getting a taxi home.
BILL: Well, get it for her.
JOY: OK.
BILL: And Joy –
JOY: Well?
BILL: Come in a minute, will you? Now.
(*She comes in.*)
Close the door a minute.
(*She does so.*)
How are you?
JOY: I'm all right. You don't look so hot.

BILL: Joy.

JOY: Yes?

BILL: Will you stay on a bit tonight?

JOY: Is it important?

BILL: Yes.

JOY: If you like.

BILL: Thank you.

    (JOY *turns to go.*)

JOY: What shall I do about Mrs Eaves?

BILL: Keep trying her.

JOY: Will you speak to her?

BILL: No. But. Say I'll be round this evening.

JOY: What time?

BILL: Tell her: to expect me when she sees me.

    (*Curtain.*)

ACT TWO

The same scene. A little grey light. An early morning taxi can be heard. Bill is lying asleep on the sofa, his collar open, an overcoat over him. He seems to be making an effort to wake as he did in Act One, and the struggle becomes gradually more frantic as he tries to escape. He is rescued by the telephone ringing. His eyes open and relief and fatigue mingle as he sits up. Then apprehension, more than apprehension. He goes to the telephone on his desk, looks at it. Peers at his watch. Can't see. Draws the curtains and some light comes in. He looks out, switches on his desk light and examines his watch. Cautiously he picks up the telephone. It has not been put through from the switchboard. He goes into the outer office and picks up the one on Hudson's desk. The ringing stops. Quiet.

BILL: *(Presently)* Yes? *(Pause.)* Hello? *(Pause.)* Who is it? Who's there? *(The line is dead and he replaces the receiver. He fumbles with the switchboard, muttering.)* How do you put this . . . thing through! *(He walks back into his room, picks up the receiver. Obviously nothing. Goes back to the switchboard. Returns with a glass of water, picks up the receiver again. All right this time. He gets his pills out of his desk drawer, and starts to dial a number. Then loses courage or strength and puts the receiver down. He takes one pill which makes him 'gag', as if he were in a dentist's chair. He goes out for some soda water, fills a glass, looks at the two pills to come and redials.)*

NOTE: *This telephone conversation and the ones that follow it, and some of the duologues should progressively resemble the feeling of dream and unreality of Bill's giving 'evidence' at the beginning of Act One. Some of the time it should all seem actually taking place at the particular moment, naturally, casual, lucid, unclouded. At others the grip of the dream grows tighter: for example, in the call that follows now, the presence of the person on the other end should be made very real indeed, but, sometimes it should trail into a feeling of doubt as to whether there is anyone to speak to at all.*

BILL: (*On phone*) Liz? Darling? Did I wake you? . . . I'm sorry
. . . it wasn't you ringing then . . . a few moments ago . . .
I wasn't sure who it was . . . Oh – I guess it must have
been Anna. Yes, I'm at the office . . . Well, it's not like
your own bed, as they say . . . Yes . . . like a gimlet, the
old thing, right up there behind the eyeballs . . . How are
you? Did you take a sleeping pill? . . . Three? You're crazy!
. . . I know, my darling, I'm sorry . . . Yes, I should have
phoned, I should have phoned . . . (*He starts to take his pill
with soda water.*) Just a minute . . . That's two . . . That's
three . . . Sorry . . . I know I said I'd come round . . . Oh,
come off it, anyway, Shirley walked out yesterday . . . Well,
I'm not surprised either . . . I know . . . Yes, well it
worried me too . . . What do you mean Joy can do the job
just as well? Look, it's too early for jokes and suspicion . . .
Look, hang on just one minute. (*He claps a hand to his
mouth.*) Just one minute. Hang on. (*He disappears into the
outer office. Sound of lavatory cistern. He comes back, wiping
his face.*) Sorry. What? No, I just lost my pills that's all . . .
Yes, now I'll have to take three more . . . I made a mistake,
I just had plain water with the first one . . . Look, I know I
should have phoned but I didn't and I couldn't. But I love
you dearly and I wanted to be with you and talk to you
more than anything . . . well, I'll tell you what happened
. . . only no more jolly, barbed jokes about Joy. Please . . .
I know, but *I'm* allowed to make them . . . All right, I
won't make them any more . . . It was a bad day, Liz, a
bad day right from the beginning . . . I was just about to
ring you because I reckoned on having a good three-
quarters of an hour before meeting Anna . . . Well, there
was a lot of work in . . . Anyhow, she turned up here
suddenly at seven thirty . . . No, the downstairs door was
locked . . . Well the caretaker always does that . . . No, she
didn't . . . Darling, I said please no more Joy jokes . . .
Well, what could I do? I couldn't ring you with her here in
the room . . . Well, I know it doesn't make any difference
at this stage, but I couldn't bring myself to do it . . . I
don't think you'd have cared much for the experience

either . . . She'd arranged for us to go out to these dreary friends of hers, the Watsons . . . that's right, they're the ones, they write books together . . . Sociology and Sex. I don't know – Natural Childbirth and CND: An Analysis . . . All tables and diagrams and unreadable . . . Yes. All it adds up to in the end is either do it or don't. We do . . . You've got it. Every time she drops one he's in there in the room with a surgical mask on and popping away with his camera . . . Yes . . . being encouraging . . . Well, it's pretty discouraging to look at them together . . . Oh, sure, *rotten* dinner . . . Oh, wooden bowls, yes, sort of *Sunday Times* Supplement Primitive . . . *very* badly cooked . . . Hullo . . . Hullo . . . Are you there? . . . Oh . . . I keep thinking you're not there . . . Well, you weren't saying anything and I suddenly . . . Hullo . . . Hullo . . . Oh, hell's bloody bells . . . Well, as I say she turned up here . . . I know, well it's not something you'd do . . . You're too clever for that . . . Well I didn't just mean . . . She pitched into the weekend thing the minute I answered the door . . . Yes – Joy answered the door . . . No, I think that quite pleased her. She felt if anything had been going on you'd have been the loser and not her . . . Which is kind of true . . . I had a drink, and told her the truth . . . just that: that you and I hadn't had any time together for weeks and we were determined to have at least three whole, clear, uncluttered days together – and Jane, well just bad luck. She's a nice girl but she's a strapping nevertheless seventeen, less than half our age and looked after and cosseted and God knows what. Besides, she's young, she's got all that youth everyone's so mad about and admires. Even if she's not very clever or pretty, she's got good old youth. I'd never use anything else if I could help it . . . Sure, she'll not get into any mess like us . . . Hullo . . . Hullo . . . I say, like *us*. Or, if she does, it won't matter, it won't overwhelm her or get the better of her . . . I promise you that's what I said . . . Yes . . . I said we just had to go . . . I love you very dearly . . . Yes, I did say it . . . Oh, what's the matter? I don't seem to hear properly . . . Yes, we went to the party,

don't ask me why, I think I'd even have rather gone home
. . . Of course I had too much booze, what do you think
. . . It was strange, as if I were there on tolerance . . . Sure,
they're sorry for Anna and think I'm a boorish old ram but
it was more, there was more to it than that . . . I don't
know . . . Liz . . . Liz . . . Hullo, Liz . . . I'm frightened
. . . It was as if I only existed because of her, because she
allowed me to, but if she turned off the switch . . . turned
off the switch . . . who knows? But if she'd turned it off I'd
have been dead . . . They would have passed me by like a
blank hoarding or a tombstone, or waste ground by the
railway line or something . . . And then there was Mrs
Garnsey . . . Mrs Garnsey, you remember her . . . I don't
know what to do about her . . . No, quite straightforward
really . . . Of course we will. What did I have the row
about then? She knows all about it. Not that she didn't
anyway . . . Believe me . . . Oh, there was a sort of row at
the table and we left early . . . Sure, she wanted to stay . . .
I took her home and, oh, it went on and I came back here.
The car was in the garage, I couldn't get a taxi, so I came
back and slept here . . . I wanted to, but I didn't want to
break in on you somehow . . . I know I should have but I
couldn't! Well . . . Look, I'll come over the minute I can.
I'm longing to see you and I can't wait and I'm dreading
today . . . Well, I'll make a hole in the day . . . Hullo . . .
Hullo . . . Stay in won't you? Stay in, I'll ring you. Bye.
(*He puts the phone down. Picks it up again several times to see
if it is alive. Gets out a razor, brush and mirror and looks at
them dully. Dials phone again. More than ever the ambiguity of
reality is marked, of whether the phone is dead, of whether the
person at the other end exists. He trails back and forth between
lucidity and near off-handedness and fumbling and fear and
addressing himself.*
*Some jokes are addressed to himself, some bravado is deflated to
himself, some is dialogue between real people. The telephone is
stalked, abused, taken for granted, feared. Most of all the fear of
being cut off, of no sound from either end.*)
(*On phone*) Anna? How are you? . . . I'm sorry . . . Didn't

you take a pill? . . . Well, it's hardly surprising then, is it?
. . . You rang me . . . oh, my dear, come off it, of course I
know it was you. You've got your own click . . . No, I
spent the night here, believe it or not . . . I couldn't get a
taxi so I walked here . . . you obviously rang up to find out
where I am not *how* I am . . . Oh, great, especially after
your little visit and then your friends . . . well, it wasn't
exactly a load of old fun was it? . . . Well, *you* were a
success, but then you always are . . . I didn't mean it
unkindly, you deserve to be. It's just that the more they
despise me the more admirable and courageous and decent
spirited you become . . . Sometimes I think you're my only
grip left, if you let me go, I'll disappear, I'll be made to
disappear, nothing will work, I'll be like something in a
capsule in space, weightless, unable to touch anything or
do anything, like a groping baby in a removed, putrefying
womb . . . No, I'll not leave you . . . I've told you. I'll not
leave you . . . *you* are leaving me . . . I told you the
weekend is out, it's out, the weekend is out . . . Yes, I am
. . . I don't know about Liz. She may be the last to pack it
in, but pack it in she will . . . Of course she's coming with
me . . . because I haven't seen her probably for six bloody
weeks and I have to be with her . . . I know I am, have I
ever denied it . . . I see Jane every day of the week and no
one could be more relieved to be rid of me when her
friends are around . . . because I'm only an inquisitive,
hostile, undistinguished square I suppose, and I bore the
jeans off her . . . must you always say 'mistress'? It's a very
melodramatic word for a very commonplace archetype . . .
you make it sound like a pterodactyl who gives you lung
cancer . . . or something . . . Yes, well she said something
almost identical about you . . . with a little more wit, I may
say . . . Well, she's quite a humorous girl . . . Oh,
something about your gold lamé hairstyle . . . and, oh yes,
your dress: what did she call it: chintz and sequin collage
. . . I don't know, someone must have described it to her –
no – not me . . . Well, you're neither of you the greatest
dressers in the world . . . I know, but mistresses, as you

call them, are usually less tolerant than wives. Mind you, they're also less patronizing but totally without generosity . . . No, I malign her about that . . . Yes, and you too. Look, has Jane left yet? Could you put her on . . . I want to speak to her, that's why . . . Listen, I'm a fairly rotten father but better than some, at least I can ask my daughter a question on the telephone. After all, she can refuse to speak to me if she wants to. But try not to prompt her? (*Pause.*)

Jane? Hullo, darling, how are you? . . . I should say I'm more or less the same as usual. Or, rather less than usual. How's the Drama then? I don't mean your personal drama, if you have one, I mean speech training and improvisation or whatever it is? . . . Good, well I'm glad. You deserve it. You see, you'll be a dame before I die. No, well by the time you're thirty . . . What I wanted to ask is could you pop in and see me today? . . . This morning, any time? . . . No, it's not all that important, but I'm just asking you if you would do me a favour and give me ten minutes of your time . . . we could have lunch if you'd . . . well, can't you cut voice production or something? You speak quite beautifully enough as it is . . . I'm not flattering you – or bribing you. Frankly that folk-song and poetry recital voice gives me the flaming pip, I'm just asking you to see me for a few minutes at least before . . . That's better! I'll buy you an air cushion for the next Aldermaston. Save you getting felt up in Trafalgar Square too . . . Sorry, well, it *is* nine o'clock in the morning and my sofa isn't very comfortable . . . Thank you, darling, very much. It won't take . . . What? All right, put her on. (*Pause.*)

Hullo . . . I honestly don't know . . . No, I really don't. It's a bit of a tough day. Hudson seems to be in court all the time nowadays. Jones is useless . . . well, the truth is I don't like him then; it's all right him working for me, but I'd feel differently if he wanted to marry my daughter. I just hope to God she wouldn't want to . . . Of course I'm not drunk, a little of last night's fire is coursing through the

gates and natural alleys of the body with my three pills,
that's all. Anyway, Jane's sure to marry an emergent
African. Perhaps I am a bit, I don't know. That is, if she
hasn't already sent her virginity to Oxfam . . . I tell you I
don't know. I've got to see Mrs Garnsey again. I'm going
to fail there, I've done it already, but she's coming in again
to lose her grip or what ever it is, and then there's Tonks
and Tonks and an indecent assault or criminal assault I
don't remember which, and some bank manager who's a
flasher and . . . Yes, I am seeing her, you must know that,
you *do* know that, now . . . I'll let you know and I'll come
back . . . as soon as I can . . . I know you do . . . I love you
. . . It just doesn't do much good does it? . . . Look, try
and take a pill and go back to bed . . . OK, please yourself.
Oh, don't talk Jane out of coming to see me. No, forget it.
If you can and you want to, well . . . Bye.
(*He puts the phone down. There is a noise from the outer office.
He calls out:*)
Joy.
(*No reply. He gets up, looks through the door. There is no one
there. He comes back, looks at his watch. Picks up phone, dials.
Waits. No reply. He waits, then looks carefully at his thumb.
Puts down the phone. Not knowing what to precipitate next.
Again, a noise from the outer office. Someone has certainly come
in this time. He waits. No one appears and he can't bear it any
longer.*)
Joy? Joy?
(HUDSON *appears, taking off his raincoat. He takes in the sofa
bed and situation.*)
HUDSON: (*Ponderously, of course*) Hullo – early bird.
BILL: Oh.
HUDSON: Where's the woman, then?
BILL: Flown.
HUDSON: How was she?
BILL: Fine.
HUDSON: Well, that's good.
BILL: Sure. Let me tell you, she could lose you in five minutes.
HUDSON: Delighted to hear it.

BILL: Tell me, what about Shirley?

HUDSON: What about her?

BILL: Do you think she'll come back?

HUDSON: No. You've seen the last of her.

BILL: Really? The last?

HUDSON: She rang Joy and asked her to send her cards off last night.

(*Another noise from outer office.*)

BILL: If that's Jones, keep him out of my way, I don't want to see him.

HUDSON: Well – sounds as if you've met your match this time.

BILL: What do you mean?

HUDSON: Perhaps you'd better take the day off.

BILL: I've too much to do.

HUDSON: What have you done to your thumb?

BILL: I keep looking at it, that's all. It's rather painful. But they're rather interesting to look at, anyway. I never did look at it properly before. Have you? I wonder if it's cancer.

(JONES *looks in.*)

JONES: Hullo.

HUDSON: Hullo. Come on your scooter?

JONES: Yes.

HUDSON: Well, you'd better go and thaw out I should think.

JONES: No Shirley then?

HUDSON: No. Not any more.

JONES: Where's Joy?

HUDSON: Overslept we believe.

JONES: Well, I'll do the post then.

HUDSON: Yes, I should if I were you.

JONES: What's that?

HUDSON: The boss has got cancer this morning.

JONES: Oh?

HUDSON: In his thumb.

(JONES *goes out.*)

BILL: Thank God for that. I suppose you're in court all day again.

HUDSON: 'Fraid so.

BILL: Why do you leave it all to me?

HUDSON: What would you like me to do?

BILL: I don't know.

HUDSON: You've got Jones.

BILL: Thanks. You can take him with you.

HUDSON: Well, I'd better leave you then. Oh, how did you get on with Mrs Garnsey?

BILL: Didn't work out at all.

HUDSON: I didn't think it would.

BILL: Eh?

HUDSON: We got the husband's reply in after she'd left.

BILL: Well?

HUDSON: Oh. I don't think she's got anything to worry about.
(BILL *stares at him and starts to laugh. Another noise in the outer office.*)
That'll be Joy.

BILL: Send her in.

HUDSON: Right.

BILL: Wally – have you thought any more about my offer?
(*Pause.*) The offer, Wally. The partnership.

HUDSON: Yes. As a matter of fact I have given it a bit of thought.

BILL: And?

HUDSON: I'd like to take a bit more time over it. If you don't mind.

BILL: And Piffards?

HUDSON: They don't seem to be in any hurry for a decision.

BILL: No? Well, they're a big firm. Right, well then.
(*Pause.*)
Joy!
(*She appears.*)

HUDSON: Ah, there she is.

JOY: D'you want me?

HUDSON: Bright as a button.

BILL: Bring in the post, will you?

JOY: Mr Jones is sorting it.

BILL: Well, bring in what he's done.

JOY: OK.

BILL: And ring Mrs Garnsey.

JOY: Which?

BILL: Which what?

JOY: Which first?

BILL: Oh – Mrs Garnsey. I want to catch her.

(*She nods and goes out.*)

HUDSON: You sound as though you think you'd lost her. Well,
see you later.

(*He goes out.* BILL *reaches for the intercom.*)

BILL: Joy! Get me Mrs Eaves.

JOY: Which?

BILL: What? Oh, you speak to Mrs Garnsey. Make another
appointment for her as soon as she can.

JOY: OK.

BILL: And what about Shirley?

JOY: What about her?

BILL: Well, isn't she coming in?

JOY: Why should she?

BILL: You mean she's really left?

JOY: Yes. Really.

(BILL *stares at his thumb. The phone rings.*)

BILL: (*On phone*) Liz? Look, I'm sorry. It's just that it's going to
be a day. I can see it only too well . . . Yes, I'm all right.
My thumb's a bit painful, that's all . . . Yes, of course it's
cancer. But, look, you will stay in, won't you. Whatever
happens, wait for me, don't leave will you? OK. Thank you
. . . But you won't leave . . . Bye.

(JOY *reappears with some letters.*)

JOY: This is all for the moment. You know how slow he is.

BILL: OK. Give them here. Did you get Mrs Garnsey?

JOY: Well, I spoke to someone. Her sister or someone.

BILL: Close the door.

(*She does so.*)

JOY: She said she'd changed her mind.

BILL: Changed her mind?

JOY: That's what she said.

BILL: But did you make it clear it was important I see her again?

JOY: Sure. She just said would you send in the account.

BILL: But I wanted to see her again.
   (*Pause.*)
JOY: Shall I send it in then?
BILL: What? Oh, yes, I suppose so. No. No, don't.
JOY: But that's crazy.
BILL: How are you this morning?
JOY: I'm fine.
BILL: Well, you look it, I must say.
JOY: Thank you, Mr Maitland.
BILL: Did you get home all right?
JOY: Well, it was only half past seven in the evening, you know.
   I didn't exactly have a night out.
BILL: I'm sorry.
JOY: For what? We enjoyed ourselves. Didn't we?
BILL: Yes, I think we did.
JOY: The draught under that door's a bit much, though. And it
   was a bit of a shock opening the door to your old woman.
BILL: But you don't regret it?
JOY: Maybe there'll be other times, other places. And if not,
   well . . . She's very attractive, isn't she?
BILL: Do you think so?
JOY: Well, don't you?
BILL: Yes. Yes. I do. So many of you are.
JOY: I've only one regret but that's more or less the usual one.
BILL: What's that then?
JOY: Bill.
BILL: Yes, Joy?
JOY: I have one flaw in my character. Well, not just one, but
   one that crops up all the time. You see I want to have
   sex constantly, I mean I'm always wanting it, I always
   have.
BILL: Joy, for a woman to make that admission is no shame,
   believe you me.
JOY: Ah, but everyone tells you differently. Right? You lose a
   man's respect, you lose your own sense of respect and all
   that old load of rubbish. Right?
BILL: Right.
JOY: So. So I've always felt guilty. There it is, daft, but I am. So

230

I have to get them to say 'I love you.' And then, then I say 'I love you.'

BILL: And then?

JOY: And then. Then, I feel better. (*Pause.*) You see.

BILL: I'm sorry.

JOY: Don't be. You don't love me. And I don't love you. But it's all right. Isn't it? (*She kisses him lightly.*) You're a funny old thing. You're scared aren't you?

BILL: Yes.

JOY: Well, Joy won't leave you. Not yet a while. What do you want doing?

BILL: I don't know. Just cope, will you?

JOY: Sure.

BILL: There's this Tonks thing. And that boy. The indecent assault. Or was it criminal?

JOY: Shall I ask Mr Jones?

BILL: No. Just hang on to that switchboard.

JOY: All right, love.

BILL: Oh, my daughter's coming in.

JOY: When?

BILL: Sometime this morning. Just send her right in.

JOY: OK. See you later. (*She goes out.*)

BILL: (*Calls out*) Oh, try and see if you can get Mrs Garnsey personally, and I'll talk to her. If not, if not remind me to send a letter.

(*Presently* JONES *looks in.*)

Well?

JONES: Joy told me to bring in the rest.

BILL: Great.

JONES: There's not a great deal.

BILL: Not a great deal. Any money in? Any business? Any problems?

(JONES *looks dull.*)

JONES: Only what you see there. Mr Hudson told me to sort it out for you.

BILL: Sort it out? Yes, I'll bet. Do you think old Wally's going to leave us?

JONES: No idea. Except he's had an offer from Piffards.

BILL: What do you think about that?

JONES: Well, they're a very respected firm? Aren't they?

BILL: Very.

JONES: Not much criminal stuff.

BILL: No.

JONES: Libel, isn't it?

BILL: Quite a lot. Would you like that?

JONES: What – libel? Not specially.

BILL: What would you like specially?

JONES: Oh, I don't know. It's all much the same when you come down to it, isn't it?

BILL: But if they – Piffards – offered you a job, you'd take it, wouldn't you?

JONES: Well, I, I'm not likely to be asked, at this stage, anyway, am I?

BILL: No.

(*Pause.*)

JONES: Have I done something wrong?

BILL: No, nothing. I admit I've tried to catch you out. But usually, you come round. Even if it takes a little time. You're pretty solid, I'd say. Solid but forward-looking, you know, a child of the jet age, a new age of fulfilment with streamlined institutions, a sense of purpose and looking forward to the new frontiers of knowledge. If Mr Hudson leaves, do you think you could take his place?

JONES: I don't know. I might.

BILL: But you might not. You might go elsewhere?

JONES: Well, I haven't had a lot of experience yet, and it doesn't do any harm to strike out a bit –

BILL: That's right. I think you should. What's this?

JONES: Tonks v. Tonks. Anderson v. Anderson and Maples. Oh, and that's the supplemental petition.

BILL: What's Maples?

JONES: Indecent assault.

BILL: Well, what are you giving him to me for?

JONES: Well, Mr Hudson thought you'd be better to deal with this one.

BILL: Yes, I see. Has this been sent to counsel?

JONES: Mr Hudson said you might like to have a word with Mr Winters about it, but he said he didn't think he'd touch it.

BILL: He'll touch it if I ask him.

(*Disbelief between them.*)

JONES: Well, if you like, I can give them to Mr Winters this morning.

BILL: No, I'll do it. But I'll see Maples first. Otherwise, if you send him straight down to Winters, he'll carve him up. What do you make of him?

JONES: Maples? Not much.

BILL: Oh?

JONES: Well, he hums and hahs. And stammers.

BILL: Perhaps he's nervous. At being prosecuted by the police.

JONES: But he's a bit affected at the same time.

BILL: Does he seem like a pouf?

JONES: (*Casually*) Yes. I should say so.

BILL: Do you believe him?

JONES: Well, it's a bit fishy, isn't it?

BILL: Yes.

JONES: I mean, put him up before old Glover, and I wouldn't give him much change. First offender and all, six months.

BILL: We'll just hope the old bastard breaks a leg. I don't think he's ever missed a day yet though. Sir Watkin Glover, VC. For Vicious Character.

JONES: And then there's Mr Simley.

BILL: Who's that? Oh, yes, the bank manager who's a flasher. Perhaps I can do something for Maples. What time's he due?

JONES: Eleven.

BILL: Try not to let me keep him waiting.

JONES: I'm going out.

BILL: Oh, yes. Well, tell Joy. All we want is one good reliable person.

JONES: What?

BILL: A witness?

JONES: Oh.

BILL: There isn't one is there?

JONES: No.

BILL: Well, we'll see. I like the sound of Maples. Better than I
    like Piffards. Ask Joy to get me a glass of water.

JONES: OK.

BILL: Most of these police jobs are decided by someone quite
    outside the event. They're not the only ones who can 'lean'
    on the evidence. You think someone's going to shop me to
    the Law Society one day, don't you? Someone will send an
    anonymous little note, and I'll get a summons to defend
    my professional conduct. I wonder who it'll be. Someone's
    sure to do it. It's surprising it's not happened before. I've
    been threatened with it, you see. Someone at Piffards
    actually. He never did. I don't know why. Milson it was,
    not the old man, he wouldn't have bothered with me. The
    young one, I wonder who it will be though. Someone –
    (*Pause.*)

JONES: I hear you've lost Mrs Garnsey.

BILL: What do you mean *I've* lost Mrs Garnsey?

JONES: Well, *we've* lost Mrs Garnsey. The firm has.

BILL: The *firm* has? I'm writing her a letter. Something went
    wrong. I scared her off. In some way. I could feel her
    withdrawing from me. I'm the wrong man for these things.
    You and Hudson should do them. *You're* the right people.
    You can handle them – I can't. They turn away from me,
    and they're probably right. (*He looks at the papers on his
    desk.*) And you really can't, either of you, do these?

JONES: You know what we've got in. Well, I'll get on. You
    wanted a glass of water, OK?

BILL: When are you getting married?

JONES: Don't know yet. I haven't really made up my mind.
    Still, there's no hurry. About these things. Is there?

BILL: No. Not if you don't feel it.

    (JONES *goes out.* BILL *picks up a divorce petition and starts
    reading in a low voice:*)
    In the High Court of Justice, Probate Divorce and
    Admiralty Division. Divorce. To the High Court of Justice
    the 27th day of January 1964. The humble petition of
    Maureen Sheila Tonks. Maureen. I remember Maureen.
    She always, well not always, but most times I went out

with her, wore hand-knitted suits, knitted by her mother. They'd always shrink and they were in horrible colours and her skirts would be too short because of it, which worried her. It worried me, but she always seemed to be in some pain, some funny pain, *physical* pain I mean. It was never any good. Which was a pity because she has the most strange blue eyes with dark hair, very dark. English beauty her mother called it. English beauty. And Sheila. Well I remember two of them. One was Scots with white, flaky skin. She rode a bicycle with a crossbar and didn't give a damn. She'd punch and go at you like a boy, but she'd cry too when it came to it.

JOY: (*Entering*) Mrs Tonks to see you.

BILL: (*Rises*) Ah, Good morning.

(MRS TONKS *enters. It is the same woman as* MRS GARNSEY. *Played by the same actress.*)

BILL: Please sit down. Would you like some tea or coffee?

MRS TONKS: No, thank you very much.

BILL: Right. Thank you, Joy.

(JOY *goes out.*)

Right. Now. I'll just give this to you, if you'd care to look at it. I want you to go over it very carefully. It's your petition, the smaller one is the supplement petition. Mr Hudson's just prepared it so there may be one or two things – (*Pause.*) All right?

MRS TONKS: (*She nods presently. She begins*) The humble petition of Maureen Sheila Tonks. That. On the 21st day of April 1958, your petitioner Maureen Sheila Tonks, then Maureen Sheila Williams, Spinster, was lawfully married to Richard George Tonks, hereinafter called the respondent, at the Parish Church of St Hilda's in the County Borough of Leicester. That. After the said marriage, your petitioner and the respondent lived and cohabited at divers addresses and from October 1960 to August 1963 or thereabouts at 42 Macwilliam Street.

BILL: Lived and cohabited.

MRS TONKS: Save and except that in the application of the petitioner by reason of the respondent's cruelty, the

Justices of the Petty Sessional Division of Kingston did on
the 12th day of August 1963 make an order that the
petitioner be no longer bound to cohabit, to live with and
cohabit, with the respondent and that he should pay her a
weekly sum of two pounds seventeen shillings.

BILL: Skip on to paragraph nine.

(*She fumbles.*)

There.

MRS TONKS: That. That the respondent is a man of excessive
sexual appetite who has habitually and constantly made
sexual demands on the petitioner which he knew she
regarded as inordinate or revolting.

BILL: Habitually and constantly. I'm sorry . . . In your
husband's answers, which, admittedly aren't very coherent,
he says. Now. Paras one to seven correct. Para eight I deny
that I have been cruel to my wife. Here we are, paragraph
nine: I deny being a man of excessive sexual appetite.
There were never sexual relations between us except by
mutual agreement.

(*Pause.*)

Are you all right?

(*She nods.*)

Right, let's get on then.

MRS TONKS: That. On many occasions, occasions insisted on
having intercourse three times and even four times a day.
He adopted a practice he termed . . .

BILL: Paragraph twelve, your husband says the allegations
contained are a gross exaggeration of the true facts.

MRS TONKS: That the respondent refused to cease from having
intercourse during the time of the petitioner's menstrual
periods at 42 Macwilliam Street and number 11 Wicker
Street, notwithstanding the petitioner's entreaties . . .

BILL: There were difficulties between us. Such that my wife
failed to reach satisfaction.

MRS TONKS: That. On frequent occasions at the said address
whilst he was having intercourse with petitioner he
did . . .

BILL: My wife visited the Marriage Guidance Council on at

least three occasions who told her they believed the difficulty was due to my wife's reluctance . . .

MRS TONKS: Notwithstanding the fact that he knew the petitioner found this conduct revolting and upsetting.

BILL: We've none of us been reluctant much have we. Well, there were girls like Maureen, and even with you there were difficulties but not revolting or upsetting. At least, not much, I don't think so. You weren't reluctant, you should be happy you didn't cling on to it like it was the crown jewels. You were generous, loving, bright, you should have been able to cope. *I* should have been able to cope.

MRS TONKS: He told the petitioner he liked to hear the noise made by . . .

BILL: To have another child. Another child. In spite of the advice given to her by the Counsel she refused to use this.

MRS TONKS: That. It was his desire to have sexual intercourse with a woman in this street to whom he referred . . .

BILL: Because she said it was nasty. Nasty and messy.

MRS TONKS: He constantly referred to as 'that great big beautiful blonde bat'.

BILL: I wonder if it was real or dyed. Not that it matters.

MRS TONKS: On at least eleven occasions during the marriage he attempted to commit . . .

BILL: I deny that I persisted.

MRS TONKS: And did in fact.

BILL: There is no truth at all in this.

MRS TONKS: Upon the person of the petitioner, compelling the petitioner with force to submit.

BILL: I respected my wife's feelings at all times and especially . . .

MRS TONKS: To these malpractices. That. In March 1961 when the petitioner was seven months pregnant with the child Laura, the respondent violently chastised the child Edward with a heavy brush of a type . . .

BILL: No truth at all in these allegations . . .

MRS TONKS: After the said occurrence on the 19th July 1961 . . .

BILL: As described, bears no relation to what actually

happened. I do admit there were many times when I failed. Many times.

MRS TONKS: The petitioner left the respondent.

BILL: I failed in giving her complete satisfaction. My wife left me on the 12th day of September 1963.

MRS TONKS: Wherefore your petitioner humbly prays that the court will exercise its discretion in her favour and decree (1) that the said marriage may be dissolved, (2) that she may be granted the custody of the children of the said marriage, (3) that the respondent be condemned in the costs of the proceedings.

BILL: All the time we have lived together she has been a very highly strung person. She has been constantly depressed and been to the doctor, but it all seems to have come to no good. I have done all I can. Signed: Richard George Tonks.

(*Pause.* JOY *enters.*)

JOY: I'm sorry, but Mrs Anderson is downstairs. What do you want me to do?

BILL: Has Mr Jones gone yet?

JOY: He's just leaving.

BILL: Well, stop him. He can't leave yet. Not yet. We need . . . Mrs Tonks, would you mind going into the other room? I think you've met Mr Jones. There are one or two things to be sorted out here, and, we really ought to get on with them. All right?

(*She smiles.*)

I've just got someone else to see. You'll be looked after. You'll be looked after. It's *not* a question of passing you on. All right? Joy will look after you. I'm sure you wouldn't mind a cup of coffee or something now?

(JOY *takes* MRS TONKS *out.* BILL *picks up another petition.*)

BILL: Audrey Jane Anderson. Audrey, I remember Audrey. Even an Audrey Jane. I thought she was a bit posh. Except she wasn't. She just took elocution and dancing and wore patent shoes. I think. I'm not sure, I thought I could remember. And I've no idea of what's to come. I can't even call to mind little details like that. If only it could be

fixed. And improved. Improved. But it doesn't, nothing
does. I can't even reassemble it. Why do I do it? Well, not
because it's good. I suppose, I suppose, because it still has
a little withered ball of interest. Somewhere. Audrey Jane
Anderson. The returns are coming in and they aren't good.
(JOY *enters with* MRS ANDERSON. *Again it is the same woman
as* MRS GARNSEY, *as* MRS TONKS.)
BILL: Ah. Please sit down. Would you like some tea or coffee?
MRS ANDERSON: No thank you.
BILL: All right. Thank you, Joy.
(JOY *goes out.*)
Right. Now. I'll just give this to you. Mrs Anderson. If
you'd like to take a look at it. It's just a rough, rough
summary of the statement Mr Jones, Mr Hudson took
down for you. So I'm sure there'll be one or two things to
clear up. All right?
(*She nods.*)
Good. Carry on them.
MRS ANDERSON: Audrey Jane Anderson will prove as follows.
BILL: What goes wrong? Nothing happens for you, I fail you,
and you're frightened and full of dislike.
MRS ANDERSON: I was married at Kidderminster Registry
Office. I was a spinster. My maiden name was Wall. My
husband was then a clerk in the local post office. Our
marriage –
BILL: Our marriage. What a phrase.
MRS ANDERSON: Our marriage seemed normal for a time and
reasonably happy. There were difficulties owing to the fact
that we were living at my mother's house, 148 Chadacre
Road, for two years.
(BILL *makes a massive effort to assemble the facts in his mind.
It is very difficult.*)
BILL: Two years. You know, you mustn't expect people to
behave well towards you, Audrey. You mustn't. I know
you have and I know you will.
MRS ANDERSON: There was discord when I was pregnant with
the little boy Patrick John.
BILL: Patrick John.

239

MRS ANDERSON: My parents persuaded me to return to him.

BILL: You must always ask yourself. Is it dangerous or is it safe? And then make your choice. If you can, if you can.

MRS ANDERSON: Things became increasingly unhappy and difficult when my husband gave up his job and became a traveller for a firm in electrical fittings. He was able to be at home most of the time, but when he was away, never more than for the odd day or two, he would accuse me of going out with men.

BILL: Well. She thinks I've got mistresses all over London. They both do. And it's not even true. Worse luck. No, thank God.

MRS ANDERSON: He said I ought to go on the streets.

BILL: You might have met me then. You might have been worse off.

MRS ANDERSON: I have never been with anyone apart from my husband.

BILL: That's what's wrong with all of you, you dim deluded little loving things. You listen to promiscuous lady journalists and bishops and your mother. And hang on to it.

MRS ANDERSON: But he's always saying these things.

BILL: He listens.

MRS ANDERSON: It's as if he can't help it. When he wanted to, he would have intercourse two or three times a day. He would, he could go as far as he could but that was all. But it's not only that, it's not even that. If it were only that I could put up with all kinds of things. Because I know he is a good man, really, and a kind man. He can be, and he has been kind to me.

BILL: I love you. He never said, he hardly ever said, he stopped saying, he found it difficult to say I love you. It has to be heaved and dropped into the pool after you, a great rock of I love you, and then you have to duck down below the surface and bring it up, like some gasping, grateful, stupid dog.

MRS ANDERSON: He loves the children, and is always making a fuss of them, and giving them things. My sister used to come in to watch TV, but I hardly ever went out while she was there. We went to the doctor and he made me go to Weymouth for two weeks for a complete rest.

BILL: I often think of my dying. And her, I mean. Of her being a widow. As opposed to a wife. A blackened wife. Of the kind of suit she would wear and wear and where she would get it from. She hasn't got a useful black suit. Liz has, but I don't think she'd get there. Which worries me. Because the idea of her not being there is disturbing. I've asked her to be there, and she's promised me, which is damned silly and a lot to ask, especially if you think of her having to face Anna in her black suit. I wonder if they'd notice what the other was wearing. In the crematorium with all that G-Plan light oak and electrical department brass fittings and spanking new magenta hassocks. And the pink curate sending me off at thirty bob a head as I go rattling on little rails behind him and disappear like a truck on the ghost train at Dreamland, in the amusement park, behind the black curtains, and all the noise.

MRS ANDERSON: I am on National Assistance. Three pounds twelve shillings a week. I am not working now, not since early May.

BILL: But did you really enjoy work? Did you? You didn't enjoy sex. Wasn't it just another effort, um? I mean an effort on your part, some way of helping, of fighting off what's going to happen to you?

MRS ANDERSON: I'm still under the doctor. The defendant has given me housekeeping all the time – barring a short period of about a fortnight. He has not touched me sexually since August Bank Holiday. He slept in another room for a few weeks, but he used to cry quite often and it kept me awake. We would both cry sometimes. He offered to leave me alone. I told him I would leave him if that's what he wanted. I still wanted some happiness for him. We are buying the house and the TV has been paid for. He said he would save for the down payment on a car and take us all out – a Mini – and take us all out at the weekends to the sea. I am quite sure he meant it. I think he wanted to, I think he really did.

BILL: There was a time when I used to speculate about *her* death. Oh, but not only Anna's. I'd be crunching back up that new path with the planks and the wet clay and the flowers. Perhaps I'd have walked out of that place on my own, there'd have been no one else, I could have done as I liked. I could have sat in Lyons and got myself a cup of coffee and a roll and butter all on my own. I might have looked around me, and my throat would have been tight and I'd have trouble with my coffee, and I'd smile sentimentally at the coloured girl who was clearing away the plates just because she was coloured, and my throat seemed to be closed up with the business of dying, and I'd kid myself we were friendly to one another. I might have gone and bought myself a new suit. Something a bit too sharp for someone my age and size, but I'd have stalked into some popular camp store and got something off the peg. And some shirts. I'd make up my mind to throw out all my old shirts and buy new ones, clean cotton shirts with that new smell, and lots of large handkerchiefs. All new. I'd have walked around, trying to remember London, trying to put it together, looking for street musicians with my pockets full of change.

MRS ANDERSON: I have often contributed to finance. Often by simply going without new things or buying things cheap from my sister.

BILL: I think I'd have gone on a bus. An 11 or a 38. All the way. Say, from Putney to Hackney.

MRS ANDERSON: When he gets in at night after work and early in the morning. Before I get up to get his breakfast.

BILL: I'd have had dinner alone, very, very, slowly. I'd have had a cigar and a Calvados or Marc de Bourgogne. Or – and – or I'd have gone to the pictures or a theatre with no one beside me except my new overcoat and a new book to read at home in bed, a new novel perhaps, by some woman perhaps. Something which might surprise me, take me by surprise a bit. Something I hadn't quite thought of, or not

242

in that way, or so well, or, but not something that
necessarily, no, something that didn't disturb me. Perhaps
something easier. Something new but old. Something. A
fat biography, perhaps something scandalous, about
Marshall Hall. Or Rufus Isaacs. Something new.

MRS ANDERSON: He says I'm not natural. He says I'm not like a
woman should be.

BILL: My death and hers. Theirs? Yours, and mine. Who first?
Um?

MRS ANDERSON: He says I've no intelligence and no brains and
no education. And I'm not fit to run anything, not even a
brothel. I have not imagined, imagined any of these things
because I may be unhappy or unwell. (*Her voice is
disappearing, but she rallies for her last speech.*)

BILL: Good. Now. Joy!

(JOY *appears.*)

MRS ANDERSON: I know I'm no good at all to him. He
humiliates me. I know he hates me. I wish I could have
done better. That I could go back.

(JOY *touches her shoulder and she follows her out. Pause.*)

BILL: Joy!

JOY: Yes.

BILL: Get me Mr Winters, will you?

JOY: OK.

BILL: Tell him it's urgent.

JOY: Mr Maples is downstairs. Shall I send him in?

BILL: No. I want to speak to Winters first. Then afterwards.
Did you look after Mrs Tonks?

JOY: She went.

BILL: Went?

JOY: That's right. Well, I'll get Winters. (*She goes out. Presently
her voice comes from his desk.*) Mr Winters is engaged at
present.

BILL: Well, of course he is. Hudson's with him isn't he?

JOY: I'll see. (*Pause.*) They say Mr Hudson's gone.

BILL: What's the matter with them all? Well, put me on to
Roberts. (*Pause.*) His managing clerk. Come on. Don't *you*
start.

243

(*Pause.*)

JOY: (*Off*) He's not available.

BILL: Not available! But that's his job – to be available. He doesn't ever have to be anything else.

JOY: Well, that's what they say.

BILL: Here: put me on to them.

JOY: What?

BILL: Put me through! Hullo. Charley! Hullo: What's going on. Can I speak to Mr Roberts, please? What do you mean? Out? He can't be out. I can hear his voice . . . I tell you, I can hear his voice . . . I see . . . All right . . . Well, please ask him . . . to ring me . . . when he can.
(*He puts down the phone.*)

JOY: (*Off*) Shall I send in Mr Maples?

BILL: No. Get me Mrs Eaves. Tell him I'm, tell him I'll be a couple of minutes. Now, get her quickly in case she's popped out. (*He waits. Very disturbed indeed. Buzz.*)

JOY: (*Off*) Mrs Eaves.

BILL: Liz! Thank God, I thought you'd gone out. What? Do I? Well, I'll tell you, I'm sorry, but I just rung up old Winters. You know . . . Well, he wouldn't speak to me. Which is all right, but he always speaks to me, even if it's only half a minute, especially if I say it's urgent, which I did. And the funny thing is I *know* Hudson was with him. They swore he wasn't but he must have been. He couldn't have finished in the time. But old Winters and I have been quite pals. I must have put more work in his way over the past . . . Exactly . . . And he's a nice, straightforward . . . a bit brusque, but forthright. He even laughs at . . . And then there was his clerk, Roberts. Charley Roberts . . . I picked up the phone and I heard him say, I heard him say quite clearly, 'Oh tell him I'm out or something. Anything.' He didn't even bother to lower his voice. It was like talking to you now . . . But, Charley. He's not like that. Bit dull, like Hudson. But – he's just a posh office boy. He's known me fifteen years . . . But why should he do that . . . Well, sorry to bother you. It was just a funny experience . . . As soon as we can – I'll ring you. Now, don't go out, will you? Eh?

Well, I'm seeing some kid for importuning. That could
take up a bit . . . Well, Jones has been doing it but he's
obviously muffed it, and I'll have to start more or less . . . I
must try and help . . . Yes, perhaps too hard, perhaps . . .
Well, I'm hoping Jane will come in . . . I'm just going to
tell her that I shan't be at her birthday weekend. That she
knows quite well it's because I'll be with you, and that to
please be honest with both of us, and own up that she
doesn't care whether I'm there or not and that she's just
letting herself be used, or rather lending herself, as a blunt
instrument by her mother . . . All right . . . Don't forget
. . . (*He rings off.*)

JOY: (*Off*) Shall I –

BILL: Yes, And keep trying Winters. And tell them I know
Charley Roberts is there . . . No, just keep ringing. And
when Mr Hudson gets in, tell him to come and see me
right away.

JOY: OK.

BILL: And say right away. Even if I have a client with me.

JOY: Yes, sir. (*Presently she appears at the door and announces:*)
Mr Maples.

(JONES *comes in.* JONES – MAPLES *has some of* JONES*'s
unattractiveness but with other elements. In place of his puny
arrogance and closed mind, there is a quick-witted, improvising
nature, not without courage. His flashes of fear are like bursts of
creative energy, in contrast to Jones's whining fixity and
confidence.*)

BILL: Mr Maples. Sorry about all this waiting about for you.
I'm afraid it's . . . Do sit down. No calls, Joy. Right?

JOY: What about Mr Winters?

BILL: Oh. Yes. Him.

JOY: And.

BILL: I don't know do I? Use your judgement. Well, try me if
you're not sure. But I must see to Mr Maples, I must see
he's looked after. We *must* get on with it.

(*Slight pause as he falters into another distraction. They watch
him. He wrenches himself out and dismisses her.*)
All right.

(JOY *goes out*.)

Now, at last. So sorry. You've . . . (*He looks for Maples's file. Flips through papers*.) You've, yes you've been seeing – Mr Jones.

(MAPLES *nods*.)

Yes, there's a fairly longish statement. And, of course, a copy of your statement to the police. And these other things . . . It doesn't make a very clear . . . at the moment, does it? Shall we start more or less . . .

(JOY *buzzes*.)

JOY: (*Off*) Your daughter's here.

BILL: Ask her to wait.

JOY: Only thing is she says she's not got very long. Shall I –

BILL: Who has? Tell her to wait. Give her a cup of tea and discuss your teenage interests together.

JOY: I'm no teenager, thank you!

BILL: No one would know it. And look – don't let her go. She's got to stay and see me. After I'm through with Mr Maples. Tell her that. (*Switches off*.) Fresh start was right. Yes, let me say to you –

(*He is thrown by the image of his daughter waiting outside. She is just visible to the audience*.)

As your lawyer, you have no, no obligations to me. Whatsoever. However, if you wish me to act in your interests, you should regard me like, the, the Queen, with the right to, to be consulted, to encourage and to warn I don't even ask for the truth. You may not be capable of it, it's difficult to retain for most of us, some of us at least, and when you're in a spot of trouble, as well, you are, let's be quite honest about it, and you feel you are gradually being deserted and isolated, it becomes elusive, more than ever, one can grasp so little, trust nothing, it's inhuman to be expected to be capable of giving a decent account of oneself. . . . Could you just shift your chair a little nearer to the desk. There, then I can see you properly. I hate to have my clients half-way across the room, having to talk to themselves. Instead of to me. Shall we see if we can't find anything that's been let out. (*Pause*.) Who *are* you?

(*When* MAPLES *replies, his delivery adopts roughly the same style as in the* MRS GARNSEY – ANDERSON – TONKS *dialogue.*)

MAPLES: How can I describe myself to you? I do seem to be very ordinary, don't I?

BILL: I don't know. I wish I could see you more clearly. This statement . . .

MAPLES: Isn't true.

BILL: Well, I knew that before you came in.

(*Presently, he gives his evidence, like* BILL *himself, mostly at speed, more polemic than reflection.*)

MAPLES: All right then. My name is John Montague, after my uncle Monty, Maples. I am married, I am quite young though I don't feel as if being younger ever happened to me. I've always been married or in the army or living with my parents. I have one child, aged six, a little girl, Daphne, Susan, my wife's choice not mine. My wife's name is Hilda. That was about the only name she didn't need to be talked out of as she hated it too. I met Hilda when I was still doing my National Service, which was a bit of a difficult time for me. But it isn't very interesting to tell anyone because I don't have any proper characteristics at all, save one, and there's not even any interest in that, any more than there is in being five feet seven or prone to hay fever. Physically I'm lazy, on the whole, that is, but it doesn't stop me being restless. I can't stop at home, but most of the time I'm scared to death of putting my nose outside the front door. But sometimes I do. I'm there somehow, on the, because of some row with Hilda, or some excuse or I get back late from one of the shops, and in twenty-five minutes I'm in the West End. I used to like to play tennis, which I'm rather good at – And badminton, that too, I played that at school. Hilda doesn't like anything like that, and I haven't bothered. But I used to be rather good and full of energy and I could beat quite a lot of the others. There were always a few, though, and we used to have wonderful, great long duels when we should have been doing our homework. And it might even end up in a bit of a fight. A couple of times I even burst into tears

247

when I was playing against someone called Shipley, his name was. He thought I was a bit mad, but it was all right. We were old friends. Nothing else. We talked about girls constantly, all the time.

(BILL *tries to take some of this in.* MAPLES *sees the effort and slows down the concentration for a few moments.*)

BILL: No. Go on.

MAPLES: Well, I met my wife, Hilda, while I was still in the Services.

BILL: Yes, I see. Let's see you're . . .

MAPLES: I'm in the drapery business. My father-in-law's business actually, but I've done a bit about building it up. He had this old shop in Richmond, you see, ribbons, buttons, calico, towels, oh – cheap lot of old stuff. He'd have lost the lot in another year. Then Hilda and I got engaged, while I was still in the forces. There was nothing much I could think of to do then, I wanted. I'd got a pass 'O' level in GCE but I didn't have a clue what to do with it. And I'd a sort of feeling for materials and I could organize a bit. I got rid of some of the old hags in the shop. Anyone could have done it, honestly. Anyway, now there's these three shops – the old one, one in Kingston and a new one just opened up in Hounslow. I'd come back late from Hounslow on this particular night.

BILL: Tell me about the arrest.

MAPLES: All right.

BILL: So I might as well throw this away.

MAPLES: I'll have to tell you about Denis.

BILL: Denis who? Oh, all right, tell me later.

MAPLES: Well, a year ago I nearly left Hilda. I fell in love. I still think it was the first time. But I couldn't bear the thought that I couldn't get over it, that it was bigger than me, however ordinary I might be. I never liked girls except my sister but she wasn't always easy to talk to. She could be suspicious and sort of unwelcoming. We all talked about girls all the time and we'd play games like seeing how we could look up their skirts when they were playing games or going upstairs on the bus.

248

BILL: I'll bet Shipley was good at that.

MAPLES: Yes. He was.

BILL: So was I, I'm afraid.

MAPLES: The only thing that excited me was playing tennis, and especially the badminton with him. I'd sweat for hours, before, during and afterwards, and I couldn't get my homework done in time for bed which scared me because I was terrified of getting into trouble or being found out in even little things, like not dubbining my football boots or never understanding what 'parsing' was. I never wanted to marry Hilda or anyone else but I was scared stupid, I was stupid anyway, not to. My mother was always going on about the rottenest thing men did was to get girls pregnant, which is what I did, of course. So did my brother. But it didn't matter for him. He's got three more now, and he's happy enough, and so's mother. No, I was never very fixed on her. My father's *much* nicer. Yes, I know you're thinking he was ineffectual and all that, but so was she, what was she so good at, at least he didn't scare anyone, or lean on anyone. He's all right. He maybe should have belted her across the chops a few times, but I doubt if anything or any of us could have changed. No, I never liked girls, but I didn't like men who didn't seem like men either. I think I believe in God. Still, I seem to let things happen to me. I have always let the others make the first advances, usually if it's possible in the dark, or with the lights turned down or something of that sort.

BILL: What about Hilda?

MAPLES: Oh, Hilda. We're getting on better.

BILL: And – she knows about this change?

MAPLES: Oh yes. One of the detectives made a big point, coming round. We even had a drink together, the three of us by the end of it. *I* was offering him a drink. And he took it. But he knew what he was doing – *I* couldn't bribe anyone, not anywhere. I suppose you'll have to get up and say 'his wife is standing by him'.

BILL: Well it often makes a better impression in court to say you're undergoing medical treatment.

MAPLES: Shall I tell you what the doctor said to me?

BILL: No. I've heard it. Did you get another doctor?

MAPLES: Yes. He agrees with *me*. But then he's the same. Just keep out of the law, keep out of the law and not to invite trouble. I don't want to change. I want to be who I am. But I stayed with Hilda, I'd even given up Denis four months ago. I hadn't spoken to him even for four months and this happened. On the way back from the new Hounslow shop. Hilda's mother tries to call it a boutique, but I think I've talked her out of that now. I used to have to get drunk, first, like I did when I forced myself into bed with Hilda and got married for it. But I haven't had to do that for a long time. Do you think I should plead guilty?

BILL: Not yet.

MAPLES: What's the advantage?

BILL: Of pleading guilty? It has the advantage of certainty, that's all.

MAPLES: That sounds very attractive at the moment.

BILL: Well, I can't even guarantee that yet.

(JOY *buzzes*.)

JOY: I'm sorry, but your daughter wants to know how much longer, because she can come back.

BILL: Tell her she's got to wait. I don't care. She's got to wait. Now tell her . . . (*Switches off.*) Can I offer you anything? (MAPLES *shakes his head.*)

MAPLES: Sometimes I would think I was unique, of course. You know, years ago. I hoped I was. But I'm not. I'm ordinary. But I wish I wasn't. I didn't have a clue. Nothing happened until after I was married, after Daphne was born. For some reason I got on the wrong train, but it was the right direction more or less and I just stayed on it, standing up, all those bodies pressed together and suddenly I felt two, maybe three, fingers touch me, very lightly. Every time the train stopped more people got out and there was more room. I was scared to look up from my paper and there wasn't any longer any excuse to be so close to anyone. A great draught of air came in from the platform and I felt cold, and it was Gunnersbury station which is not too far from me, so I looked up and got out. I didn't dare look back but I heard the footsteps behind me. That was the first time and I'd had a few drinks first and I was very cold, at the back of some row of shops called something Parade, by the Midland Bank. About half past seven at night. That's about all I remember of it. When I got in, my dinner was all overcooked and simmering on a plate over the gas stove with the gravy gone hard round the edge of the plate, which is a bit like the way Hilda does things, spills them or upsets them or does them too much and she wasn't feeling well and couldn't get the baby to sleep. I went out into the garden, put my fingers down my throat and then buried it all with a trowel. If I wasn't married I'd have done it all the time, one to another, I suppose, but I don't think so. That's never been what I wanted. Oh, not that I haven't behaved . . . They're right to get me, people like me. There was a young fellow, a sales manager at a store in Kingston. Do you know what I did? He was married. Nice girl. Rather attractive, not long married. Well, I set my sights and one night the three of us went out, got drunk, and while, all the time, while his wife was in the front –

BILL: Driving?

MAPLES: Driving –

BILL: Actually in the back?

MAPLES: And she never knew. We were so damned sharp, she never knew from beginning to end. Still doesn't know. Like Hilda, she never knew about Denis, about giving him up. I gave him up, you see. He wanted me to leave Hilda and take on a new life altogether. He begged me. He threatened to phone up or write to me. But he hasn't. He kept his promise. I longed to break the whole thing, and I think I would have done this particular night.

BILL: Do you still want to give him up?

MAPLES: No.

BILL: Do you think he's given you up?

(*Pause.*)

MAPLES: Yes. Probably. What's going to happen to me?

BILL: I don't know enough yet. I need to know more than that. I should think Sir Watkin Glover, QC, is sure to apply the full rigour of the law and send the both of us down. What about the police?

MAPLES: I've only had one brush with the police before. Late one night by Turnham Green. He flashed his torch on us. He let the other one go, but he took my name and address and made me meet him the next night. Only about three times. I know you think I haven't tried. I can't make any more effort, any more, I want to plead guilty.

BILL: Well, you can't, now go on!

MAPLES: He asked me for a light, this policeman.

BILL: In plain clothes?

MAPLES: Naturally.

BILL: Look, try to help me, will you. Where?

MAPLES: Piccadilly tube station.

BILL: You're crazy.

MAPLES: I know. But I knew it was going to happen. Sounds camp, but then the truth so often is. He was quite young, younger than I am, with lots of fair, wavy hair, like mine used to be, when I just went in the Army, before I met Hilda, before it started to go. He looked up. In the usual way. His eyes were pale and his cheekbones looked sharp and frail as if you could have smashed them with a knock from your finger, but when he walked away, you could see how really strong he must be. He walked straight into the cottage at number one entrance, you know, by the Regent Palace. And that was it. There was another one in there and they both of them grabbed me. Savile Row station. Oh, quite gently. And no surprise to any of us. Denis and I had often talked about it happening. They seemed nice enough at first. I began to feel better and relaxed, as if I was being loved openly and attended on, and then, then the pressure turned on. What I ought to do. What the magistrate would say. What they knew. The one who had asked for the light had seen me with Denis. He said they knew all about him. About both of us. I had to keep him out of it. I knew nothing could be worse. So I, I signed this statement. And there it is. In front of you. So. Are you all right?

BILL: (*Just audible*) Yes.

MAPLES: You haven't taken anything down. Was it . . .

BILL: Don't worry, we'll go through it all again with Hudson.

MAPLES: No. I don't think so.

BILL: You haven't seen me, my friend, you haven't seen me, cross-examining coppers is my speciality. But we'll get Winters in on this. Was there anybody else there? It's a pity nobody saw you.

(MAPLES *rises.*)

BILL: Joy! What's happening about Winters?

JOY: (*Off*) I tell you, I keep trying.

BILL: Well, Hudson'll be in soon. Tell him to come straight in. (*Switches off.*) Don't move. It's only my daughter outside. It's a pity about nobody seeing you. Oh, well – perhaps there was.

(*Pause.*)

Don't worry – we'll get someone.

(*They look at each other.*)

MAPLES: Thank you. (*Pause.*) In the meantime, maybe you'd better see your daughter.

(*He goes out. Presently* JANE *comes in.* BILL, *barely seeing her, waves her to the chair* MAPLES *has been sitting in. Slowly he takes her in. He buzzes* JOY.)

BILL: Joy!

JOY: (*Off*) Well?

BILL: Joy.

JOY: (*Off*) Yes?

BILL: Don't let Mr Maples go.

JOY: (*Off*) Well, I'm sorry –

BILL: All right. No. Wait.

JOY: (*Sympathetically. Off*) Yes?

BILL: Get me another glass of water.

(*He looks across at his daughter. She fidgets. Slowly.*) You can wait just one more minute –

(*Fade. Fade up on* JANE *and* BILL *together. Bill's speech must be started at the full flood. When he fails it is with his*

253

longing. His daughter is cool, distressed, scared.)
They're all pretending to ignore me. No they're not
pretending, they are! And that'll be the going of you except
that it's happened already. Of course, it has, ages ago.
Look at me. Why you can't have looked at me and seen
anything, what, not for years, not since you were a little
tiny girl and I used to take you out and hold your hand in
the street. I always used to think then that when you're the
age you are now, I'd take you out to restaurants for dinner,
big restaurants like I used to think posh restaurants were
like, with marble columns and glass and orchestras. Like
Lyons used to be before you knew it. And I thought we'd
behave like a rather grand married couple, a bit casual but
with lots and lots of signals for one another. And waves of
waiters would pass in front of us and admire us and envy
us and we'd dance together. (*Holds her to him*). Very
slowly. (*Pause.*) And when we got back to our table, and
when it was all over, we'd lean forward and look at each
other with such, such oh, pleasure – we'd hardly be able to
eat our dinner. (*Releases her.*) So that when we got up, after
a bit too much champagne, we'd have to hang on to each
other very tightly indeed. And then, go home . . . I always
wish I'd been brought up in the country you know. Won't
be possible much longer. There isn't any place for me, not
like you. In the law, in the country, or, indeed, in any place
in this city. My old father lives in the country, as you know,
but he doesn't want to see me these days. Can't say I
blame him. When I went to see him the other day –
whenever it was, do you know, I tried to remind him of all
sorts of things we'd done together, but he simply wouldn't,
he wouldn't remember. And then the old devil got mad
and told me I was imagining it. I had to go in the end. He
was tired and he wanted me to go. When I bent down and
kissed him, he didn't look up . . . Your other grandparents
can hardly bring themselves to acknowledge me. The old
woman crossed to the other side of the street once when I
was pushing you in the pram so as to avoid speaking to me.
With you, I mean. They have you over there and your

254

mother goes, I know, and they still give you generous presents Christmas and birthday, but do you know when they write to your mother, they never even mention me by name, love to Bill, how's Bill, nothing, not for ten years, and they only did it in the early years after you were born because they thought they had to if they were going to be able to see you! And then they discovered that they didn't even have to mime that genteel little courtesy. How much do you think your safety depends on the goodwill of others? Well? Tell me. Or your safety? How safe do you think you are? How? Safe?

(*She turns away, increasingly frightened.*)

Do you want to get rid of me? Do *you*? Um? Because I want to get rid of you.

(*She moves to the door. He is toweringly cool for a while.*)

Just a moment, Jane. You can't go yet. Till I tell you. About this famous weekend.

(*She shrugs impatiently.*)

Oh, I know it's none of your fault. But you should know I shan't be with you, or, at least, your mother then, just because I shall be with Liz – a subject that bores you, I know, as much as it's beginning to her, if you see – I'll be with her for three whole days or something, if she'll have me. I don't know that she will, but I'll be with her instead of you on your seventeenth – is it seventeen? – anyway, birthday and the reason for that is because I know: that when I see you, I cause you little else but distaste or distress, or, at the least, your own vintage, swingeing, indifference. But nothing, certainly not your swingeing distaste can match what I feel for you. (*Small pause as he changes tack.*) Or any of those who are more and more like you. Oh, I read about you, I see you in the streets. I hear what you say, the sounds you make, the few jokes you make, the wounds you inflict without even longing to hurt, there is no lather or fear in you, all cool, dreamy, young, cool and not a proper blemish, forthright, unimpressed, contemptuous of ambition but good and pushy all the same. You've no shame of what you are, and, very little,

255

well, not much doubt as to what you'll become. And quite right, at least so I used to think. They're young, I said, and for the first time they're being allowed to roll about in it and have clothes and money and music and sex, and you can take or leave any of it. No one before has been able to do such things with such charm, such ease, such frozen innocence as all of you seem to have, to me. Only you, and girls like you, naturally, could get on that poor old erotic carthorse, the well-known plastic mac and manage to make it look pretty. Pretty, mark you! Chic. Lively. You've stopped its lumbering, indecent, slobbering ancient longing and banged it into the middle of the *Daily Express* – where they're only allowed to say the word 'rape' if a black African's involved. Or perhaps a nun. *You* don't even, not moved, to wear make-up any longer. Your hair looks like a Yorkshire terrier's come in from out of the monsoon. And, yet, somehow, perversely, you are more beautiful and certainly more dashing than any of the girls I used to know and lust after from morning to night, with their sweety, tacky lipsticks and silk stockings on coupons and permanent waves and thick-hipped heavy skirts. I don't know what you have to do with me at all, and soon you won't, you'll go out of that door and I'll not see you again. I am quite sure of *that* by this time if nothing else. You hardly drink except for some wine and pintfuls of murky coffee. You'll go anywhere and more or less seem to do anything, you've already permanent sunless, bleached stains beneath your breasts and two, likewise, crescents, on your buttocks. You'll read any menu without bothering, order what you want, and, what's more, get it. Then maybe leave it. You'll hitchhike and make your young noises from one end of Europe to the other without a thought of having the correct currency or the necessary language. And you're right. And you dance with each other, in such a way I, would never have been able to master. (*He gazes longingly across.*) But, and this is the but, I still don't think what you're doing will ever, even, even, even approach the fibbing, mumping, pinched little worm

of energy eating away in this me, of mine, I mean. That is, which is that of being slowly munched and then diminished altogether. That worm, thank heaven, is not in your little cherry rose. You are unselfconscious, which I am not. You are without guilt, which I am not. Quite rightly. Of course, you are stuffed full of paltry relief for emergent countries, and marches and boycotts and rallies, you, you kink your innocent way along tirelessly to all that poetry and endless jazz and folk worship, *and* looking gay and touching and stylish all at the same time. But there isn't much loving in any of your kindnesses, Jane, not much kindness, not even cruelty, really, in any of you, not much craving for the harm of others, perhaps just a very easy, controlled sharp, I mean 'sharp' pleasure in discomfiture. You're flip and off hand and if you are the unfeeling things you appear to be, no one can really accuse you of being cruel in the proper sense. If you should ever, and I hope you shan't, my dear, I truly do for I've leapt at the very idea of you, before you were ever born, let alone the sight and smell of you. If you should one day start to shrink slowly into an unremarkable, gummy little hole into a world outside the care of consciousness of anyone, you'll have no rattlings of shame or death, there'll be no little sweating, eruptions of blood, no fevers or clots or flesh splitting anywhere or haemorrhage. You'll have done everything well and sensibly and stylishly. You'll know it wasn't worth any candle that ever burned. You will have to be blown out, snuffed, decently, and not be watched spluttering and spilling and hardening. You know what God is supposed to have said, well in Sunday School, anyway? God said, He said: Be fruitful and multiply and replenish the earth. And *subdue* it. It seems to me Jane, little Jane, you don't look little any longer, you are on your way at last, all, to doing all four of them. For the first time. Go on now. (*She waits. They elude each other. She goes out. Fade. Fade up on* BILL.)
Joy! Joy! What's going on out there? Joy! Where are you? What is it then? Joy!

(JOY *enters in her overcoat.*)

JOY: So he's gone?

BILL: Oh, there you are. Who?

JOY: Hudson.

BILL: Yes.

JOY: Oh? Is he going to Piffards then?

BILL: Apparently.

JOY: I always thought he would.

BILL: So did I.

JOY: Well . . .

BILL: Are you going home?

JOY: There's not much to stay for, is there?

BILL: I don't think so. Did you try Winters again before –

JOY: They've all gone home now. Which is where I should be.
Is the Law Society really on to you?

BILL: Did Jones say so?

JOY: Yes.

BILL: Then I'm sure he's right.

JOY: Aren't you going to see Mrs Eaves?

BILL: Do you know what a client said to me today?

JOY: No, who?

BILL: Oh, I don't know. One of them. She said when I go out
to the shops, I go to the ones furthest away so that I can be
out of the house and away from him longer. Then I get
angry when the shopping is so heavy, and I can't carry it on
my own.

JOY: Crazy.

BILL: Stay a little longer.

JOY: What for?

BILL: Have a drink.

JOY: No thanks.

BILL: Well, stay and talk.

JOY: No.

BILL: I promised not to say 'please'.

JOY: What do you want me to do? Press myself in a book for
you? You know what? I think they're all right. I don't like
you either.

BILL: I know.

258

JOY: Well, I'm off. Like I should have done . . .

BILL: I'm still surprised to hear you say it though. I always am. And I shouldn't be . . . Why does it shock me? Why? I myself, am more packed with spite and twitching with revenge than anyone I know of. I actually often, frequently, daily want to see people die for their errors. I wish to kill them myself, to throw the switch with my own fist. Fortunately, I've had no more opportunities than most men. Still, I've made more than the best of them. Will you come in tomorrow?

JOY: I'll see.

BILL: Try to.

JOY: I have to take the day off.

BILL: Oh?

JOY: I've not been feeling so good lately. I think maybe I need a bit of a rest.

BILL: I see.

(LIZ *enters*.)

LIZ: Hullo.

JOY: Hullo, Mrs Eaves.

LIZ: (*Nods to* BILL) How's your thumb?

BILL: Painful. A fat little tumour. On the end of another.

LIZ: In his usual state of catatonic immobility, are we?

BILL: Yes. (*To* JOY.) That's her way of saying I don't seem to be able to hold on, on to, to anything. She talks in that funny way because her father is a don and is what is called a conceptual thinker, which, it's all too clear, I am not. No, darling, it's not something in a rubber goods shop, it's what her father is. One of those little intellectual monkeys who chatter on the telly about Copernicus at two hundred words a minute. And don't ask me who Copernicus is. I don't know the name of the Prime Minister, at this moment. He's a very cold fish, Joy. Her father I mean. He's probably the only man living whose unconscious desires are entirely impersonal.

JOY: Well. I'll be off. Goodnight, Mrs Eaves.

LIZ: Goodnight, Joy.

BILL: Goodnight.

JOY: Bye.

BILL: Joy.

(*She goes out.* LIZ *goes over to him.*)

LIZ: My darling, are you all right?

BILL: Splendid.

LIZ: Why don't you come home?

BILL: Yes.

LIZ: I'm sorry, I had to come. You didn't answer the telephone.

BILL: Didn't I?

LIZ: I wasn't interrupting anything was I?

BILL: No.

LIZ: Oh, come along. I don't know why you don't admit you knock off that girl –

BILL: Because I don't need to.

LIZ: I keep giving you opportunities.

BILL: Well, I don't want them. I don't want to be cued in by you –

LIZ: It's a lot to ask, you know.

BILL: Yes. I see that too.

(*Pause.*)

LIZ: You do ask a great deal of both of us, you know. It's unnecessary and it diminishes you.

BILL: True.

LIZ: I do love you.

BILL: Your assessment's impeccable. As usual.

LIZ: You're a dishonest little creep.

BILL: Why the 'little'? Because you seem to have more authority than I have. (*Pause.*) You're not *bigger*. You're cleverer. More accomplished, more generous. And more loving.

LIZ: I've always managed to avoid guilt. It's a real peasant's pleasure, you know. For people without a sliver of self-knowledge or courage.

BILL: There *are* other qualities besides courage.

LIZ: Well?

BILL: Cowardice, for instance. For example.

LIZ: I've not seen you since Thursday. I thought somehow we'd managed to resolve the pain of that particular evening. Even on the telephone.

BILL: So did I. So we did. Till the next time.

LIZ: I love you so dearly. I can't think what to say to you.

BILL: I think you will.

LIZ: Why can't you trust me? Please?

BILL: It isn't easy.

LIZ: I know.

BILL: It isn't easy to trust someone: you're busily betraying. Sit down. I can't see you over there. I don't like my clients sitting half-way across the room talking to themselves.
    (*She sits. Pause.*)

LIZ: What do you want to do?

BILL: Do?

LIZ: Yes, my darling . . . do.

BILL: I don't know. I haven't given it much thought.

LIZ: Did you see Jane?

BILL: Yes.

LIZ: How was that?
    (*He looks at her.*)
    I see. So. What's going to happen?

BILL: Liz!

LIZ: What!

BILL: I'm tired of being watched. I'm tired of being watched by you, and observed and scrutinized and assessed and guessed about.

LIZ: Who gives a damn!

BILL: You do, you did. But you won't.

LIZ: What are you saying? Do you want me to go – Really?

BILL: Well, you're the one who insisted on what you called an ethic of frankness.

LIZ: Believe me, the last thing I would insist on is an ethic like that. I can't think of anything more destructive.
    (*Phone rings.*)

BILL: Hullo – No, everyone's gone.

LIZ: Well, we know who that is.

BILL: I'm just clearing up . . . I told you, everyone's gone . . . Just me . . . Yes, she *is* here . . . Because I couldn't be bothered to tell the truth . . . Listen, now's not a very good time, is it? Look, I'll ring you back.

(*Pause.* LIZ *looks slightly mocking, but doesn't exploit it. She is too concerned for him.*)

When I leave you sometimes and I get in, deliberately, of course, about three or four a.m. and Anna's lying there in bed, pretending to be asleep. After making love to you and the drive back, I'm so tired and there's the following morning a couple of hours away only, but I pretend to sleep because I can't to begin with. We both just lie there. And if I'm lucky or drunk enough and I go to sleep, she lies there choking in silence unable to sleep again till she wakes me in the morning. Do you know I can't remember one detail of what she looks like, not since I left this morning and we'd had the row about the weekend. I sat down to read the *Charterhouse of Parma* while you were away at Christmas. You said I'd like it. So I started. It took ten days and I gave up round about the middle somewhere. I can't tell you what it's about. I can't grasp anything. I used to be good at my job because I had what they called an instinct and a quick brain. Quick! I can't get through the Law Reports. I leave everything to Hudson and now he's gone, and I wouldn't leave a camel's breakfast to Jones even if he *were* still here.

LIZ: Bill. What are we going to do?

BILL: Go away. I suppose.

LIZ: But where?

BILL: Far away, as far away as possible from this place. There's no place for me here.

LIZ: (*Half humouring*) I never think of you as a traveller.

BILL: Meaning?

LIZ: Well, you never seem to enjoy it much, do you? (*Pause.*) Well, do you?

BILL: Damn it, I've, I've travelled thousands of miles in the past few years for various clients in the last –

LIZ: Oh yes, flights to New York and Amsterdam and Geneva. They're just business men's bus rides.

BILL: What do you want then? What should I be? Lady Hester

Stanhope with a briefcase of legal documents perched on a
camel?

LIZ: I just don't think of your business trips as travel –

BILL: Oh, travel –

LIZ: They're just for getting from one place to another for a
particular purpose.

BILL: (*Bitterly*) Well, what do *you* call travelling?

LIZ: Well, like, like going in a boat round the Isles of Greece.

BILL: Yes. With a lot of tight-lipped, fast-shooting dons on the
look out for someone else's wife or crumpet.

LIZ: When you're anywhere, you're always desperately
miserable. You want to get back.

BILL: Yes?

LIZ: Oh, to your clients. Or something. I was thinking, on my
way here, and now . . .

BILL: Well?

LIZ: I was thinking, perhaps you'd rather I didn't come away
for the weekend.
(*Silence. He faces her.*)
I just thought you seemed . . . as if . . . you might . . .
want to be alone.
(*Pause.*)

BILL: I was only waiting, from the moment you came in, for
you to say that.

LIZ: I'm sorry to be so predictable. One often is, you know,
when someone knows you well and loves you.

BILL: As I do. As I certainly do.

LIZ: I was trying my hardest to be honest. It's a failing –

BILL: Well, why don't you take something for it.

LIZ: I don't care what you are or what you do –

BILL: Or who I am.

LIZ: I need you.

BILL: Not that word, please.

LIZ: You pretend to be ill and ignorant just so you can escape
reproach. You beggar and belittle yourself just to get out of
the game.

BILL: Whenever I do it, I enjoy, I think you do know, being
some, some sort of, sort of good and comfort and pleasure

263

to you because I love you. I don't love you for the sake of that pleasure. I can get it anywhere.

(*She touches his shoulder and kisses the back of his head. He won't look up.*)

LIZ: You can always ring me.

BILL: But you won't be there.

(*She can't reply.*)

You do know that I love you?

LIZ: Yes.

BILL: And I shall never forget your face or anything about you. It won't be possible. I think, I'm quite certain, not that it matters, I loved you more than anyone.

LIZ: More than Jesus?

BILL: Yes.

LIZ: Goodbye.

(*She goes out.* BILL *takes a pill with a glass of water. He dials a number on the telephone.*)

BILL: Anna? Anna, what time is it? I can't see very clearly . . . Do you think I should come home . . . I don't think there's much point, do you? . . . Please don't cry, love . . . I, I think it must be better if you don't see me . . . don't see me . . . yes . . . don't. Please don't don't . . . I'll have to put the receiver down . . . I think I'll stay here . . . Well the Law Society or someone will, sometime . . . I think I'll just stay here . . . Goodbye.

(*He replaces the receiver and sits back waiting.*
Curtain.)